MASTERING THE SAT

Neil R. Chyten

Mastering the SAT

Copyright © 2011

Printed in the United States of America

ISBN 978-0-9905085-1-9

From the Author

Yet another SAT Study Guide. One might ask, "What did we do to deserve this fate?" Aren't the bookstores already cluttered with these tedious testaments to the ingenuity of test busters across the land? I asked myself these same questions before starting this book, and had any book worthy of parental trust existed, I would not have begun this all-consuming project. But when parent after parent asked for a recommendation of a study manual for the SAT, I could not in good conscience recommend any that existed. Not that any of them did not have some merit, but not a single one got everything right. In some cases, the question banks were good, but the strategies were not very helpful. Some books just got it all wrong, either miscalculating the difficulty levels, or making dangerously wrong suggestions about omitting. In all cases, something was missing or something was just plain wrong. The maestros of matriculation had fallen flat. Someone had to pick up the baton (or in this case, number 2 pencil) and create a book with real strategies that went beyond "read carefully" or "just guess C."

So, creating this book was not an act of pride or politics. It was an act of necessity. As both an SAT instructor and as a parent, I was taken aback by the realization that such a gap existed in preparation for such a high-stakes test as the SAT. I feel strongly that when my students dedicate their time to an endeavor, that time should be meaningful and productive. I created this manual to capture the skill-building exercises and strategies that have enabled my students to master the SAT for the past 20 years. Over that time, I have seen thousands of students gain hundreds of thousands of points. An SAT score many not be the most important thing in the world. Nevertheless, it is important and one's time and efforts should be rewarded.

About our Strategies

This book is full of strategies. Yet the word "strategies" is both overused and misunderstood. Exactly what role do strategies play in test preparation? Strategies fall into two categories: technique strategies and guessing strategies. Technique strategies offer a better way of going about something, whereas guessing strategies enable students to increase their odds of making an educated guess. This book has an abundance of both types. From the Zig Zag Method[SM] for Critical Reading and the Adaptable Essay Strategy[SM] for Writing, to the Spy[SM] and Double Agent[SM] Methods, this manual teaches students that omitting is entirely unnecessary and, in fact, hurt one's score. No matter how hard a question is, this manual makes clear that the odds are always in your favor!

We view it as our responsibility to develop effective methods/strategies to solve problems and to identify predictable tendencies in tests and scoring techniques. To do any less is to defy the trust our students have placed in us. This is my charge and my promise to all my tutors, teachers, coworkers and students. Chyten will always be the best it can be and will serve our students to the best of its ability, in honor and recognition of the trust they have placed in us.

Sincerely,

President
Chyten Educational Services

Mastering the SAT

Table of Contents

Introduction

SAT Reading

SAT Writing - Grammar

SAT Writing - Essay

SAT Math

Table of Contents

Mastering the SAT

Written by Neil Chyten

with contributions from
Chyten's Tutors

Introduction

A Brief History of the SAT

In the Beginning

In a fierce, fiery flash the universe was born. Within microseconds, space-time was ablaze with brilliant white-hot, expanding gasses that slowly cooled and coagulated into the bits of solid and quasi-solid matter that were to become the stars and planets we see from our windows.

In a miniscule moment, when time could only be measured in millionths of seconds, a universe sprang up, sprouted kinetic wings and spread itself in all directions. Seconds later, it had magnified its own existence from a local anomaly to something that could only be measured in tens of millions of units, each equal to the distance traveled by light in a terrestrial year. Still, it was impossibly hot and dense. The cataclysmic, cosmic event that created our universe still defies any rational explanation or interpretation.

For 15 billion years, the universe has continued to expand and evolve, carrying time on its back like a headless horseman, pitching and rolling along magnetic and gravitational waves. Welcome to your universe: a dynamic entity, born in a flash and in a state of constant flux ever since.

The Rise of the Intelligentsia

What was to follow was equally astounding. 15 billion years later, a small rocky planet in the outer arm of a rather ordinary galaxy gives rise to intelligent life. This life form develops a language with which to express feelings and ideas. It crawls out from caves and crevasses to build structures that protect it from the elements. It builds factories that furnish it with heat and light. It creates print to store language and ideas. It creates books to store print. It reads the books and accumulates information. It invents the wheel and draws detailed sketches so that it would never have a need to reinvent the wheel – the designs were saved in books. It devises a numerical system to explain concepts like shape and speed. Over time, new information builds geometrically upon the old. Reading each other's ideas, they then build upon those ideas. They have discovered knowledge. Eventually, knowledge creates Intelligence. Then, in a blazing flash of creation, Intelligence spawns the Intelligentsia.

The Intelligentsia builds hallowed halls. Within these halls, it feels free to explore the deeper meanings of life, including its own origin and eventualities. In doing so, it foresees its own demise, and seeks the means to avoid such an event. The fraternity of the Intelligentsia realizes that if it is to survive, it will need to refresh and augment its membership. Within this primordial soup of ultimate Intelligence, a savior arises - a test that promises to measure the immeasurable, a test to identify potential successors who would occupy the halls of knowledge. The year is 1926 A.D. The S.A.T. is born.

The Origin of the S.A.T.

It took 15 million years to develop the first S.A.T. (Scholastic Aptitude Test), a test that could purportedly measure aptitude – the likelihood of success at Harvard, or Yale or Smith. That was the idea anyway, as it was first administered in 1926 to approximately 8000 students. When it was introduced, Calvin Coolidge was president, the Great Depression had not yet occurred and the Model T was the most popular car in the world. Approximately 80 years and seven revisions later, the SAT (now just a trade name whose initials stand for absolutely nothing) is taken by millions of college hopefuls. What was once a requisite test for the elite is now a prerequisite test for the masses.

Chyten's Laws

Chyten Educational Services will introduce you to a series of effective strategies and logical systems that will make it possible for you to tackle the SAT and other standardized tests. However, these strategies and systems depend on you to carry them out.

Chyten's First Law:

An object at rest tends to stay at rest, until acted upon by another force.

Interpretation: Higher SAT scores don't just happen – they result from hard work and application. Start the process now. Once in motion, don't stop thinking about your success and what it will take to achieve it until the very moment your test is over.

Chyten's Second Law:

The greater the mass of an object, the greater the amount of force needed to accelerate the object.

Interpretation: How high can your SAT scores go? The answer is up to you. Hard work yields high scores. That axiom applies to your studies and to your actions on the actual test. Work hard leading up to the test, then work hard on the test. The greater the improvement you desire, the more effort you must put into the process.

Chyten's Third Law:

For every action, there is an equal and opposite reaction:

Interpretation: Hard work yields results. The amount of work you apply to this project will ultimately determine the magnitude of your success.

SAT Quiz:

1): What do the letters S-A-T stand for?

    A) Nothing at all, SAT is merely a trademark
    B) Scholastic Assessment Test
    C) Scholastic Achievement Test
    D) Scholastic Aptitude Test
    E) Scholastic Archdiocese Test

2) The first SAT was administered in 1926 to how approximately many students?

    A) 80
    B) 8000
    C) 80,000
    D) 800,000
    E) 8,000,000

3) The SAT essay is graded by two readers. Approximately how long does each reader take to grade an essay?

    A) 2 minutes
    B) 5 minutes
    C) 7 minutes
    D) 9 minutes
    E) 14 minutes

4) The new SAT is nearly four hours long. According to the College Board's research, performance on standardized tests is not adversely affected by length of test time until total test time reaches. . .

    A) 17 hours
    B) 9 hours
    C) 6 hours
    D) 5.5 hours
    E) 5 hours

Answers: 1) A. 2) B. 3) A. 4) D

New PSAT & New SAT Length and Question Types

	New PSAT/NMSQT	New SAT
	2 hours 5 minutes	3 hours 45 minutes*
Critical Reading	50 minutes: Two 25-minute Sections. Short and Long Reading Passages Sentence Completions	70 minutes: Two 25-minute sections plus one 20-minute section. Short and Long Reading Passages Sentence Completions.
Math	50 minutes: Two 25-minute sections. Multiple choice and grid-ins.	70 minutes: Two 25-minute sections plus one 20-minute section. Multiple choice and grid-ins.
Writing	25 minutes: One 25-minute Multiple-choice grammar	60 minutes: One 25-minute plus one 10-minute grammar section plus one 25-minute writing sample. Multiple-choice grammar section. Writing response to a prompt.

*The SAT contains an additional 25-minute experimental section that does not count toward the score.

Start Your SAT Engines

Check your supplies

- Manual?
- #2 Pencils?
- Cool eraser?
- Calculator? (A graphing calculator is preferred.)

Plan for Success

1) Set your sights high.
2) Create a plan that will allow you to reach your objective.
3) Follow that plan until you reach your objective.

Once you have established your plan, you'll need to follow through. The following three qualities are essential to success.

Determination

Assiduous work and dogged determination are essential to success on the SAT.

Motivation

You may see the SAT as a challenge to your intellect, as a gateway to college or as a hurdle to overcome. You may see it as your friend or as your enemy. Any view is acceptable, as long as you pick the one that best motivates you to succeed. One thing you must never do is take the SAT for granted. It is worthy of your attention. You can learn to master it, but first you must acknowledge and respect it.

Evaluation

With each step forward, you should evaluate your performance. Or, have someone close to you evaluate your performance. Dedicate yourself to reaching a point of desirable excellence and consistency.

The Shampoo Concept

Practice. Evaluate. Repeat.

General SAT Information

The SAT is a standardized test written by Educational Testing Service (ETS) and administered by the College Board to more than a million students each year. It is designed as an objective test of scholastic aptitude, a quality thought to contribute to continued educational success. Thus, the SAT is a tool intended to measure and compare the relative academic abilities of students from different schools and backgrounds and to predict which of these students are likely to be productive in college.

The SAT is offered seven times per year. Students are allowed to take it as many times as they wish (our general recommendation is to take the SAT no more than three times). It consists of <u>ten distinct sections:</u> two twenty-five minute reading sections plus a twenty-minute reading section, two twenty five-minute math sections plus a twenty-minute math section, one twenty five-minute and one ten-minute writing skills section and a twenty five-minute writing sample. One of the ten sections is experimental, either reading, writing (grammar) or math. That section does not count toward your score; it is used to pretest questions for future tests. You will not know which section it is.

The SAT is used by colleges as one of a handful of defining characteristics of an applicant. In general, the larger the college, the greater is the importance of the SAT. Other factors highly regarded by colleges are a student's grades, personal profile (a summary of interests and activities, thoughts and concerns), application essays and SAT essay.

Any College to Which you Apply Can Get a Copy of Your Essay

Yes, colleges can see your actual SAT essay. They can, and many have indicated they will, use it as an additional admission factor. They can access your essay with the click of a mouse, and can use it any way they please. Many have said they will use it as a factor in admission, while others will use it to compare with your application essay or as a placement tool once you have been accepted.

The Key to Success

The fact is that you will be most successful if you consider the SAT a challenge, rather than a burden. It is more like a jigsaw puzzle or a mystery novel than any test you'll take in school. A positive view of the test is far preferable to that of a disinterested participant.

Chyten's Strong Suggestions:

A) Don't take the SAT lightly! Treat each and every question as though it were your key to success. Treat each question like a micro-version of the SAT, actively seeking its unique tricks, traps and/or clues. Solve one at a time, giving each and every question a solid, thorough and thoughtful effort. If you come out of the SAT thinking it was easy, then most likely you have not applied maximum effort and thus have not done as well as you can. If you come out feeling like you've just been through a series of battles - then you have probably done your best!

B) Don't let fear overcome you. Nervousness is natural, but you must learn to manage and harness your fear. Perhaps this is easier said than done. Try taking actual practice tests in a group setting, and convincing yourself that this is your "real SAT." Sounds a bit too simple, but it can really help.

C) Expect surprises. You can count on the fact that the real SAT will have some tricks up its proverbial sleeve. You might encounter a hard question where you didn't expect it. You might even see something familiar used in an unfamiliar way (like a common word used in an uncommon way). If you expect surprises, then you will not be surprised. Don't let anything shake you from your mission.

D) Watch your time. Do not spend too much time on any one question. Do not hesitate to skip a question and come back to it if you have time. If you do skip a question, don't forget to match your answer to the proper space in the answer key!

E) With all the hours of study, the lessons, the strategies and suggestions, the key to success is you! Your solid effort and smart decision making will ultimately determine your SAT score.

Specific Breakdown of SAT Section Contents
(Not in test order)

The SAT has 10 Distinct Sections

Two 25-minute <u>Reading</u> sections	➤ sentence completions, short and long passages
One 20-minute <u>Reading</u> section	➤ sentence completions and one long passage
Two 25-minute <u>Math</u> sections	➤ one with multiple choice; one with multiple choice *and* student-produced response
One 20-minute <u>Math</u> section	➤ multiple choice
One 25-minute <u>Writing</u> section	➤ written essay
One 25-minute <u>Writing</u> section	➤ grammar
One 10-minute <u>Writing</u> section	➤ grammar
One 25-minute Experimental section	➤ could be Reading, Writing or Math

Number of Each Type of Question

Reading
Sentence Completions:	Blocks of 5, 8 and 6 questions	19
Short Reading Passages:	1 set of paired passages (4 questions)	8
	2 individual passages (2 questions each)	
Long Reading Passages:	1 set of paired and 3 individual passages	40

67 Total Reading Questions

Writing
Identifying Sentence Errors:	18
Improving Sentences:	25
Improving Paragraphs:	6

Essay
1

49 Total Writing Questions
Plus an Essay

Math
Multiple Choice:	Blocks of 20, 16 and 8	44
Student Produced Response:	1 Block of 10	10

54 Total Math Questions

How Colleges Use your SAT Score

The SAT is viewed by colleges as one of the three most important measures of a student who is applying (or who has applied) for admission. In general, the larger the school the greater the importance of the SAT. In addition to the SAT, colleges look at a student's grades and his or her personal profile (a summary of interests and activities, thoughts and concerns). Not all colleges require the SAT, and many accept the ACT as an option, instead of the SAT.

Mental Preparation

Successful students approach the SAT as a challenge, rather than as a problem or a burden. It is more like a jigsaw puzzle or a mystery novel than any test you'll take in school. Like a puzzle, you have to find the piece that fits. So try to view the test in a meaningful way, either as a friend or an adversary. But don't be neutral. Once you learn the inside information contained within these pages, you'll know what it takes to truly master the SAT. Attend to each question as you would to a task you enjoy, such as catching a baseball, hitting a tennis ball, shooting a basketball, passing the puck, acting in a play, playing piano or answering a riddle. In other words, concentrate; give your full attention to every minute of this very important exam. Do not take the SAT lightly. Taking the SAT is a task not unlike a competition against your greatest rival. You must bring your "A" Game! But don't dread the SAT. Be ready to work hard and compete against a test that can be mastered – but only with hard work and focused effort.

Be an Active Test Taker

Preparation can get you ready for the questions on the SAT, but may not fully prepare you for the experience of taking of the test. Think of taking the SAT as going into Lambeau field, to face the Green Bay Packers on the Frozen Tundra in mid December. Not a football fan? Walking into the test center is like walking straight into a room of strangers. You may be nervous. You'll certainly be curious as to what or whom you'll encounter when you walk through the door. Opening to page one of the SAT is like that. When you turn that page, remember to think about all the lessons you have learned in creating and writing an essay. The same advice holds when you get to the math sections, the grammar sections and the reading sections. Do not allow the test to dictate to you which answer you'll choose, or the subject you'll write about. Think actively about each question. Work methodically through each set of answers, being more skeptical than accepting. Think, "why is this answer wrong'" rather than, "could this answer be correct." Never be afraid to choose an answer that contains a word you don't know. These are often correct answers. Be an active tester. Work as hard as you can for the time you are there, and don't be afraid of guessing. The SAT is a guessing test – but make sure to put yourself in a position to make the best possible guess!

Timing

Time need not be a student's greatest adversary. Many think it is unfair to time such an important test. But there is a reason the SAT is timed – and that reason may surprise you. Limiting the time you can spend on a question makes you predictable. In turn, your predictability makes the test consistent. How does this work?

Students react predictably when told to answer a question in a short period of time. On the SAT, a student under time pressure might guess something that merely sounds "right," rather than analyzing a question-and-answer pairing more carefully. The College Board counts on this fact to help them maintain consistent results from test to test.

To counteract this effect, you must simply manage your time. This is one reason why practice is so important. Use these guidelines to help you.

Correct Timing for SAT Completion

Reading

Sentence Completions	36 seconds per question
Passages	70 seconds per question (includes reading)

Writing

Identifying Sentence Errors	30 seconds per question
Improving Sentences	45 seconds per question
Improving Paragraphs	60 seconds per question

Math

All Types	60 seconds per question

(less time for easy questions – more for hard questions)

Questions Blocks:

Sentence Completions and Math Only

The term *question block* refers to any single group of similar question types. For example, a question block might consist of eight sentence completions or twenty math questions.

Within any question block, questions are organized from easy to medium to difficult. You can estimate that the first-third are easy, the middle-third are medium and the final-third are difficult. ETS determines where a question will appear within a question block based on the percentage of students who correctly answered the question in an experimental question from a previous SAT. Usually, the last third were answered correctly by fewer than 30% of the students who responded. Responses to questions in your experimental section will determine where these questions will appear in a future SAT.

Dumping the Trash
(Eliminating Bad Answers)

Among the five answer choices you can almost always locate one, two or even three answers that are ridiculous, impossible or improbable. They don't answer the question, they contain a word or words that are inaccurate, or they are just obviously incorrect. These answers we refer to as *trash*. One very effective SAT strategy involves dumping the trash, thereby dramatically increasing your chances of selecting (or guessing) the correct answer.

Guessing vs. Omitting

It is always to your mathematical (and logical) advantage to guess; therefore guessing is a much better strategy than omitting. Those who suggest otherwise have apparently not thought this through very well!!!!

The Wrong Thinking:

"Since there are 4 wrong answers and only 1 correct answer, I should omit when I am not sure, since I am more likely to guess wrong than right!"

The Mathematical Proof of the Advantages of Guessing:

- Each correct answer earns 1 point. Each incorrect answer loses ¼ point.
- Since there are 5 answer choices per question, the odds are 1 out of 5 that a random guess will be correct (random guessing is a worst-case scenario).
- That means that 5 random guesses will yield, on average, 1 correct answer and 4 incorrect answers.
- The 1 correct answer yields 1 point. The 4 incorrect answers lose a total of 1 point combined.

Random guessing does not really affect your SAT scores. However, in truth, random guessing seldom occurs, since you can always eliminate 1-3 answers from any set of answers. This is because the SAT is designed to have answers that are very wrong – so wrong that you can be 100% sure that they can be eliminated. Once you eliminate these really bad answers, the odds turn in your favor to guess.

Omitting is the easy (read: lazy) way out and can limit your potential SAT score. There is no reason for routine omitting. Occasional omitting of a very difficult question is understandable and acceptable. However, the practice of intentional omitting to hit a target score is preposterous.

Remember – just one correct answer earns back the point that four incorrect answers cost you.

Intentional Omitting is Bad Advice

Even worse are those who suggest that you should omit a certain number of questions <u>AS A STRATEGY</u>! No mincing words - this is horrible advice. By intentionally omitting a certain number of questions, you lower your ceiling and thus your potential score! Instead, we will show you how to answer these questions correctly. Don't intentionally omit! Don't buy into that lazy-student mentality. It is not better to omit than to guess! It is just easier!

Selecting the Best Answer

Among the five answer choices, usually two or three stand out as possible choices. It is up to you to select the best answers from those that remain after the initial dumping process. In order to increase the chances of selecting the correct answer, learn from past tests what kinds of answers are usually correct. These will vary from question type to question type and will be covered in the pages that follow.

Mining for Gold

Did you ever think of how many tons of dirt and rock must be painstakingly removed by miners in their quest for small amounts of gold? Did you ever think of the hours of relentless work and diligent effort on the part of the assiduous workers day after day, month after month as part of their normal working routine? When you put it in perspective, three-and-three-quarters hours of digging out correct answers from among the rubble of traps and trash seems embarrassingly easy. Yet, the tasks are very similar in nature. But remember - all that shines is not gold! Answers that appear to be correct may be designed to trap you. So be careful, be diligent and, above all, be resourceful as you mine for gold among the trash.

SAT Reading

Building your Vocabulary
Sentence Completions
Short Reading Passages
Long Reading Passages

Building your Vocabulary

Memorizing Words

With the past two changes to the SAT, the College Board has removed much of the need for vocabulary building. However, SAT Sentence Completions and SAT Reading questions still have built-in vocabulary. While spending endless hours memorizing words is not a particularly profitable venture, it can boost already high scores by 20-30 points and average to slightly above average scores by 30-40 points. If you feel that this is a reasonable payoff for 10-20 hours of your time, then by all means memorize.

Perhaps a more reasonable alternative is to memorize prefixes and word roots. Learning prefixes and word roots can help you identify clues in words that will help you determine that a particular choice is a likely or unlikely answer.

Learning Prefixes and Word Roots

One quick way to improve your chances of making a correct guess on a sentence completion or reading question that contains unknown words is to learn how to determine the nature of the word. Often, the College Board includes words that contain internal clues, such as prefixes, roots or suffixes, or words that just "sound" good or bad. All these things are legitimate clues. Looking for a negative word? Which is the better choice?

- confluence
- disdain

Con is a positive prefix that means with or together, and
Dis is a negative prefix that means away.

So, disdain is the better choice.

Memorizing words or learning prefixes and word roots - both can improve your SAT score. The pages that follow have valuable lessons which can assist you in doing both. It is best to learn prefixes and roots by association with words you know.

For example: mis = wrong (think: mistake)

For learning words, association is also important, but in a different way. Learning groups of associated words is a powerful memorization technique.

For example: curmudgeon and misanthrope are both bad people. Memorize both words' meanings by making a mental connection between them.

SAT Prefixes and Word Roots

Prefix/Root	Meaning	Example 1	Example 2	Example 3	Example 4	Example 5
a/ab(s)	away	abstain	absolve	abdicate	abhor	adopt
ad	towards	advance	adhere(nt)	adulation	adoration	adamant
ante	before	antecedent	anteroom	antediluvian	antebellum	anterior
bell	war	belligerent	antebellum	bellicose	rebellion	bellow
bene	good	beneficial	benefactor	beneficent	benevolent	benign
bi	two	biped	bimodal	bisect	binary	bipartisan
circuit	around	circumference	circumspect	circumlocution	circuitous	circumvent
co/com/con	with/together	cooperate	confluence	communal	composite	accomplice
de	lessen(neg.)	delete	deleterious	denounce	defrock	degrade
dic/dit	say/speak	dictate	benediction	diction	malediction	dictum
dis	away	disappear	distend	disdain	disband	discursive
eu	good	eulogy	euphonious	eugenics	euphemism	euthanasia
ex	out	exit	extract	extricate	excommunicate	exculpate
extra	out/beyond	extrasensory	extraneous	extrovert	extravagant	extrapolate
in/im/il/ir	not	impossible	impropriety	irreverent	intransigent	impervious
in	in	internal	inquisitor	innate	invoke	intrinsic
inter	between	interfere	intercede	interspersed	interlocutor	interim
intra/intro	within	intramural	introspective	intramuscular	introvert	intravenous
loc/log/loq	speak	locution	eloquent	loquacious	eulogy	monologue
magna	large	magnify	magnanimous	magnificent	magniloquent	magnitude
mal	bad	malpractice	malefactor	malapropism	malcontent	malignant
mis	wrong	mistake	misanthrope	miscarry	misappropriate	misconceive
ob	against	obscene	obstinate	obdurate	obfuscate	obtrusive
pac/peac	peace	pacifist	pacific	pacify	peaceable	peaceful
para	similar/above	parachute	paradigm	paragon	parable	paradox
peri	around	perimeter	peripheral	peripatetic	perigee	perinatal
phon	sound	telephone	cacophonous	euphonious	phonic	phonology
post	after	postbellum	posthumous	postulate	posthaste	postdiluvian
pro	for/towards	propel	propensity	proclivity	projectile	propose

pre	before	prepare	predestined	predicate	precipice	preamble
re	again/back/bad	retract	renege	rebuke	rebuttal	remonstrate
retro	backwards	retroactive	retrospective	retrofit	retroversion	retrocede
son	sound	sonar	consonance	dissonance	sonority	resonance
sub	under	submarine	subterranean	subjugate	subversion	subtle
super	above	superimpose	supersede	supercilious	superfluous	superlative
trans	across	transatlantic	transient	translucent	transcend	transgress
tract	movement	traction	tractable	intractable	retract	contract
vi(v)	life	vitality	vivacious	convivial	vim	vigorous

Learning to recognize vocabulary clues in questions and answers can help you increase your SAT score. For example, let's assume you don't recognize any of the answer choices in an SAT question. This condition is created below where you are shown only the first few letters of each answer to the following example.

Because Leroy had not completed several assignments, his teacher informed him that he was to be _____ from the class.

a) *ad* (toward)
b) *ex* (out)
c) *dis* (away)
d) *pro* (for, toward)
e) *con* (with, together)

The most likely choices are *b* or *c*, because *ex* means *out,* and *dis* mean *away,* each of which seems to convey the meaning of the missing word. He was _____ *from* implies that he was removed. If the answer were *criticized* or *rebuked,* for example, the word *from* would not be correct. You are not *criticized from* nor are you *rebuked from.*

Categorized Vocabulary Words

Color Words

<u>Red</u>
scarlet, vermilion, crimson, magenta, ruddy, fuchsia or cerise.

<u>Yellow</u>
flaxen, saffron, jasmine, tawny or sallow

<u>Blue</u>
azure, indigo, sapphire, turquoise or aqua

<u>Green</u>
emerald, jade, chartreuse, sage

<u>Purple</u>
lilac, mauve, heliotrope, magenta, plum or lavender

<u>Black</u>
ebony, somber, raven

<u>Grey</u>
ashen, grizzled, dusty or smoky

Multiple-Meaning Words

Each of the following words is a strong candidate to be on your SAT.
The College Board loves to test you on alternative meanings of common words.

Word	Meaning One	Meaning Two
Fathom	(v.) To measure	(v.) To get to the bottom of and to understand
Divert	(v.) To distract	(v.) To amuse or entertain
Champion	(n.) One that holds first place in a contest	(v.) To fight for or defend
Diner	(n.) One that dines	(n.) A restaurant
Arrest	(v.) To detain in legal custody	(v.) To stop the progress or spread of
Warrant	(n.) A written order that serves as authorization for something	(v.) To justify or deserve
Conviction	(n.) The process of proving guilty	(n.) A fixed or strong belief
Discriminate	(v.) To differentiate or to make a clear distinction	(v.) To act on the basis of prejudice
Legion	(n.) A large number; a multitude	(n.) An organization
Articulate	(adj.) Capable of, speaking in a clear , expressive language	(v.) To pronounce distinctly and carefully; to enunciate
League	(n.) An association of sports teams or clubs that compete among themselves	(n.) A unit of distance/large number
Knot	(n.) A fastening made by tying together lengths of material	(n.) A nautical unit of speed
Sage	(n.) A cooking herb or spice	(n.) A person well-known for his or her wisdom
Sanction	(n.) A penalty to ensure compliance	(v.) To authorize or to legitimize
Asylum	(n.) An institution for the mentally ill	(n.) Protection or immunity
Retiring	(v.) Withdrawing from work at a certain age	(adj.) Shy and modest
Swagger	(n.) A strut	(v.) A boastful or conceited expression
Juvenile	(adj.) Characteristic of youth or children; immature	(n.) A young person
Expire	(v.) To come to an end; to terminate	(v.) To die
Deliberate	(adj.) Done or said on purpose	(adj.) Leisurely or slow
Discount	(n.) A reduction of price	(v.) To disregard
Beacon	(n.) A lighthouse or signaling device on the coast	(n.) Someone or something that guides
Reclaim	(v.) To claim again	(v.) To renovate or to make suitable for living
Anxious	(adj.) Worried or distressed	(adj.) Eager

Word	Meaning One	Meaning Two
Marshal	(n.) The head of police or fire department	(v.) To gather or to arrange
Glacial	(adj.) Extremely cold or icy	(adj.) Lacking friendliness or warmth
Tonic	(n.) A carbonated beverage	(adj.) Something that refreshes and restores
Buoyant	(adj.) Able to float	(adj.) Animated or easily excited
Table	(n.) A piece of furniture	(v.) To postpone or put aside
Watershed	(n.) The region draining into a river or body of water	(n.) A critical point or turning point
Rider	(n.) One who rides a horse	(n.) An addition to a document or record
Qualified	(adj.) Competent or able	(adj.) Limited, restricted or modified
Static	(adj.) At rest	(n.) Electrical charge
Parochial	(adj.) Supported by local church	(adj.) Narrow-minded
Cause	(n.) Something producing an effect	(n.) A belief that someone is dedicated to
Exhaustive	(adj.) Tiresome	(adj.) Thorough or complete
Deduction	(n.) Subtraction	(n.) Drawing a conclusion by reasoning
Prize	(n.) A reward	(v.) To value
Founder	(n.) A person who starts something; an originator	(v.) To sink

People Words
(with Simplified Definitions)

Word	Definition	Word	Definition	Word	Definition
Curmudgeon	Mean	Demagogue	Leads the Weak	Nomad	Wanderer
Dolt	Idiot	Firebrand	Troublemaker	Bungler	Screws Up
Philanthropist	Generous	Detractor	Negative	Stalwart	Strong
Mentor	Guide	Malingerer	Shirks Duty	Reveler	Partier
Neophyte	No Experience	Transient	No Home	Entrepreneur	Business Minded
Scapegoat	Blamed	Colleague	Same occupation	Figurehead	Symbolic Leader
Debunker	Disproves	Collaborator	Works together	Compatriot	Countryman
Mediator	Settles Disputes	Proponent	Supporter	Raconteur	Story Teller
Nit-picker	Picky	Libertarian	Likes Liberty	Insurgent	Rebel
Sage	Wise	Malefactor	Wants to harm	Pacifist	Peaceful
Miser	Cheap	Sycophant	Flatterer	Sybarite	Likes Luxury
Pariah	Outcast	Hedonist	Seeks Pleasure	Hermit	Lives Alone
Pedagogue	Teacher	Charlatan	Fraud	Progenitor	Ancestor
Hector	Annoying	Dupe	Gets Fooled		
Heckler	Jeers	Iconoclast	Against Tradition		
Mercenary	Loyal to Money	Inquisitor	Strict Questioner		
Misanthrope	Hater of Man	Martinet	Tyrant		
Pugilist	Fighter	Cynic	Cynical		
Despot	Tyrant	Antagonist	Trouble Maker		
Ingrate	Not Grateful	Usurper	Steals Power		
Paragon	Model/Example	Interlocutor	In a Conversation		
Gourmand	Lover of Food	Meddler	Interferes		
Protagonist	Main character	Idol	Looked Up To		
Utopian	Believes in Utopia	Procrastinator	Delays		
Anarchist	Hates Laws	Magnate	Powerful		
Benefactor	Generous	Glutton	Overindulges (as in eating)		
Beacon	Guide	Orator	Speaker		
Pundit	Expert/gives opinions	Hypocrite	Says One Thing - Does Another		

Vocabulary Words in Groups
(with memory phrases)

Category: Bad People

CHARLATAN   -   A fake or fraud
Memory Phrase -   "A *charlatan* posed as King *Charles.*"

MALEFACTOR   -   A person who harms another
Memory Phrase -   "A *malefactor* is a *bad factor* in your life."

CURMUDGEON -   A crude and mean spirited person
Memory Phrase -   "A *curmudgeon* throws *mud* at children."

MERCENARY   -   A person who has loyalty only to money "A
Memory Phrase -   *mercenary* soldier is a paid assassin."

ICONOCLAST   -   A person who goes against traditional values "An
Memory Phrase -   *iconoclast* breaks *icons.*"

DILETTANTE   -   A person who does things on a superficial level (for show)
Memory Phrase -   "A *dilettante* learns one song on the piano to impress her
                      friends."

Category: Good People

BENEFACTOR -
Memory Phrase -

A person who offers financial or other kinds of assistance
"A *benefactor* is a *good factor* in your life."

MENTOR -
Memory Phrase -

A personal guide or teacher
"A *mentor meant* to teach me about life."

CONSTITUENTS -
Memory Phrase -

A group of people represented by someone
"My *constituents* believe in the *constitution*."

PHILANTHROPIST -
Memory Phrase -

A person who generously donates money to a cause
"*Phil(anthropist)* was very generous."

AESTHETE -
Memory Phrase -

A person who loves beauty
"An *aesthete* loves art."

UTOPIAN -
Memory Phrase -

A person who believes in the perfect society
"A *utopian* believes in the perfect society called *Utopia*."

Category: Stubborn

OBSTINATE -
Memory Phrase -

Stubborn or difficult to convince (<u>Ob</u> means against)
"Stubborn B*ob* is *obstinate.*"

OBDURATE -
Memory Phrase

Stubbornly wicked or hardhearted (<u>Ob</u> means against)
"Stubborn B*ob* is *Obdurate.*"

DOGMATIC -
Memory Phrase

Stubbornly adhering to false beliefs
"*Dogs* are stubborn." Also Dogma, Dogmatism, Dogged

DOCTRINAIRE -
Memory Phrase -

Stubbornly adhering to a belief or action (doctrine = belief)
"Stubborn *Doc* was *doctrinaire.*"

INTRACTABLE -
Memory Phrase -

Unyielding or unchangeable (<u>Tract</u> means movement)
"The *intractable tractor* wouldn't move."

INCORRIGIBLE -
Memory Phrase -

Not capable of being reformed
"*Incorrigible Cory* couldn't be reformed."

Category: Submission

OBSEQUIOUS -   Willing to serve someone
Memory Phrase -   "Remember that *sequi* means to follow as in sequence"

SERVILE -   Willing to serve
Memory Phrase -   "The servant was *servile.*"

GROVELING -   Begging for favor
Memory Phrase;   "The *groveling* groupie begged for an autograph."

SYCOPHANT -   Ridiculous flatterer
Memory Phrase: "*Syd Sycophant* constantly flatters."

ACQUIESCE -   To give in peacefully, without contest (*qui* means *quiet*)
Memory Phrase: "Remember that *qui* means quiet."

CAJOLE -   To coax gently
Memory Phrase: "The cat was *cajoled* into the *cage.*"

Category: Showy or Arrogant

HAUGHTY -
Memory Phrase:
Arrogant
"Some people considered 'hotties' are often *haughty*."

BOMBASTIC -
Memory Phrase:
Pompous (speech or writing)
"The *bombastic* speech hit the audience like a *bomb*."

SWAGGER -
Memory Phrase:
A way of walking/talking that indicates confidence.
"You don't *stagger* when you *swagger*."

GRANDILOQUENT -
Memory Phrase:
Pompous speech (grand means large, loq means speech)
"Remember *grand* and *loq*."

FLAMBOYANT -
Memory Phrase:
Highly decorated, colorful or rich
"The flamboyant *boy* was colorfully dressed."

POMPOSITY -
Memory Phrase:
Extreme arrogance
"Pompous Pam was arrogant."

Category: Entertain

REGALE -	To Entertain
Memory Phrase:	"*Gale* entertained her guests with her singing."
DIVERT / DIVERSION	To entertain / A form of entertainment
Memory Phrase:	"Everyone needs a form of diversion."
REVELRY -	Wild excessive partying
Memory Phrase:	"Before his wedding, he had a night of revelry."
RACONTEUR -	A story teller
Memory Phrase:	"The raconteur recounted great stories of old France."
JOLLITY -	Great happiness or merrymaking
Memory Phrase:	"Jollity Sounds like *Jolly*."
VIRTUOSO -	An expert in an art (such as music)
Memory Phrase:	"Violet is a virtuoso on the violin."

Category: Praise

EXTOL -   To Praise
Memory Phrase: "Extol the virtues of the victor."

KUDOS -   Praise
Memory Phrase: "Kudos candy bars deserve praise."

LAUD / LAUDABLE -   Praise / Praiseworthy
Memory Phrase: "Remember app*laud*."

EULOGY -   A Praising speech in tribute to someone who has dies
Memory Phrase: "*Eu* means good, *log* means speech."

REVERE -   To praise or look up to.
Memory Phrase: "Paul Revere is a much revered hero."

CELEBRATE -   To praise
Memory Phrase: "We celebrate holidays to praise our heros."

Category: Good Speech/Good Sound
(often with loc, loq, phon, son)

ELOQUENCE -
Memory Phrase:

Good speech
"Loq means speak."

EUPHONY -
Memory Phrase:

A pleasing sound
"*Eu* means good, *phon* means sound."

LOQUACIOUS -
Memory Phrase:

Talkative
"*Loq* means speak."

CONSONANCE -
Memory Phrase:

Harmonious
"*Con* means with or together, *son* means sound."

ORATION -
Memory Phrase:

Speaking
"*Oration* means speaking, as in a public orator."

COLLOQUIAL -
Memory Phrase:

Common or everyday speech
"His colloquial style made his speech easy to understand."

Category: Bad Sound

DISSONANCE -   A disharmony or disagreement
Memory Phrase: "*Dis* means away, *son* means sound."

CACOPHONOUS -   Disharmonious
Memory Phrase: "*Caco* sounds bad, *phon* means sound."

RAUCOUS -   Loud and Displeasing (Ruckus is the noun -ex. to make a ruckus)
Memory Phrase: "The rowdy kids made a raucous sound."

STRIDENT -   Shrill and harsh, as in a strident voice
Memory Phrase: "Stan Strident has a shrill voice."

HECKLE -   To jeer or to voice disapproval in a disrespectful manner
Memory Phrase: "Harry Heckler hissed at the history teacher."

DISCORDANCE -   Disharmony or disagreement
Memory Phrase: "*Dis* means away, *cord* is like a musical chord."

Category: Angry Speech

TIRADE -	An abusive, sometimes violent speech or lecture
Memory Phrase:	"Ty 's tirade angered the team."
INVECTIVE -	An abusive speech
Memory Phrase:	"Victor's invective angered the team."
DIATRIBE -	A bitter and abusive criticism
Memory Phrase:	"*Di*'s diatribe angered the *tribe*."
CONTENTIOUS -	Argumentative
Memory Phrase:	"Contentious is the opposite of content."
REBUKE -	A sharp reprimand
Memory Phrase:	"Mean Luke's rebuke was no fluke."
CENSURE -	To chastise or criticize
Memory Phrase:	"His censure was so mean that it had to be censored."

Category: Prefix Re
Usually is "bad" in harder words

REBUKE	Reprimand
REBUTTAL	Counter-argument
RENEGE	Break a word, bet or promise
RECALCITRANT	Stubborn, resistant to authority
REMONSTRATE	Protest
REVILE	Denounce
REVOKE	Null or void
REPUDIATE	To reject or to refuse to honor

Category: Prefix De
Strongly Negative

DEARTH   Scarcity

DEBACLE   Disaster

DECLIVITY   Downward slope

DEBILITY   Weakness

DECRY   Criticize

DEFILE   To make dirty or impure

DEFROCK   To remove the right to practice a profession

DERELICT   Neglectful

Category: Prefix Co/Con/Com
With/Together

COLLABORATE   Work together

COMMUNION   A sharing or common experience

CONCERT   Work together

COMPREHENSIVE   Complete, all-inclusive

COHESION   Sticking together

COALESCE   To form a union or bond

CONGEAL   To form, as in Jell-O

CONVIVIAL   Lively, sociable

Category: Prefix Chron/Ante/Post/Pre/Temp
Time

CHRONOLOGY   Time list

CHRONIC   Permanent

ANACHRONISTIC   Existing in the wrong time period

ANTEBELLUM   Period of time before a war

ANTEDILUVIAN   Old fashioned (literal: before the biblical flood)

POSTHUMOUS   After death

PRELUDE   Something coming before an event

CONTEMPORANEOUS   Occurring or existing simultaneously

Category: Prefix Tract/Trans/Ab/Ad
Movement Toward and Away

INTRACTABLE	Immovable, stubborn
TRANSIENT	Passing through, having no place to stop
ABHOR	To hate
ABDICATE	To give up a position of power
ADULATION	Attraction or admiration
ADORATION	A strong liking or love
TRANSCEND	Moving beyond
TRANSLUCENT	Allowing light to pass through

Category: Prefix Mis/Mal/Ben/Eu
Good and Bad

MISANTHROPE	Hater of mankind
MISBEGOTTEN	Wrongly conceived
MALEDICTION	A curse
MALEFACTOR	A person who does harm
BENEFACTOR	A person who helps
BENEVOLENT	Kind
EULOGY	A praising speech
EUPHONIOUS	A pleasing sound

Sentence Completions

A sentence completion question consists of a sentence with one or two parts missing. It is your job to determine which of the five answers best fits the blank(s). In order to be able to do so, you must develop the ability to recognize the clues within a sentence. Often, a blank will be simply and clearly defined for you, as in the case when a blank is followed by a comma (*he was a -----man, not afraid of any challenge*). Otherwise, you'll be looking for other clues to identify a missing word. Clues may be as large as an entire sentence or as small as a single word. Two-blank questions are in some ways easier than one-blank questions, especially if you have caught on to the concept of <u>clues</u> in SAT questions. Two blanks means that there are twice as many clues that should help you eliminate twice as many answers.

The Spy

Sentence Completion Tip 1:

Read the sentence carefully. Identify the <u>Spy</u> to help you determine the general nature of the missing word(s). A Spy is a word or phrase that tells you that the missing word (words) is (are) positive, negative, different (antonyms), same (synonyms),or that they have to do with time, space, distance, etc. A Spy can even go so far as to help you <u>anticipate</u> the correct word so you can then look at the answers to find a word that is similar.

1) Find the <u>Spy</u>.
2) Determine the *nature* of the missing word. Circle it below the sentence.

A: (easy case)

He was a ---- man, taking pleasure in the suffering of others.

What is the nature of the missing word?   Positive?   Negative?   Size?   Emotion?   Place?

B: (medium case)

The ---- of the thermometer proved the ---- care with which it had been constructed.

What is the nature of the missing words? Negative? Positive? Strong? Weak? Scientific?

C: (hard case)

An allusion can be highly ----; like an evanescent thought or tepid breeze, it can trigger a remembrance of something once cherished.

What is the nature of the missing words?   Negative?   Positive?   Time?   Money?   Age?

Answers:

A: Negative ("taking pleasure in the suffering of others" is the Spy).
B: Positive/Positive ("care" is the Spy).
C: Positive ("cherished" is the most obvious Spy – though tepid breeze is a positive Spy phrase as well).

Sentence Completion Exercise Two:

Circle <u>The Spy</u>, then mark the correct answer.

<u>Example:</u>

> Biswell's relentless attack was the climax of the ---- heaped on sculptures that today seem astonishingly ----
>
> (A) criticism..imaginary   (B) ridicule..refined   (C) aggression..amateurish
> (D) indifference..sacrilegious (E) acclaim..praiseworthy
>
> Spy: attack
> Answer: (B) ridicule..refined
>
> Explanation: "attack" could only be the climax of "criticism" or "ridicule," thus eliminating the other three answers C, D and E.   The words "that today seem" indicate that the second blank will be opposite to the first, which eliminates A.

1: (easy case)

Food can be ---- factor in family life, bringing us closer in times of turmoil and in times of joy.

(A) an additive (B) a conflicting   (C) a unifying   (D) a residual   (E) an inconsistent

2: (medium case)

Sympathetic from the start, the board of executives listened to the employee's grievances with ---- and then began to ---- the conditions that caused them.

(A) trepidation..exacerbate   (B) remorse..enunciate

(C) disdain..improve (D) concern..rectify   (E) interest..restate

3: (hard case)

Although Mr. Morrison's music is by far the most interesting and imaginative I have seen, it nonetheless contains some ---- features.

(A) candid   (B) absorbing   (C) discerning   (D) tangible   (E) dubious

Answers: 1. (C) "bringing us closer" is The Spy   2. (D) "Sympathetic" is The Spy   3. (E). "Although," "interesting,"
"imaginative," and "nonetheless" are The Spies.   Note: though discerning sounds negative - dis prefix - it actually
means perceptive.

Oil and Vinegar (Don't Mix)

Sentence Completion Tip 2:

Certain words match up exactly. Others cannot reasonably exist side by side. Plug in answer choices and identify those pairs of words that cannot exist side by side. Eliminate those answers.

Sentence Completion Exercise Three:

The following chart contains words from actual SAT Sentence Completions. Eliminate the choices that form unlikely pairs and match those that form likely pairs.

phrase	(A)	(B)	(C)	(D)	(E)
Example: 1. ---- thirst	unsolvable *(not likely)*	envious *(not likely)*	unquenchable *(very likely)*	inconsequential *(not likely)*	awesome *(not likely)*
2. ---- the wounds	heal	soothe	avenge	magnify	shatter
3. ---- and neglect	happiness	praise	treason	falsehood	abuse
4. ---- and ----	aloof..honest	wary..sincere	sly..shy	open.. honest	candid..hidden
5. ---- game, full of surprises	creative	magical	unpredictable	omnipotent	stalwart
6. ---- origin, they were all from China	predictable	ancient	common	wild	obscure
7. ---- the ravages	imperil	perpetuate	belittle	forestall	protect
8. gradually ---- thouqh seldom ----	ostracized.. published	approached.. accosted	accepted.. applauded	copied.. imitated	idolized.. glorified

Answers: 1. (A) "thirst" and "unquenchable" naturally go together
2. (A) Best choice. Weaker case for soothe. You soothe pain, not wounds.
3. (E) A,B make no sense. C,D are not nearly as plausible as E.
4. (D) "...and..." indicates that the two words are similar. Note: Candid means honest, not hidden.
5. (C) Clear choice, because something unpredictable is "full of surprises."
6. (C) "all from China" indicates a common origin. Note: Not all things from China are ancient!
7. (D) "Ravages" means damage. You don't imperil, perpetuate, belittle (speak down to) or protect ravages.
8. (C) A,B don't really make sense. Word pairs D and E are synonyms, which can't work.

Sentence Completion Tip 3:

Expanding your search for the Spy to a larger portion of the sentence can often lead you to the correct answer. This is often very effective with sentences that are long and/or confusing.

Sentence Completion Tip 4:

In a two blank question, you can often find Spies for each part of the sentence. One Spy can help you eliminate some answer choices, then another Spy can help you find the answer from among the remaining choices.

Sentence Completion Exercise Four:

Find the right word to complete the phrase:

Note: The two boxed rows with the arrows represent a single, two blank question that has been divided into two parts. The first row is the first part of a question and the second row is the second part **of the same question.** Using the first row ("Like most. . ."), eliminate three answer choices. This will also eliminate three answer choices below, in the row that begins ("represents a..."), since they are part of the same answer. Next, use the second row to choose between the two remaining answer choices.

Phrase	(A)	(B)	(C)	(D)	(E)
1. Example: a certain---**in his acceptance** of . . .	defiance *(opposites)*	apathy *(possible)*	**complacency** *(this fits very well)*	orderliness *(no relation)*	deceptiveness *(opposites)*
2. ---in which nothing was any longer considered sacred.	heresy	fantasy	preservation	hoax	relic
3. Like most political ----, this newly coined phrase . . . 4. represents a---of groups whose parts do not fit together seamlessly.	labels ⇕ mosaic	parties ⇕ discord	entities ⇕ violation	symbols ⇕ symmetry	slogans ⇕ milestone
5. the---link between cigarette smoking and lung disease ...	unusual	causal	meager	questionable	residual

Answers: 1. (C) Acceptance and complacency go together.
2. (A) Heresy (not hearsay) is the opposite of "sacred."
3. (A) or (E) Has to be a "phrase," which rules out B, C, and D.
4. (A) With only A and E to choose from, "traits do not always seem linked" points to A, rather than E.
5. (B) Did you get fooled? B says causal (as in causes), not casual.

51

A Sheep in Wolf's Clothing

They may look mean and nasty, but appearances aren't everything. The College Board knows that those nasty looking words will scare lots of people away. Underneath the surface, though, these cantankerous-appearing words are as tame as sheep - and are often the correct answer! Why does the College Board do this? Simple. These words scare people away. Because they scare people away, few people actually answer the question correctly, thus making it a hard question and deserving of its place at or near the end of a sentence completion section or anywhere in a hard reading passage.

Sentence Completion Tip 5:

In all blocks of Sentence Completion questions, the last few questions are rated as difficult. When selecting an answer to these questions, give greater consideration to SAT-type words (unusual or difficult words that often contain prefixes and/or word roots).

Sentence Completion Exercise Five:

Determine a possible or likely answer based on the fact that these are answers to questions found at the end of question blocks (you may select more than one answer per row).

	(A)	(B)	(C)	(D)	(E)
Example: Answer Set	construing..intolerance	distorting..spirituality	inflate..methodology	**debunking..credulity**	reproving..rationalism
Answer Set 1	chimerical	indispensable	historical	cynical	inharmonious
Answer Set 2	tyrant..eliminate	traitor..avoid	dilettante..broach	firebrand..evade	coward..delegate
Answer Set 3	deterrent	moratorium	vindication	harbinger	scapegoat
Answer Set 4	decorous	iconoclastic	intense	precise	ingenious

Answers: 1. (A) Reason: Best "SAT word."
2. (C) or (D) Reason: Both contain good "SAT words."
3. (D) There is a somewhat weaker case for B.
4. (B) Reason: Great "SAT word."

Sentence Completion Review Page

Sentence Completion Tip 1:

Read the sentence carefully. Identify the <u>Spy</u> to help you determine the general nature of the missing word(s). A Spy is a word or phrase that tells you that the missing word (words) is (are) positive, negative, different (antonyms), same (synonyms),or do they have to do with time, space, distance, etc. A Spy can even go so far as to help you <u>anticipate</u> the correct word so you can then look at the answers to find a word that is similar.

Sentence Completion Tip 2:

Certain words match up exactly. Others cannot reasonably exist side by side. Plug in answer choices and identify those pairs of words that cannot exist side by side. Eliminate those answers.

Sentence Completion Tip 3:

Expanding your search for the Spy to a larger portion of the sentence can often lead you to the correct answer. This is often very effective with sentences that are long and/or confusing.

Sentence Completion Tip 4:

In a two blank question, you can often find Spies for each part of the sentence. One Spy can help you eliminate some answer choices, then another Spy can help you find the answer from among the remaining choices.

Sentence Completion Tip 5:

In all blocks of Sentence Completion questions, the last few questions are rated as difficult. When selecting an answer to these questions, give greater consideration to SAT-type words (unusual or difficult words that often contain prefixes and/or word roots).

Long Reading Passages

If you just look at the numbers, you'll realize that if you hope to have high scores on SAT Reading, you'll need solid strategies for SAT reading skills. Below is a breakdown of the average number of questions per passage you will encounter.

Overall, spread across three sections, you'll have three single reading passages and a set of paired, related passages than run between 450 and 850 words each. There are a total of 40 questions total relating to the passages, broken down exactly or approximately as you see in the above illustration.

Some of these reading passages and questions are difficult, while others are easy or medium. In general, the shortest passage tends to be the easiest, while the longer ones tend to be harder. But whether the passage is easy or hard, long or short, the best method is the Zigzag Method. ™

Other Methods are Not Nearly as Effective

There are many theories as to how one should approach long critical reading passages. Some companies and individuals recommend that you read the passage quickly, like a "once over." Others, including the College Board, recommend a thorough first reading, followed by regular returns to the passage to answer specific questions. At least one company recommends you read only parts of the passage, while still others recommend that you read the questions first. None of these approaches makes sense. Even worse, none of these approaches takes advantage of a very important factor: the order in which information is presented is similar to the order of the questions. Based on that fact alone, either reading the questions or the entire passage first diminishes one's ability to do one's job correctly – that is if one really understands what that job is!

Mission: Ridiculous

Memorize these sets of numbers

	A	B	C	D	E	F	G
Set 1	242	568	215	996	342	8811	1723
Set 2	1876	675	1477	1707	365	954	112
Set 3	3359	145	877	196	5452	7413	6647
Set 4	123	468	557	8474	1386	8256	9917

No way, dude!

Having to memorize any of the rows above is, at best, a difficult exercise.

Now, let's imagine that these numbers are, instead, facts. Could you memorize seven facts about a reading passage well enough to answer multiple choice questions about all seven?

Probably not. In order to answer these questions, you'd need to return to the passage – exactly what the College Board and others recommend!

That is crazy, and an incredible waste of your valuable and limited time!

The Wrong Ways

Here is a list of the four basic reading strategies of other companies and individuals, followed by short explanations about why each is not the most effective strategy:

1) Read all the questions first.

   With 6 – 13 questions per passage, there is simply TMI – <u>too much information</u>. This can cause confusion that can actually make you do worse than if you had not read the questions.

2) Read the passage carefully first.

   Again, <u>TMI</u>. Reading a whole passage actually makes it harder to answer any one specific question.

3) Read the passage quickly, answer the general questions, and then go back over the parts of the passage to answer specific questions.

   Reading a passage quickly does not allow you to effectively answer general questions. Only a careful reading does that. Furthermore, if you are going to go back and read parts of the passage again – why read it in the first place?

4) Answer line-specific questions one at a time, by starting to read a few lines before and reading through a few lines after the referenced lines. Then, answer general questions at the end.

   Skipping parts of the passage is confusing. It also makes it much harder to answer the general questions.

The Zigzag Method [TM]

The Zigzag Method is a system of reading and answering questions while you read the passage. The name "zigzag" refers to the pattern you follow in reading and answering questions. The big advantage that the Zigzag Method gives you is that it allows you to answer one question at a time, reading only the part of the passage that pertains to that question. You can do this because the questions are asked and answered in order.

With other methods. . . .

You get one large daunting task:

"Learn the passage then answer all the questions."

With the Zigzag Method. . . .

You get one small task:

"Read one part of the passage then answer one question."

Followed by another small task:

"Read the next part of the passage and then answer the next question. "

After you have answered all the specific questions, you can go back to answer the general questions.

But there is more to the Zigzag Method. In fact, there are a series of steps that go by the acronym SQR^4

The Zigzag Method ^{TM}
$\underline{S\ Q\ R^4}$

(1) SURVEY – A BRIEF INITIAL SCAN OF THE PASSAGE

Read the italicized opening statement, topic sentences, words that stand out and the last five lines of the passage. Try to identify a flow, a tone and a point of view. Is the content consistent, or does it change? Survey is a brief 30–45 second overview that serves the same function as consulting a roadmap before traveling by car to a distant destination.

---

(2) QUESTION

Read the first question. If it is specific, find <u>The Spy</u> – the part of the questions that identifies <u>where</u> in the passage that question will be answered (could be line numbers or an easily identifiable word, phrase or concept). If it is a general question, circle it in your test booklet, skip it, and then come back to it after you have answered the specific questions.

(3) READ

Read up to <u>and through</u> the part of the passage in which the identified subject is found. Continue reading until you have enough information to answer the question, or until the identified subject changes (could be the end of a paragraph). Do not read only the lines referenced in the question. Continue to the end of the specific identified subject of discussion.

(4) RETURN

Return to the answers. Look for the choice that best answers the question, focusing only on the information contained in the section you just read to answer each question.

(5) RESIST

Have a negative attitude! Resist each answer, looking for its <u>Double Agent</u> - the part of the answer that makes it wrong. When you eliminate, put a slash through the letter only! In case you eliminate all choices, you need to be able to return to the answers, this time being less critical! The <u>Double Agent</u> can be a specific word, type of word or phrase. If you cannot find the <u>Double Agent</u> move on to the next answer, repeating the process until all four wrong answers have been eliminated. If two or more answers remain, compare one against each other until you determine the most likely answer. Remember, look for what is wrong – not what is right. By approaching SAT Reading answers this way, correct answers become more clearly visible.

---

(6) REPEAT

Repeat steps 2-5, until all specific questions have been answered. With each successive portion of the passage you read, start out where you left off. Do not skip any part of the passages.

For example: If you have read to the end of line 14 to answer question 1, then start reading at sentence 15 to answer question 2.

Finally, return to the circled, general questions in order to answer them.

Survey

Think of a Survey the same way you would think of looking at a road map before driving cross country. You would look at the major highways, but not the side roads. You would try to get a general sense of the time involved. In short, you would try to gain an overview of the drive. That way, each detail of the drive would have a context; you'd perceive it as part of a larger whole, rather than an isolated stretch of road.

<u>That is what a Survey is – an overview.</u>

It is important not to spend too much time on a Survey: 45 seconds at the most. In that 45 seconds, you should learn as much about the passage as you can.

The following passage is an excerpt from a book about proper speech. In it, the author makes a point about the use of language.

Read the introduction

It is very easy to learn how to speak and write correctly, as for all purposes of ordinary conversation and communication; only about 2,000 different words are required. The mastery of just twenty hundred words, the knowing where to place them, will make us not masters of the English language, but masters of correct speaking and writing. Small number, you will say, compared with what is in the dictionary! But nobody ever uses all the words in the dictionary or could use them did he live to be the age of Methuselah, and there is no necessity for using them.

Survey = 30-45 seconds only!

Read the first sentence of each paragraph

There are upwards of 200,000 words in the recent editions of the large dictionaries, but the one-hundredth part of this number will suffice for all your wants. Of course you may think not, and you may not be content to call things by their common names; you may be ambitious to show superiority over others and display your learning or, rather, your pedantry and lack of learning. For instance, you may not want to call a spade a spade. You may prefer to call it a spatulous device for abrading the surface of the soil. Better, however, to stick to the old familiar, simple name that your grandfather called it. It has stood the test of time, and old friends are always good friends.

Read the last five lines to see if they summarize or if they change the focus

To use a big word or a foreign word when a small one and a familiar one will answer the same purpose, is a sign of ignorance. Great scholars and writers and polite speakers use simple words. Of course the parrot, being a creature without reason, cannot comprehend; it can simply repeat what is said to it, and as it utters phrases and sentences of profanity with as much facility as those of virtue, so by like analogy, when we do not understand the grammar of the language, we may be making egregious blunders while thinking we are speaking with the utmost accuracy.

Specific and General Questions

Critical Reading Tip 2:
Learn to recognize the difference between general questions and specific questions. Specific questions may be answered as you read the section in which the answer occurs. General questions require an overall understanding of the passage. General questions should be circled and saved for last.

Critical Reading Exercise One:

Circle "S" if the question is specific. Circle "G" if the question is general.

A: According to the author..   S   G
B: The author's tone is best described as..   S   G
C: The author's main purpose is..   S   G
D: In lines 22-27, which point about tigers is being emphasized...................   S   G
E: With which statement would the author of passage one most likely agree....   S   G
F: In the third paragraph, the discussion of education focuses on..................   S   G
G: The author probably quotes Robert Frost in order to ....   S   G

Answers:

A: According to the author . . .
Specific: "According to" indicates that the answer is specifically stated, rather than generally implied.

B: The author's tone is best described as . . .
General: "tone" is usually implied through descriptions that are found throughout the passage.

C: The author's main purpose is . . .
General: The purpose of a passage becomes clear only after one reads the entire passage.

D: In lines 22-27, which point about tigers is being emphasized . . .
Specific: The line reference and the words "which point about tigers" make it clear that this question has a specific answer.

E: With which statement would the author of passage one most likely agree . . .
General: Answering this question requires you to make an inference based on your understanding of the entire passage.

F: In the third paragraph, the discussion of education focuses on . . .
Specific: This question asks you to determine the area examined within a specific part of a passage.

G: The author probably quotes Robert Frost in order to . . .
General: You are required to guess the author's reason for selecting a passage to include in his or her work.

Finding the Spy

It is sometimes easy to find The Spy - the word or words that you'll focus on when reading for the answer. In the case of line reference questions (ex. *"In lines 22-25"*) it is easy because you are already given the location of the relevant information. The same is true of vocabulary-in-context questions (ex. *In line 34, rapacious speculation means . . .*). The Spy is important because it helps you determine the location of the answer. Therefore, being able to identify the Spy is significant in solving critical reading questions. The Spy could be a concept, a word, a name or an idea. The Spy is anything in a question that helps you determine where that question is answered.

Critical Reading Exercise Two:

Find the Spy

1. The author believes that the main difference between quasars and galaxies is that quasars . . .

2. Kreiger's theory departs from accepted scientific norms in its treatment of . . .

3. When she left home for good, the author gained a sense of . . .

4. In what way was the third experiment different . . .

Answers:

1. difference between quasars and galaxies

2. Kreiger's theory

3. left home for good

4. third experiment different

The Double Agent

Yes, he is nefarious and nasty, deceptive and deadly. The College Board thought they had found a malleable mercenary to do their dirty work. But once identified, their spy became a Double Agent secretly, covertly, stealthfully, working for you!

A Double Agent is a word or phrase, contained within an SAT Reading answer that makes the answer wrong. Being a Double Agent, it was often overlooked as it lurked inconspicuously next to dark conjunctions or in verbs' shadows. But, you can identify this Double Agent and use it to eliminate incorrect answers. The only tool you need – is a keen and skeptical eye. Look at every word within an answer to make sure each is correct. If even one word is wrong – the answer is wrong.

Example 1:

Question:

<u>Which statement best describes the passage</u>:

One possible answer:
c) a catalog of historical events that have led to the current view of Catholicism.

- Was the passage a <u>catalog</u> (a list)?
- Did it talk about <u>historical events</u>?
- Did those events lead to the <u>current view</u> of Catholicism?

(Three possible Double Agents)

Example 2:

Question:

<u>The primary purpose of the passage is to...</u>

One possible answer:
a) explain a traditional idea in terms of newly established examples.

Was it a <u>traditional</u> idea
Were the examples <u>newly</u> established?

(Two possible Double Agents)

Be Suspicious of Strong and Absolute Words

Critical Reading Tip 5:

Correct answers are usually mild and open to interpretation, (using words such as can be, might be, and could be) rather than harsh and absolute (using words such as always, every and never). Stronger words or absolute words are other examples of Double Agents.

Critical Reading Exercise Three:

Can you find the absolute words or words that are too strong (Double Agents) in these phrases?

1. All species of animals have an internal clock
2. They were always considered to be outsiders
3. The scientist employed every known method
4. He never saw the consequences of his action
5. No species had become extinct prior to this
6. No one knew of Banneker's work prior to
7. They are exactly the same (indistinguishable)
8. His methods were the best available
9. The worst of all possible worlds
10. He was the only politician ever accused
11. They cannot exist outside the human body
12. Ridicule the parents' lack of
13. Condemn the policies of those.
14. Demand a change
15. Deliberately ignores the facts

Note: These words do not always indicate that an answer is wrong, and in fact there are some exceptions. For example, two absolute words can effectively cancel each other out.

"Cannot always," is a good example of this. This is actually good wording.

So use this strategy wisely, not absolutely!

Answers: 1) all, 2) always, 3) every, 4) never, 5) no (species), 6) no one, 7) exactly, 8) best, 9) worst, 10) only, 11) cannot, 12) ridicule, 13) condemn, 14) demand, 15) deliberately.

Identify as many incorrect answers as possible based on the strategy that every word must be correct, that strong or absolute words are usually incorrect and that correct answers are usually mild, soft, general or nonspecific in nature.

1. If it can be assumed that Morison has been accurately represented in passage two, what would the authors of passage one conclude about his work?

(A) It does not record humanity's progress toward a better society.
(B) It deals with the same topics as their work does.
(C) Its approach to history can be described as Whiggish.
(D) It is not sufficiently researched.
(E) It represents the best of its kind in historical writing.

_____

2. Guy's attitude during the months following his injury was one of. . . .

(A) spiritual renewal
(B) patient optimism
(C) open defiance
(D) bitter regret
(E) morbid contemplation

_____

3. The author suggests that drawing conclusions about an ancient ecological community from any assemblage of fossils is a complex task primarily because.
. . .

(A) only the most durable parts of the animals remain, and these give a misleading sense of the animal's hardiness
(B) the animals were not necessarily associated with each other while alive
(C) animals that lived underground will become fossilized
(D) so much information is lost that all conjectures are pointless
(E) different scientists will interpret the information differently

Answers: 1 (C). Reason – "can be" 2 (B). Reason - C,D,E are too strong. A is not an attitude 3(B). Reason – "were not necessarily."

Critical Reading Exercise Five:

Each of the following SAT critical reading questions is followed by the portion of the passage in which it is answered.   Circle the word or words in each of the four incorrect answers that is not supported by the passage. Then select the remaining (correct) answer.

1. Flooding is mentioned in line 50 as an example of

From Passage: These investigations show that we cannot assume that animals lived in the environments in which they were fossilized; (50) those living in upland areas may have washed down into the lowland areas during flooding, for example.

(A) one of the causes of extinction
(B) a natural event that increases the possibility that animal remains will become fossilized
(C) a process that might provide misleading evidence about where an animal lived
(D) a particular danger to burrowing animals
(E) a danger to those who study fossils

2. The author focuses on the feet and limbs of animals living in swampy terrain in order to:

From Passage: One quick way to calculate how well a dinosaur would cope with swampy terrain is to calculate the area of its hind foot available to support the downward thrust of its hind leg. Thus if you want to move speedily over mud or soft earth, you need to use devices such as snowshoes which expand the foot's area.

(A) indicate ways in which swamp-dwelling dinosaurs could have reached food plants
(B) suggest that dinosaurs were too heavy to walk on swampy ground
(C) estimate how frequently swamp-dwelling dinosaurs would have entered deep water
(D) judge how effectively certain dinosaurs could have moved in such terrain
(E) reconstruct why certain dinosaurs might have failed to swim effectively during a flood

3. <u>To the author, Marianne Moore's poetry was</u>

From Passage: I had not known poetry could be like that: her treatment of topics as diverse as glaciers and marriage struck me, as it still does, as a miracle of language and construction. Why had no one ever written about these things in this clear and dazzling way before?

(A) reminiscent of poems by other great poets
(B) subtly satirical
(C) too scholarly for most readers
(D) inspiring and well crafted
(E) difficult but rewarding

4. <u>If modern cities are so terrible, why, according to Passage 2, do people continue to live in them?</u>

From Passage: Those who do not reject modern cities are conditioned not to see, hear, feel, smell, or sense them as they are. The greatest obstacle to seemly cities has become our low expectations, a direct result of our having become habituated to the present environment and our incapacity to conceive of any better alternative.

(A) Cities provide more varied employment opportunities than other places
(B) People see cities for what they are and actually enjoy living in such places
(C) The cultural opportunities available in cities are more varied than those in rural areas
(D) Despite their drawbacks, cities have a quality of life that makes them desirable as places to live
(E) As a consequence of living in cities, people have become unable to think objectively about their environment

Answers: 1. (C)   2. (D)   3. (D)   4. (E)

Long Reading Passages Review Page

Critical Reading Tip 1: Learn to perform a brief Survey of a reading passage. In 30-45 seconds only, look at the italicized introduction, the first sentence of each paragraph, the last five lines of the passage and anything else that stands out. Try to gain a basic understanding of the subject, bias, and flow of the passage. Does the perspective change at the end? Is the language subjective or objective?

Critical Reading Tip 2: Learn to recognize the difference between general questions and specific questions. Specific questions may be answered as you read the section in which the answer occurs. General questions require an overall understanding of the passage. General questions should be circled and saved for last.

Critical Reading Tip 3: Learn to identify The Spy – the part of the question that helps you identify the location of the answer within the passage.

Critical Reading Tip 4: In order for a critical reading answer to be correct, each and every word in the answer must be correct. Therefore, you can eliminate many answers that contain a word or words that are not accurate. A word, phrase or concept that is not correct is called a <u>Double Agent.</u> Find the <u>Double Agent</u> and use it to eliminate as many answers as possible.

Critical Reading Tip 5: Correct answers are usually mild and open to interpretation, (using words such as can be, might be, and could be) rather than harsh and absolute (using words such as always, every and never). Stronger words or absolute words are other examples of Double Agents

Critical Reading Tip 6: A specific critical reading answer will be supported within one clearly defined place in the passage. Read only the part of the passage that pertains to the question you are answering, then answer that question. Eliminate answers that appear to be irrelevant or incorrect.

Short Reading Passages

Each SAT will have two individual short passages and one set of paired passages.

There will be a total of 8 questions

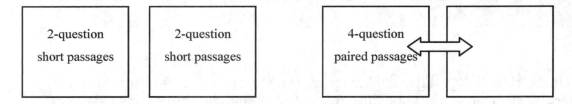

Similarities and Differences to Long Passages

Since these passage are only around 100 words long and have so few questions, the Zigzag Method should not be used.

However, identifying The Spy and the Double Agent are very important. Also many of the strategies for Long Reading Passage apply to Short Reading Passages as well. These are reprinted below.

Short Reading Passage Tip One: Preread the two questions to each short passage, or the four questions to the set of paired short passages. Pay attention to, and underline, key words within the questions. These key words are <u>Spies</u> that can help you indentify where an answer is found within a short passage.

Short Reading Passage Tip Two: In order for a critical reading answer to be correct, each and every word in the answer must be correct. Therefore, you can eliminate many answers that contain a word or words that are not accurate. A word, phrase or concept that is not correct is called a <u>Double Agent.</u> Find the <u>Double Agent</u> and use it to eliminate as many answers as possible.

Short Reading Passage Tip Three: Correct answers are usually mild and open to interpretation, (using words such as can be, might be, and could be) rather than harsh and absolute (using words such as always, every and never). Stronger words or absolute words are other examples of Double Agents.

Sample Short Passages

A complete man is so uncommon that when he appears he is looked upon with suspicion, as if there must be something wrong about him. If a man is content to deal vigorously with affairs, and leave art, religion, and science to the enjoyment or refreshment or enlightenment of others, he is accepted as strong, sound and wise; but let him add to practical sagacity a love of poetry and some skill in the practice of it; let him be not only honest and trustworthy, but genuinely religious; let him be not only keenly observant and exact in his estimate of trade influences and movements, but devoted to the study of some science, and there goes abroad the impression that he is superficial.

The hideous noise always considered necessary in those ships when calling the watch, roused me effectively at midnight, "eight bells." I hurried on deck, fully aware that no leisurely ten minutes would be allowed here. "Lay aft
5   the watch," saluted me as I emerged into the keen strong air, quickening my pace according to where the mate stood waiting to muster his men. As soon as he saw me, he said, "Can you steer?" in a mocking tone; but when I quietly answered, "Yes, sir," his look of astonishment was
10   delightful to see. He choked it down, however, and merely telling me to take the wheel, turned *forward** roaring frantically for his watch. I had no time to chuckle over what I knew was in store for this salty sailor, getting those poor greenies collected from their several holes and
15   corners, for on taking the wheel I found a machine under my hands such as I never even heard of before.

toward the front

1. The author's attitude could best be described as

    (A) discriminatory
    (B) resilient
    (C) angry
    (D) depressed
    (E) concerned

2. It may be implied that the author believes that a "complete man"

    (A) should be viewed suspiciously because there might be something wrong with him
    (B) is a myth perpetuated by science
    (C) should be superficial
    (D) may be viewed suspiciously by those who have preconceived notions about what a man should be like
    (E) should only be taken seriously if he studies science or religion

3. The sentence that begins "I had no time. . . (lines 12-16) indicates that the author

    (A) felt the same about the crew as did the sailor
    (B) respected the crew more than did the sailor
    (C) believed that the sailor could not easily gather the crew onto the deck
    (D) felt a special kinship with the sailor
    (E) thought that he could do a better job than the sailor in steering the ship

4. The author's attitude toward the sailor could best be described as
    (A) confused ambivalence
    (B) utter disdain
    (C) quiet disrespect
    (D) flagrant aggression
    (E) embittered hatred

Answers and Explanations:
1)E. The author is expressing her concern. A,B, and D make no sense, and C is too strong.
2)D. The other answers do not express the author's view.
3)C. This is clearly indicated by the phrase that begins "getting those poor greenies....".
4)C. His tone is mocking, though he does not openly disrespect the sailor.

Questions 5 and 6 are based on the following passage

A singular fatality has ruled the destiny of nearly all the
most famous of Leonardo da Vinci's works. Two of the
three most important were never completed, obstacles
having arisen during his life-time, which obliged him to
5   leave them unfinished; namely the Sforza Monument and
the Wall-painting of the Battle of Anghiari, while the
third--the picture of the Last Supper at Milan--has suffered
irremediable injury from decay and the repeated
restorations to which it was recklessly subjected during the
10   XVIIth and XVIIIth centuries. Nevertheless, no other
picture of the Renaissance has become so well known and
popular through copies of every description.

5)   In his description of the restorations of one of da
Vinci's paintings, the author's tone can best be
described as one of

A) disapproval
B) understanding
C) objectivity
D) extreme confusion
E) bitter regret

6)   In context, the author's use of the word *obliged*
(line 4) most nearly means

A) obfuscated
B) caused
C) demanded
D) promised
E) enunciated

Questions 7 and 8 are based on the following passage

The flying abilities of pterosaurs have never been fully
appreciated. Although pterosaurs have been represented
traditionally as clumsy gliders, with leathery curtain-like
wings, new evidence suggests that they were strong and
5   graceful fliers. Unlike bats' wings, those of pterosaurs
were narrow and gull-like and extended along the body
wall only to the limits of the pelvis. The bones of the
upper arm are also well developed to support flight
musculature, and are perforated at their ends by tiny
10   pores, as in birds. (These pores, called pneumatic
foramina, allow the expansion of the respiratory surface
of the lungs into the bones, to increase the animal's
ability to receive oxygen and breathe out carbon dioxide,
thus maintaining the high metabolic rate that flight
requires.) Far from being clumsy gliders, pterosaurs
must have been among the most graceful of all airborne
creatures the earth has ever witnessed.

7. The passage as a whole attempts to
    (A) distinguish the flight paths of pterosaurs from
    those of birds and bats
    (B) revisit the conventional view of the pterosaur's
    airborne ability
    (C) introduce an new strategy for studying flight
    physiology
    (D) determine the body composition required for
    flight capabilities
    (E) support the view that all winged creatures had a
    common ancestor

8. The discussion of the "pneumatic foramina" (line 11)
suggests that flying is an activity that
    (A) requires a large expenditure of energy
    (B) places great stress on the wings of flying
    creatures
    (C) is an efficient means of locomotion
    (D) involves still-obscure physiological processes
    (E) has reached a point of no return

Poetry is not like reasoning , a power to be exerted
according to the determination of the will. A person
cannot say, "I will compose poetry." The greatest poet
even cannot say it: for the mind in creation is as fading
5   coal, which some invisible influence, like an inconstant
wind, awakens to transitory brightness: this power arises
from within, like the color of a flower which fades and
changes as it is developed, and the conscious portions of
our natures are unprophetic either of its approach or its
10   departure.

9. The main point of the passage can be summarized as

(A) Once a poet's mind is committed to writing, nothing
can stop it.
(B) Poets, like flowers, have different phases through
which they pass in the course of their lifetimes.
(C) The creation of poetry occurs at unpredictable
moments
(D) One cannot write poetry for an extended period of
time without stopping for breaks
(E) Not even poets can predict how successful their poems
will be.

10. The comparison of "the mind in creation" to "a fading
coal" touched by the wind (lines 4-5) emphasizes which of
the following:
(A) The infinite variety of the intellect
(B) The inability of the mind to reason consistently
(C) The nourishment that poetry gives the mind
(D) The fleeting nature of inspiration
(E) The passionate quality of poetry

Answers and Explanations:
9)C. This is implied by the "inconsistant wind." A is just incorrect. B is a throw away answer. D and E are not supported
10)D. The fading coal is touched by the wind of inpiration, then fades. This is what D indicates. The other answers may
be true, but are not supported in the passage.

Sample Short Paired Passages

The passages below are followed by questions based on their content; questions following a pair of related passages may also be based on the relationship between the paired passages. Answer the questions on the basis of what is stated or implied in the passages and in any introductory material that may be provided.

Passage 1

There is no campaign in the history of the
world which has left such a deep impression upon
the heart of the people than that of Napolean in
Russia, Anno 1812. Of the soldiers of other wars
5 who had not come home it was reported where
they had ended on the field of honor. Of the great
majority of the 600 thousand who had crossed the
Niemen in the month of June Anno 1812, there
was recorded in the list of their regiments, in the
10 archives "Disappeared during the retreat" and
nothing else.

Passage 2

When the few who had come home, those hollow
eyed specters with their frozen hands, were asked
about these comrades who had disappeared during
the retreat, they could give no information, but they
would speak of endless, of never-heard-of
sufferings in the icy deserts of north, of the
cruelty of the Cossacks, of the atrocious acts of the
Moushiks and the peasants of Lithuania, and, worst
of all, of the infernal acts of the people of Wilna.
And it would break the heart of those who listened
to them.

11. Of the following, which best describes the relationship between the two paragraphs?
    (A) The first is more descriptive than the second
    (B) The first is subjective while the second is objective
    (C) The second is metaphoric, while the first is literal
    (D) The second is less accurate than the first
    (E) The first provides an official view, whereas the second provides the soldier's view

12. In the context of the passage, the use of the words "and nothing else" (line 10-11) implies that the author believes that
    (A) the quote "Disappeared during the Retreat" is insufficient in capturing the scope of the tragedy
    (B) hopelessly little will ever be known about the tragedy
    (C) most soldiers were unaware that the retreat had occurred
    (D) most people know only what they have read about the soldiers' retreat
    (E) nothing else needs to be known about the soldiers' retreat

13. The primary purpose of Passage 2 is to
    (A) rebuke a popular misconception
    (B) explain the purpose of an event
    (C) attack those who would justify a situation
    (D) provide a unique perspective
    (E) provide a critical response to a disparate view

14. Both passages indicate that
    (A) the soldiers suffered needlessly and excessively
    (B) the loss of life was inevitable
    (C) the impact of the battle was felt beyond the battlefield
    (D) the soldiers faced unspeakable horrors
    (E) the soldiers should be honored for their service

Answers and Explanations:
11) E. A, both are descriptive. B, the second passage is not objective (detached) C, the second passage is not metaphoric. D, not supported
12) A. This is clear from the rest of the passage in which it is indicated that soldiers killed in other battles were honored, but that these soldiers were not so honored.
13) D. A, not supported. B, "explain the purpose" is not the intention. C, a throw away answer E, no evidence of another view.
14) C. A, not supported in passage 1. B, "inevitable" is not supported. D, not supported in passage 1. E, not supported by passage

SAT Writing

Grammar Simplification
Writing the Perfect SAT Essay

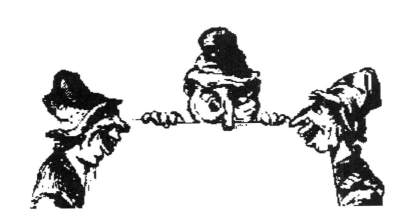

Introduction to SAT Grammar

The Definition:

Grammar (n.) The science which treats the principles of language; the study of forms of speech, and their relations to one another; the art concerned with the right use and application of the rules of a language, in speaking or writing.

(n.) The art of speaking or writing with correctness or according to established usage; speech considered with regard to the rules of a grammar.

The Interpretation

Grammar is an explanation and guide for language. In some cases it leads, setting the table for proper speech and writing. In other cases it follows, adjusting for accepted changes in speech and written and spoken language. Either way, grammar is the essence of clear communication.

The Fear

Grammar. The very word can cause hives. Fear of Grammar is prevalent and can spread fear like wildfire through fertile fields of doubt. It has no boundaries. It crosses borders of universities and school campuses as easily as locust ingest crops. It has the power to turn colleagues into rivals and students into writhing jelly. It is a chimerical metamorph whose appearance is at once transparent and opaque. It is concrete and fluid. It is still and restless. It is eternal and ephemeral. It moves methodically and erratically across time and space on outspread wings of change. It is the human genome project of language. Gaining mastery over Grammar has been the lifelong pursuit of millions, and the bane of those same millions, none of whom have ever succeeded at reining in the wild stallion. Master Grammar? You shrug and recoil. You laugh and shudder. You cower in a corner, disappearing until special relativity or microbiology or calculus BC, resurface – cute and playful puppies compared to the Grammar the Ogre. You can't see it. You can't capture it. You can't even understand it. So, then, how does one learn to master Grammar? The answer is simple: you simplify it.

The Solution:

In order to master SAT grammar, one must first:

  I) Understand the grammar of the times.
 II) Understand the bias of the entity charged with judging your performance.
III) Understand the scope of the project.

Note: A mere five concepts make up 99% of the SAT Writing section. You can learn to master each of these concepts by using the examples in this book to recognize the issues, then the practice tests to help you recognize them under test conditions.

Understanding the Grammar of the Times

If Bob Dylan was right and "*The times, they are a changing*," then grammar is changing right along side. You need look no further than the Constitution of the United States to see how dramatically grammar has changed in two and a quarter centuries. A year from now, "they" might be accepted as a singular pronoun representing an ambiguous gender case, as in:

> Your child must study hard if *they* are to succeed.

Today, the solution to this problem is the awkward "he or she," as in:

> Your child must study hard if *he or she* is to succeed.

Change is even more apparent in the case of idioms, expressions that have gained acceptance through regular usage. For example, the question of whether a place is

> in a map   or
> on a map,

seems to be changing even as this manual is being written, (*or* shall we say, as we write this manual). So, this manual represents current grammar, at least as it is defined by those who will judge your performance – the College Board.

The College Board's Preferences

The College Board is a private company with enormous power – powerful enough even to guide the very grammar we speak and write. It is judge and jury. It alone has changed curricula both across the nation and around the world. What the College Board says – goes! Don't question its authority over grammar. Rather, learn to understand it. For example, did you know that the College Board prefers that you not use *gerunds* (verbs used as nouns)? They much prefer standard form, even at the expense of requiring the word *because* to begin a sentence.

<u>Having to study for the calculus test was the hardest thing I had to do.</u>

(Correct, but not preferred)

<u>The hardest thing I had to do was to study for the calculus test.</u>

(Correct and preferred)

Understanding the Scope of the Project

There are whole books just on idioms and others on every grammatical issue you can imagine. Our goal in this program is to simplify grammar into five basic areas, then to drill those areas. These are the only five areas deemed important enough to be included in the SAT.

SAT Grammar Question Types

Identifying Sentence Errors

14 Questions on PSAT
18 Questions on SAT

Sample Question:

Many of the people <u>which</u> were <u>attending</u> the
                A   B

meeting were <u>moved</u> as they listened to story
                C

after <u>story of the</u> survivors of the plane crash.
           D

<u>No error</u>
   E

SAMPLE ANSWER A B C D E
Correct Answer: A

Grammar Tip One - Identifying Sentence Errors

There are just as many "E" (no error) answers as there are other answers. That means one out of five answers will be "no error." Don't be afraid to choose "E" if the sentence sounds right as is!

Improving Sentences

20 Questions on PSAT
25 Questions on SAT

Note: "A" = No Error.
Choice "A" repeats the original sentence. Choose "A" if the original sentence is correct.

Sample Question:

When riding a bicycle, <u>people always should be wearing a helmet and should obey</u> traffic laws.

A. people always should be wearing a helmet and should obey
B. one should always wear a helmet and obey
C. people wearing helmets and obeying
D. a helmet must be worn and you should obey
E. one must be wearing helmets and obeying

SAMPLE ANSWER A B C D E
Correct Answer: B

Reason: A and C are wrong because "a bicycle" is singular and thus requires a singular-person pronoun or noun, such as "one".
D is wrong because it does not have a proper subject after the dependent clause – "when riding a bicycle...". As it stands, answer D implies that "a helmet" is riding a bicycle.
E is wrong because "one" is wearing plural "helmets".

Grammar Tip Two – Improving Sentences:
Unlike the questions in Identifying Sentence Errors, the correct answer is among the choices. Sound out all answers to determine which one sounds best.

Improving Paragraphs

1 Passage with 5 Questions on PSAT
1 Passage with 6 Questions on SAT

The paragraphs on the SAT writing section are early drafts of essays. The questions differ from those on the SAT Reading because they focus on grammar and structural issues. Many questions address sentences or parts of sentences, which need to be rewritten in order to improve sentence structure, organization, or word choice.

Sample Passage and Question:

(1) I never thought I'd be interested in volunteer work. (2) My friends volunteered. (3) I never did. (4) Our school instituted a program to get students to volunteer. (5) They sent a list of ideas to the students. (6) I have lots of brothers and sisters. (7) I'm used to being around children. (8) When I saw the Big Brothers Big Sisters charity listed, it caught my interest. (9) Their motto is "Every kid needs a hero." (10) It wasn't easy to become a big sister. (11) You have to be eighteen. (12) You have to be interviewed and trained. (13) But, soon, my caseworker calls to tell me that I had been assigned a little sister. (14) The night before I was to meet Janie, my "little", I could hardly sleep. (15) I took the bus to her apartment. (16) We went to the park and spent a quiet day feeding the ducks and talking. (17) That night, I went to sleep knowing that I had begun to make a difference in one person's life.

Which of the following would be the best way to combine sentences 2 and 3 (reproduced below) into one?
My friends volunteered. I never did.
(A) My friends volunteered and I never did
(B) My friends volunteered, but I never did
(C) My friends volunteered, but unlike them, I never did
(D) My friends volunteered, so I, unlike them, never did
(E) My friends volunteered, while I didn't ever

Correct Answer: B

Reason: The conjunction "but" shows contrast. Answer "B" is more concise (less wordy) than "C".

Grammar Tip Three: Improving Paragraphs:
Usually four of the six questions are very easy. However, the remaining two are challenging. Pay close attention to grammatical rules when solving all these questions.

SAT Grammar is not simple.
(However, it is limited in scope)

All Grammar questions on the SAT can be placed into five categories:

I. Comparisons:

Are things similar or different (or can they be compared at all)?

II. Agreement:

Does each part of the sentence agree with each other part?

III. Verb Tense:

When do actions take place (sometimes in relation to other actions)?

IV. Diction and Idiom:

Memorizing expressions and looking out for sound-alike words.

V. Word Order and Sentence Structure:

Does the sentence make sense or does the order of some of the words or phrases make the meaning unclear or ambiguous.

The following pages contain a categorical breakdown of all five grammar categories into subcategories. Each subcategory has 10 examples to help you become familiar and to recognize the issue, then five "improving-sentences" and five "improving-paragraphs" questions for practice.

I. Comparison

A. Unequal Comparison
B. Equal Comparison
C. Logical Comparison
D. Comparative/Superlative Degrees of Comparison

I. Comparison

Mixed Examples:

Examples:
Each first sentence is incorrect. Each second sentence corrects the problem.
Compare and contrast each set.

1. Jen is the **slowest** of the **two** runners on the team.
   Jen is the **slower** of the **two** runners on the team.

2. Some people think that **Boston** is the **better** city in which to live.
   Some people think that **Boston** is the **best** city in which to live.

3. My cell phone plan is the **least** expensive of the **two** plans offered.
   My cell phone plan is the **less** expensive of the **two** plans offered.

4. Due to the nice weather, there were **less runners** in the race than anticipated.
   Due to the nice weather, there were **fewer runners** in the race than anticipated.

5. The participants in the "Survivor" reality television show were given **fewer rice** than they needed to satisfy their hunger.
   The participants in the "Survivor" reality television show were given **less rice** than they needed to satisfy their hunger.

6. There is **fewer pollution** in Los Angeles this year than there was last year.
   There is **less pollution** in Los Angeles this year than there was last year.

7. Some specialty drinks at Dunkin' Donuts have **as much calories as** cheeseburgers at McDonald's.
   Some specialty drinks at Dunkin' Donuts have **as many** calories **as** cheeseburgers at McDonald's.

8. Mike lives on the **same** block **that** Larry does.
   Mike lives on the **same** block **as** Larry.

9. G-rated movies are not **as** violent **like** R-rated movies are.
   G-rated movies are not **as** violent **as** R-rated movies.

10. Her gymnastics routine was **so** good **to** warrant a gold medal.
    Her gymnastics routine was **so** good **as** to warrant a gold medal.

I. Comparison

A. Unequal Comparisons

Fewer/Less - Amount/Number

Rule: Use the comparative word <u>fewer</u> when the subject is plural, such as people, raindrops, ears of corn, cars, lights, accidents, readers, etc. Use the comparative word <u>less</u> when the subject represents a singular unit or concept such as pollution, rain, land, interest, memory, etc. Use the term <u>amount</u> when applied to a singular concept (see above) and <u>number</u> when discussing a plural subject (see above). Note: A comparative rule also applies to the words <u>greater</u> and <u>more</u>, though improper use often sounds better than proper use, so this concept is rarely tested

Examples:
Each first sentence is incorrect. Each second sentence corrects the problem. Compare and contrast each set.

1. There were **less readers** at the library than I had expected.
   There were **fewer** readers at the library than I had expected.

2. **Greater interest** in humanity might spur a new revolution in philanthropy.
   More interest in humanity might spur a new revolution in philanthropy.

3. **Lesser** wine was consumed in those days, as is indeed apparent in the prevalent literature of the time.
   Less wine was consumed in those days, as was apparent in the prevalent literature of the time.

4. A **smaller amount of people** makes for a smoother town meeting.
   A **smaller number of people** makes for a smoother town meeting.

5. **Greater glass** is required to make a beverage container than to make a window.
   More glass is required to make a beverage container than to make a window.

6. The Olympic Stadium had, unfortunately, **less spectators** than anyone had expected.
   The Olympic Stadium had, unfortunately, **fewer spectators** than anyone had expected.

7. The mission has led to a great **amount** of new **discoveries.**
   The mission has led to a great **number** of new **discoveries.**

8. The press now prints in a day **a greater number of** discussion and declamation about the condition of the working man than was published during the entire prior decade.
   The press now prints in a day **a greater amount** of discussion and declamation about the condition of the working man than was published during the entire prior decade.

9. Willy the wildebeest could eat **over** twice his weight in food in a single week.
   Willy the wildebeest could eat **more than** twice his weight in food in a single week.

10. In Mary Shelley's <u>Frankenstein</u> the title character has **less scary qualities** than one would imagine.
    In Mary Shelley's <u>Frankenstein</u> the title character has **fewer scary qualities** than one would imagine.

I. Comparison

Unequal Comparisons

Identifying Sentence Errors

1. Five <u>people were</u> walking <u>upon the beach</u>, but <u>less than</u> three of them
           A   B   C
    <u>were involved in</u> the conversation.   <u>No error</u>
           D   E

2. As he looked out <u>over the crowd</u> that <u>had gathered</u> <u>to witness</u> the celestial
                              A   B   C
    event, he estimated <u>that over</u> two hundred people had gathered at the
                              D
    observatory.   <u>No error</u>
                              E

3. Generally an <u>exemplary</u> student, she <u>struggled with</u> the <u>most difficult</u> of the
                       A   B   C
    <u>final two parts</u> of the SAT.   <u>No error</u>
           D   E

4. The <u>slowest</u> of the two swimmers <u>nonetheless</u> managed <u>to turn</u> in a better time
              A   B   C
    in the <u>shorter</u> event .   <u>No Error</u>
                 D   E

5. Some <u>whimsically refer</u> to it as Montezuma's Revenge, but diarrhea is a <u>grave</u>
                  A   B
    medical condition that kills <u>no less than</u> 10,000 <u>otherwise healthy</u> people each
                                        C   D
    year.   <u>No error</u>
                  E

I. Comparison

Unequal Comparisons

Improving Sentences

1. Popular "rapper" Eminem originally gained <u>greater notoriety for his controversial lyrics than</u> for his musical talent.
   A. greater notoriety for his controversial lyrics than
   B. more notoriety for his controversial lyrics than
   C. his notoriety more for his controversial lyrics and not
   D. notoriety more for the lyrics, controversial though they were, than
   E. his notoriety for controversial lyrics other than

2. <u>This new and largest crop circle holds more mystery</u> than does the last one found on a Mexican farm in 1967.
   A. This new and largest crop circle holds more mystery
   B. This new and larger crop circle holds more mystery
   C. This new and largest crop circle hold more mystery
   D. The newer and largest crop circles that holds more mystery
   E. This new and the most large crop circle holds more mystery

3. Heating oil is <u>more in short supply now more than ever</u>.
   A. more in short supply now more than ever
   B. more and more in shorter and shorter supply
   C. is less and less supplied
   D. in shorter and shorter supply
   E. more shorter in supply

4. Perhaps the greatest rock and roll drummer of our era, Ginger Baker joined Eric Clapton and Jack Bruce to form Cream, a band that infused rock and roll with jazz and blues for <u>greater than a decade</u>.
   A. greater than a decade
   B. a time greater than a decade
   C. more than a decade
   D. a decade, give or take
   E. years as well as decades

5. <u>No fewer than twenty people</u> stood on the shore to wish the travelers a grand farewell.
   A. No fewer than twenty people
   B. No less than twenty people
   C. Not less than twenty people
   D. Twenty less people
   E. Not likely twenty people

I. Comparison

B. Equal Comparison

As . . . as / So . . . as / Same . . . as / Such as

Rule: Each of the first three sets of words is to be used together when two or more similar things are being compared. "Such as" helps to give examples or further explanation.

Examples:
Each first sentence is incorrect.   Each second sentence corrects the problem.
Compare and contrast each set.

1.   Apples are **as** different from oranges **than** oranges are from tennis balls.
     Apples are **as** different from oranges **as** oranges are from tennis balls.

2.   The Hamm twins are **as** talented **than** any American gymnasts of the past century.
     The Hamm twins are **as** talented **as** any American gymnasts of the past century.

3.   The Allman Brothers' "Eat a Peach" album derived its name from the fact that Duane Allman died when he crashed his motorcycle into a peach truck. Ironically, their bass player Butch Trucks died in the **same** type of accident **than** Duane's.
     The Allman Brothers'"Eat a Peach" album derived its name from the fact that Duane Allman died when he crashed his motorcycle into a peach truck. Ironically, their bass player Butch Trucks died in the **same** type of accident **as** Duane's.

4.   When his dog died, his love for animals made him want another, **so** much **as** he dreaded the thought of losing another friend.
     When his dog died, his love for animals made him want another, **as** much **as** he dreaded the thought of losing another friend.

5.   When she opened her present, she was **so pleased such that** she forgot to thank he guest.
     When she opened her present, she was **so pleased that** she forgot to thank her guest.

6.   Run **so fast as** you can, so you can get away from your oppressors.
     Run **as fast as** you can, so you can get away from your oppressors.

7.   Her behavior was exemplary **as** to warrant an increase in her allowance.
     Her behavior was **so** exemplary **as** to warrant an increase in her allowance.

8.   When she arrived at school, Rachael was surprised to find that Holly was wearing the **same** outfit **than** she!
     When she arrived at school, Rachael was surprised to find that Holly was wearing the **same** outfit **as** she!

9.   Daniel Boone was said to be **as strong than** a mighty oak tree.
     Daniel Boone was said to be **as strong as** a mighty oak tree.

10. Many problems **as** those we face today, were also faced by ancient man in prehistoric days.
     Many problems **such as** those we face today, were also faced by ancient man in prehistoric days.

I. Comparison

Equal Comparison

Identifying Sentence Errors

1. I <u>agreed with</u> the statement, <u>and said</u> so again <u>as directly as</u> I could, with the same
      A   B   C
   purpose <u>from</u> before. <u>No error</u>
          D   E

2. "Wise" and "smart" <u>are</u> <u>as different</u> from each other <u>than</u> carrots <u>and</u>
                           A   B   C   D
   celery. <u>No error</u>
          E

3. The King demanded <u>to have</u> his wife, Anne, delivered up <u>to be tried</u> in
                        A   B
   the same court and in the <u>same</u> way <u>as</u> any other murderer. <u>No error</u>
                            C   D   E

4. He shivered <u>as</u> violently <u>than</u> if he <u>were caught</u> in a soaking rain storm <u>without a coat</u>.
                A   B   C   D
   <u>No error</u>
     E

5. <u>All this time</u> I was <u>working at</u> Murdstone's in the same common way, with the same common
       A   B
   companions, and with the same sense of unmerited <u>degradation as</u> <u>like</u> always. <u>No error</u>
                                                        C   D   E

I. Comparison

Equal Comparison

Improving Sentences

1. Despite the dire and frightening diagnosis, it seems I'm doing <u>as better than ever</u>.
A. as better than ever
B. more better than ever
C. better than ever
D. most better than ever
E. as well than ever

2. If you would be <u>so good so as</u> to read to them, it would be a kindness indeed!
A. so good so as
B. so good enough
C. as good so as
D. so good as
E. just so good enough so as

3. Our ancestors were not by any means <u>as much aware as we are</u> of the importance of great general rules.
A. as much aware as we are
B. as aware as we are
C. as much aware such as we are
D. so full of awareness as we are
E. equally as much aware as we are

4. It was, therefore, by no means unusual to see in high office, at the same time, men who avowedly differed from one another <u>as widely as Pulteney differed than Walpole</u>, or Fox from Pitt.
A. as widely as ever Pulteney differed than Walpole
B. as widely as Pulteney differed than Walpole
C. as widely as Pulteney differed from Walpole
D. so widely so Pulteney differed than Walpole
E. more widely as ever Pulteney differed more than Walpole

5. Johnson declared that a tavern chair was the throne of human felicity; and Shenstone gently complained that no private roof, however friendly, gave the wanderer <u>so warmest a welcome</u> as that which was to be found at an inn.
A. so warmest a welcome
B. so warm as a welcome
C. so warmer a welcome
D. so warm a welcome
E. such warm a welcome

I. Comparison

C. Logical Comparison

Rule: In standard English, comparisons should be logical and complete. Make sure both parts of the comparison are equal and parallel. Ask yourself what is being compared to what and make sure the comparison makes grammatical sense! Note: In common speech, we often accept illogical comparison, since we understand what is being compared and do not care to correct one another. In written English, strict rules of comparison apply.

Examples
Each first sentence is incorrect.   Each second sentence corrects the problem. Compare and contrast each set.

1. **Jake's SAT scores** were higher than **all the other kids** in his class.
   Jake's SAT scores were higher than **those of** all the other kids in his class.

2. **Playing lacrosse,** unlike **some other sports,** requires great speed and strength.
   Playing lacrosse, unlike **playing some other sports,** requires great speed and strength.

3. **America's military budget** is much larger than **Costa Rica.**
   America's military budget is much larger than **that of Costa Rica.**

4. Some people believe that **living** in outer space would be much better than **here on Earth** because there would be no problem of overpopulation.
   Some people believe that **living** in outer space would be much better than **living** here on Earth because there would be no problem of overpopulation.

5. My grandfather thinks that people who talk on cell phones are annoying because **these people** talk louder than **regular phones,** but I think he is wrong.
   My grandfather thinks that people who talk on cell phones are annoying because **these people** talk louder than **the people who use regular phones,** but I think he is wrong.

6. **Going to summer school** is not fun, but it is better than **TV at home.**

   Going to summer school is not fun, but it is better than **watching TV at home.**

7. The *Harry Potter* **series of books** arguably has been more influential in motivating children to read than has **reading previous children's classics.**
   The *Harry Potter* **series of books** arguably has been more influential in motivating children to read than have **previous children's classics.**

8. It is better **to back up** one's computer files rather than **hoping and praying** that nothing will go wrong with the computer.
   It is better **to back up** one's computer files rather than **to hope and pray** that nothing will go wrong with the computer.

9. In the novel *The Color Purple,* by Alice Walker, Celie ultimately is influenced more by **Shug's passion for life** than by **her father** who mistreated her.
   In the novel *The Color Purple,* by Alice Walker, Celie ultimately is influenced more by **Shug's passion for life** than by **her father's mistreatment of her.**

10. **A large choir with 200 members has** a greater capacity to fill a large hall **than smaller choirs.**
    A large choir with 200 members has a greater capacity to fill a large hall than **do smaller choirs.**

I. Comparison

Logical Comparison

Identifying Sentence Errors

1. Unitarian Universalist churches, which are <u>the result of</u> the unification of the Unitarian
                                                  A
   and Universalist denominations, often <u>openly</u> accept people with alternative life styles,
                                            B
   which alone makes them <u>more liberal</u> than most <u>churches</u>. <u>No error</u>
                             C   D   E

2. The Big Dig construction project, which <u>has been</u> a lengthy and often <u>cumbersome</u>
                                              A   B
   undertaking, <u>is costing</u> the state more money than <u>paying for</u> all the state's public schools.
                   C   D
   <u>No error</u>
      E

3. The winters <u>in New England</u>, especially <u>the northernmost states</u>, <u>last longer than</u> any
                  A   B   C
   other season and often are <u>bitterly</u> cold. <u>No error</u>
                                 D   E

4. <u>Because</u> of the economic <u>recession</u>, teenagers are having <u>more difficulty</u> finding
      A   B   C
   summer jobs <u>than in</u> prosperous times. <u>No error</u>
                  D   E

5. <u>Censoring profanity</u> on television is arguably more important <u>than radio</u> because
      A   B
   young children, who need to be <u>protected</u> from hearing swear words, are more likely to
                                     C
   watch television <u>than to listen to radio</u>. <u>No error</u>
                       D   E

91

I. Comparison

Logical Comparison

Improving Sentences

1. <u>Writing letters by hand, as opposed to the computer,</u> is not as popular today as it was just ten years ago.
A. Writing letters by hand, as opposed to the computer,
B. Writing letters by hand, as opposed to using the computer,
C. By writing letters by hand, as opposed to using the computer,
D. Writing a letter by hand, as opposed to the computer,
E. A letter written by hand, as opposed to the computer,

2. Taking Advanced Placement courses in high school may have a greater benefit for students who want to finish college in less than four years than <u>finishing in more than 4 years.</u>
A. finishing in more than 4 years.
B. for those who don't.
C. those who don't.
D. for those finishing in much more time than that.
E. those not taking the courses at all.

3. <u>Hip-hop music, like jazz music, is an example of a cultural innovation which initially was developed</u> within African-American communities and then spread throughout American society.
A. Hip-hop music, like jazz music, is an example of a cultural innovation which initially was developed
B. Being like jazz music, hip-hop music is an example of a cultural innovation which initially was developed
C. Hip-hop music, like jazz music, are examples of cultural innovations which initially were developed
D. Hip-hop music is like jazz music as an example of a cultural innovation which initially was developed
E. Hip-hop music, more than is jazz music, is an example of a cultural innovation which initially was developed

4. The popular book *The Da Vinci Code*, by Dan Brown, <u>contains more twists and turns than reading most other mystery books.</u>
A. contains more twists and turns than reading most other mystery books.
B. is containing more twists and turns than reading most other mystery books.
C. contains more twists and turns than do most other mystery books.
D. contains more twists and turns than is found in most other mystery books.
E. contained more twists and turns than does most other mystery books.

5. In 1991, people protested against the Gulf War, but the media coverage of these protests <u>was not as extensive as the people who supported the war.</u>
A. was not as extensive as the people who supported the war.
B. were not as extensive as the people who supported the war.
C. was not as extensive as those who supported the war.
D. was not as extensive as the coverage of the people who supported the war.
E. were not as extensive as the coverage of the people who supported the war.

I. Comparison

Logical Comparison

Mastery Exercise

How might one improve the following sentences?

1. I enjoy the pizza at Pizzeria Regina much more than at Santarpio's.

2. Our teenage club members contribute fewer hours than your club.

3. The results of the research done in 2004 were better received than 2003.

4. Woodward's quiet influence and spirited energy encouraged as much quality and teamwork as Johnson and his brash verbal flogging.

5. Can you even compare Starbuck's coffee to Dunkin Donuts?

I. Comparison

D. Comparatives and Superlative Degrees of Comparison

> Rule: The comparative degree of an adjective – often identified by an <u>er ending</u> - is used to compare two things. The superlative degree of an adjective - often identified by an <u>est ending</u> - is used to compare more than two things. Note: A number can merely be implied, rather than stated. For example: "He was the fastest player on the team." Is correct even though no specific number of teammates is given.

Examples:
Each first sentence is incorrect. Each second sentence corrects the problem. Compare and contrast each set.

1. She was the **youngest** of the **two** daughters of an affectionate, indulgent father.
   She was the **younger** of the **two** daughters of an affectionate, indulgent father.

2. Of the **three** brothers, he was the **younger**.
   Of the **three** brothers, he was the **youngest**.

3. John is the **worse** swimmer on the **team**.
   John is the **worst** swimmer on the **team**.

4. **No more superior** prankster **than** John exists anywhere.
   No better prankster **than** John exists anywhere.

5. She was the **taller and fairer** of the **three** maidens, according to the popular fairy tale.
   She was the **tallest and fairest** of the **three** maidens, according to the popular fairy tale.

6. British adventurers who visited Asia found the **more** splendid empire that existed anywhere in the world at that time.
   British adventurers who visited Asia found the **most** splendid empire that existed anywhere in the world at that time.

7. He was the **less** apprehensive of the **climbers**, since he had the most rock-climbing experience.
   He was the **least** apprehensive of the **climbers** since he had the most rock-climbing experience.

8. Frankly how you feel about me is the **lesser** of my **concerns** (assumes there are more than two concerns).
   Frankly how you feel about me is the **least** of my **concerns** (assumes there are more than two concerns).

9. One might be surprised and disappointed to learn that the biggest companies often hire the **less** qualified **teachers**.
   One might be surprised and disappointed to learn that the biggest companies often hire the **least** qualified **teachers**.

10. Without a doubt, John Hannah, former lineman for the Patriots, was the **stronger man** I have ever seen!
    Without a doubt, John Hannah, former lineman for the Patriots, was the **strongest man** I have ever seen!

I. Comparison

Comparatives and Superlatives

Identifying Sentence Errors

1. Jim's pet Slim is the <u>largest</u>, <u>heaviest</u>, <u>and definitely</u> the <u>most awkwardest</u> frog in Swamp
                          A   B   C   D
County. <u>No error</u>
        E

2. It is said that The Mississippi River is <u>older than</u> the hills, <u>longer than</u> a railroad track,
                                        A   B
   <u>more enticing</u> than an invitation, and a <u>more good</u> listener than your best friend.
       C   D
   <u>No error</u>
     E

3. The <u>politest</u> man at the party <u>sat upon</u> the highest stool at the end of the <u>longest</u> table in
     A   B   C
the <u>more exquisite</u> ballroom in the hotel. <u>No error</u>
      D   E

4. One purpose of the spine, that <u>most basic</u> part of the <u>anatomy</u>, is to act as a spring bending
                                 A   B
in <u>any</u> direction at the <u>most slight movement</u>. <u>No error</u>
   C   D   E

5. Bingley had never met with <u>more pleasanter</u> or <u>more accommodating people</u> in his life;
                            A   B
everybody had been <u>most kind</u> and <u>quite attentive</u> to him. <u>No error</u>
                  C   D   E

I. Comparison

Comparatives and Superlatives

Improving Sentences

1. <u>No less</u> than one hundred and fifty of the principal noblemen and gentlemen on the Lancaster side were declared traitors.
   A. No less
   B. Not less
   C. Not a smaller number
   D. No fewer
   E. Few fewer

2. The actor had cultivated his skill in mimicry <u>to the most high degree</u>.
   A. to the most high degree
   B. to a high degree
   C. to the highest degree
   D. highly, to a degree
   E. the most to a high degree

3. Climbing a great mountain, we must walk correctly, as nature intended and <u>in the fullest accordance with her laws</u>.
   A. in the fullest accordance with her laws
   B. in fuller accordance with her laws
   C. full accordance with her laws
   D. in the most highly full accordance with her laws
   E. fully in high accordance with her laws

4. People often malign and make fun of one of the <u>most complex and important</u> parts of the human body - the foot.
   A. most complex and important
   B. most complex and more important
   C. seemingly complexer and more important
   D. complex and most important
   E. complexer and importanter

5. Though my history teacher is severe and exacting, they say Mr. Battle is <u>even severe and more exacting</u>.
   A. even severe and more exacting
   B. even more severe and exacting
   C. severer and more exacting
   D. more severer and exacting
   E. both severer and exacting

I. Comparison

Assorted Comparisons Questions

Identifying Sentence Errors

1. Lillian is from the Dominican Republic <u>where</u> she was the <u>more</u> prestigious
   A   B   C
   pediatrician in the country <u>and came to the aid of</u> thousands of children. <u>No error</u>
                          D   E

2. Sarah, <u>who</u> is Danish by heritage, traveled to Denmark <u>with the hope of</u> meeting her future
         A   B
   husband because she thought there <u>would be a greater number of</u> available single men there
                                    C
   <u>than there were</u> in her home town of Indianapolis. <u>No error</u>
        D   E

3. Franklin collects <u>less</u> antiques <u>than does</u> his brother John <u>who</u> collects clocks,
                   A   B   C
   children's toys, rocking chairs and <u>many other items</u>. <u>No error</u>
                              D   E

4. On the whole, the students from the Boston public schools <u>have not scored</u>
                                                  A
   <u>as well</u> on the MCAS tests as the students from the Boston suburban schools, but some
     B   C
   individual students <u>from both types of schools</u> have done very well. <u>No error</u>
                      D   E

5. Kristin is <u>the weakest</u> of the two finalists in the tennis tournament, <u>which will be</u>
                 A   B
   <u>televised nationally</u>, and she has the added disadvantage of <u>having recently sprained</u> her
       C   D
   ankle. <u>No error</u>
         E

I. Comparison

Assorted Comparisons Questions

Improving Sentences

1. <u>Administrators do not realize that these programs such as in the arts of music, theater and dance, offer to their students educational value, and so they are cutting them out of the budgets.</u>

A. Administrators do not realize that these programs such as in the arts of music, theater and dance, offer to their students educational value, and so they are cutting them out of the budgets.
B. Arts programs such as music, theater, and dance are being cut from public school budgets because many administrators do not realize the educational value that these programs offer to their students.
C. Arts programs such as music, theater, and dance are being cut from public school budgets because many administrators do not realize the educational value that these programs offers to its students.
D. Such arts programs like music, theater, and dance are being cut from public school budgets, because many administrators do not realize the educational value that these programs offer to their students.
E. It is the educational value of the arts programs in the public schools such as music, theater, and dance which are not appreciated by the administrators, and so they are cutting them from their budgets.

2. Driving to work during rush hour can take just as long <u>than biking</u> because on a bike, one can take the back roads and avoid traffic.
A. than biking
B. than to bike
C. as if you bike
D. as biking
E. as it does when biking

3. Despite the fact that Al Gore had <u>the most</u> popular votes in the 2000 presidential election, he did not win the presidency.
A. the most
B. the most number of
C. the more greater number of
D. many more
E. more of the

4. These paintings are <u>the worse</u> pieces of art I have ever seen!
A. the worse
B. the worst
C. the worser
D. worse than the
E. the most bad

5. Most young children do not have <u>as great an attention span as do most adults.</u>
A. as great an attention span as do most adults.
B. a great attention span whereas do most adults.
C. an attention span like most adults do.
D. paying attention like most adults.
E. compared to adults, as great an attention span.

II. Agreement
All parts of a sentence must agree in terms of
gender, number, structure and form

A. Noun/pronoun
B. Singular/plural
C. Parallelism
D. Subject pronoun/object pronoun
E. Unclear/incorrect pronouns
F. Adverb-to-verb/adjective-to-noun
G. Pronoun noun/verb
H. Subject/verb

II. Agreement

A. Noun/Pronoun Agreement

Rule: A pronoun must agree with its antecedent in number, person, and gender.

Examples:
Each first sentence is incorrect.   Each second sentence corrects the problem.
Compare and contrast each set.

1. The police officers' **union** is threatening to picket the Democratic National Convention because **they** have not gotten the pay and benefits they feel they deserve.
    The police officers' **union** is threatening to picket the Democratic National Convention because **its members have** not gotten the pay and benefits they feel they deserve.

2. There is often a correlation between **the government's** taking the country into war and **their** raising of taxes.
    There is often a correlation between the **government's** taking the country into war and **its** raising of taxes.

3. Bill likes to spend time with John, but **he** is not **his** best friend.
    Bill likes to spend time with John, but **John** is not **Bill's** best friend.

4. The management **team** laid off some of **their** best employees.
    The management **team** laid off some of **its** best employees.

5. A reality television **show** does not have the high quality acting of fictional dramas, but **they** can still be entertaining.
    A reality television **show** does not have the high quality acting of fictional dramas, but **it** can still be entertaining.

6. **The program** consists of after-school activities, sports teams, and music classes, and consequently, **they** attract many children.
    The **program** consists of after-school activities, sports teams, and music classes, and consequently, **it attracts** many children.

7. **Casinos** are designed so that overall **it** wins money, while overall the players lose money.
    Casinos are designed so that overall **they win** money while overall the players lose money.

8. **Greta** takes care of **her little sister,** but **she** doesn't like it.
    Greta takes care of **her little sister,** but **her little sister** doesn't like it.

9. **An "alternative" medical practice** like massage, acupuncture or chiropractic is more likely to be covered by insurance companies today than **they** were ten years ago.
    An "alternative" medical practice like massage, acupuncture or chiropractic is more likely to be covered by insurance companies today than **it** was ten years ago.

10. The official Costa Rican currency is *colones,* but **they** accept dollars in most establishments.
    The official Costa Rican currency is the *colones,* but **most establishments accept dollars.**

It vs. They

100

II. Agreement

Noun/Pronoun Agreement

Identifying Sentence Errors

1. <u>They that</u> <u>run away</u> from fights <u>should not</u> <u>necessarily be</u> considered cowards.   <u>No error</u>
    ___A___   B   C   D   E

2. Members of the committee disagreed <u>with itself</u> about the key <u>issues</u>, and as a result, of the
                                              A   B
    <u>several</u> motions on the table, <u>none</u> was passed.   <u>No error</u>
       C   D   E

3. Neither Tom nor Dick <u>will pitch</u> for the team <u>or any</u> of <u>its</u> farm teams unless
                                A   B   C
    he improves.   <u>No error</u>
       D   E

4. The <u>foaming</u> waves <u>dashed over</u> the islands' cliffs, and the <u>bleak</u> winds blew over <u>its</u>
         A   B   C   D
    forests.   <u>No error</u>
               E

5. <u>Some</u> of the tall ships have landed: <u>one</u> of them has <u>their sails</u> flying <u>at half-mast</u>.
      A   B   C   D
    <u>No error</u>
      E

II. Agreement

Noun/Pronoun Agreement

Improving Sentences

1. Shane, <u>whom most people believed</u> would challenge Fletcher, was generally calm and self-possessed.
   A. whom most people believed
   B. who most people would believe
   C. whom most of them believed
   D. who most people believed
   E. whom, most people believed

2. My mother always takes James to the store, <u>but today we are going alone</u>.
   A. but today we are going alone
   B. but today they are going alone
   C. but today she is going alone
   D. but today alone she will go
   E. alone is how she will go today

3. <u>The movie theatre was too dark for Cara, so they carefully walked out to find their friend</u>.
   A. The movie theatre was too dark for Cara, so they carefully walked out to find their friend.
   B. The movie theatre was too dark for Cara, so she carefully walked out to find their friend.
   C. The movie theatre was too dark for Cara, so they carefully walked out to find her friend.
   D. The movie theatre was too dark for Cara, so she carefully walked out to find her friend.
   E. The movie theatre was too dark for Cara, so carefully was the way she walked out to find her friend.

4. My principal requested a meeting with my teacher and me; <u>little did he know what I was about to tell him</u>.
   A. little did he know what I was about to tell him
   B. little did my teacher know what I was about to tell him
   C. little did my teacher know what I was about to tell the principal
   D. little did my principal know what he would be told by I
   E. little did he know that which I was to tell him

5. Any man who chases tornadoes should take out a good insurance policy <u>on their truck</u>.
   A. on their truck
   B. on its truck
   C. on his truck
   D. on his or her truck
   E. on they're truck

II. Agreement

B. Singular/Plural Agreement

Rule: Connecting parts of sentences must agree in terms of their being singular or plural. Note: These questions appear frequently on the SAT Writing section.

Examples:

Each first sentence is incorrect. Each second sentence corrects the problem. Compare and contrast each set.

1. **Neither** Marlena nor Joan scored as high as **they** would have liked on the SAT test.
   Neither Marlena nor Joan scored as high as **she** would have liked on the SAT test.

2. In the film *Rabbit-Proof Fence,* the **governmental bureau** claims that **they are** helping the Aboriginal children by removing them from their families.
   In the film *Rabbit-Proof Fence,* the **governmental bureau** claims that **it is** helping the Aboriginal children by removing them from their families.

3. **The group** of students who were in wheelchairs waiting for the bus **were** not the group that the bus driver was expecting.
   The group of students who were in wheelchairs and were waiting for the bus **was** not the group that the bus driver was expecting.

4. **Either** my older brother or my older sister **are** going to help me with my algebra homework.
   Either my older brother or my older sister **is** going to help me with my algebra homework.

5. **Each** member of my family has **their** own version of who **they** think is in charge.
   Each member of my family has **his/her** own version of who **he/she thinks** is in charge.

6. In "Star Trek IV: The Voyage Home" the mutinous **crew** of the Starship Enterprise **decide** to return home to face possible court marshal.
   In "Star Trek IV: The Voyage Home" the mutinous **crew** of the Starship Enterprise **decides** to return home to face possible court marshal.

7. The **group** of people on the shore **were** clearly visible through the San Francisco fog.
   The **group** of people on the shore **was** clearly visible through the San Francisco fog.

8. My **book**, which is full of games and puzzles, **are** useful on rainy days and long car trips.
   My **book**, which is full of games and puzzles, **is** useful on rainy days and long car trips.

9. **Both** Carlos and Jose **has** attended every single class meeting.
   Both Carlos and Jose **have** attended every single class meeting.

10. My **collection** of CD's is so extensive that **they include** almost every musical genre in existence.
    My **collection** of CD's is so extensive that **it includes** almost every musical genre in existence.

II. Agreement

Singular/Plural Agreement

Identifying Sentence Errors

1. The list of people <u>whom</u> Jan <u>plans to invite</u> to her birthday party <u>are posted</u> <u>on</u> her refrigerator
                   A   B   C   D
    door. <u>No error</u>
           E

2. Jordan <u>knows</u> <u>that</u> either an essay question or a set of multiple choice questions <u>are</u>
            A   B   C
    <u>going to be</u> on the exam. <u>No error</u>
       D   E

3. Neither of the two swimmers <u>are</u> likely <u>to qualify</u> for the state competition because neither
                                   A   B
    <u>has</u> <u>had</u> consistent access to a pool. <u>No error</u>
     C   D   E

4. My Dad's drawer <u>full of power tools</u> <u>are</u> locked, <u>and only</u> my Dad <u>has</u> the key. <u>No error</u>
                           A   B   C   D   E

5. In 2003, some members of the United States government <u>did not like</u> France's
                                                     A
    <u>position on</u> the Iraq war, <u>so it</u> <u>encouraged</u> American consumers to call their favorite fast
       B   C   D
    food "freedom fries" instead of "French fries." <u>No Error</u>
                                                 E

II. Agreement

Singular/Plural Agreement

Improving Sentences

1. From a cat's point of view, a fly is neither a nuisance nor a threat; <u>they are just a snack.</u>
A. they are just a snack.
B. they are just some snacks.
C. it is just some snacks.
D. it is just a snack.
E. they will be just a snack.

2. <u>Maya's two-year-old daughter Ella loves to swing from my arms as if it were a trapeze</u>.
A. Maya's two-year-old daughter Ella loves to swing from my arms as if it were a trapeze
B. Maya's two-year-old daughter Ella loves to swing from my arms as if a trapeze
C. Swinging from my arms is Maya's two-year old daughter, as if it was a trapeze
D. My arms, as if a trapeze were swung on by Ella, Maya's two-year old daughter
E. Maya's two-year-old daughter Ella loves to swing from my arms as if they were a trapeze

3. New York University and Wesleyan University both have great dance departments, <u>but each program differ from the other: NYU focuses on building outstanding technique, while Wesleyan focuses on encouraging creative choreography.</u>
A. but each program differ from the other: NYU focuses on building outstanding technique, while Wesleyan focuses on encouraging creative choreography.
B. but each program differ from the other: NYU focus on building outstanding technique, while Wesleyan focus on encouraging creative choreography.
C. but each program differs from the other: NYU focuses on building outstanding technique, while Wesleyan focuses on encouraging creative choreography.

D. but each program differ from the other: NYU focuses on building outstanding technique, while Wesleyan encourages creative choreography.
E. but both programs differ from the other: NYU focuses on building outstanding technique, while Wesleyan focuses on encouraging creative choreography.

4. A newspaper article described a Hindu man, <u>accompanied by a group of his disciples who walk beside him, who literally rolls through the streets of India as a form of spiritual practice.</u>
A. accompanied by a group of his disciples who walk beside him, who literally rolls through the streets of India as a form of spiritual practice.
B. being accompanied by a group of his disciples walking beside him, who literally rolled through the streets of India as a form of spiritual practice.
C. who literally rolls through the streets of India as a form of spiritual practice, accompanied by a group of his disciples, each of whom walks beside him.
D. that was accompanied by a group of his disciples who walk beside him, who literally rolls through the streets of India as a form of spiritual practice.
E. and a group of his disciples and while the man literally rolls through the streets of India as a form of spiritual practice, the disciples walk.

5. <u>In Western music, each of the notes in a major scale follows a uniform pattern of intervals,</u> so that the distance between the first and fifth notes of a C scale is the same as the distance between the first and fifth notes of a G scale.
A. In Western music, each of the notes in a major scale follows a uniform pattern of intervals,
B. In Western music, each of the notes in a major scale follow a uniform pattern of intervals,
C. In Western music, the notes in each major scale follows a uniform pattern of intervals,
D. In Western music, every major scale has notes and the notes are following a uniform pattern of intervals,
E. In Western music, the notes in each major scale can be found to be following a uniform pattern of intervals,

II. Agreement

C. Parallelism

> Rule: Parallelism may be thought of as balancing nouns with nouns, verbs with verbs and prepositions with prepositions. When balancing verbs, nouns and prepositions, each should be offered in the same form.

Examples:

Each first sentence is incorrect. Each second sentence corrects the problem. Compare and contrast each set.

1. When confronted with a bad idea, it's usually better to respond to it rather than **hiding** or **to run away**.
   When confronted with a bad idea, it's usually better to respond to it rather than **hiding** or **running away**.
   ("Running" is parallel to "hiding", not "to respond".)

2. **Clyde's puppy's tricks** are much more clever than **Danny's puppy.**
   Clyde's puppy's tricks are much more clever than **those of Danny's puppy**.

3. Theologians might argue that **to give** is more blessed than **receiving**.
   Theologians might argue that **to give** is more blessed than **to receive**.

4. Modern authors work hard to express themselves, **hold** the reader's attention, and **they try to be** entertaining as well.
   Modern authors work hard to express themselves, **hold** the reader's attention, and **entertain** as well.

5. There's **no** place like home, **no** time like the present, and there **isn't any path** but forward.
   There's **no** place like home, **no** time like the present, and **no path** but forward.

6. What wouldn't the traveler have given to have **a house** within her view, **for warm, dry clothing**, and **a bottle of water.**
   What wouldn't the traveler have given to have **a house** within her view, **warm, dry clothing**, and **a bottle of water.**

7. In show business, a 'triple-threat' performer is someone who excels at **songs**, **acting**, and **dancing**.
   In show business, a 'triple-threat' performer is someone who excels at **singing**, **acting**, and **dancing**.

8. Our conscience must reform itself through **the strengthening of our reason**, not through **our appetites getting weaker**.
   Our conscience must reform itself through **the strengthening of our reason**, not through **the weakening of our appetites**.

9. Socrates may not even have been aware of his condemnation, **being** seventy and **suffered** from a dimming of his fabulous mind.
   Socrates may not even have been aware of his condemnation, **being** seventy, and **suffering** from a dimming of his fabulous mind.

10. If it is true that dogs love to run, to play **and barking**, then my dogs must be happy for they have been known to bark all night!
    If it is true that dogs love to run, to play and **to bark**, then my dogs must be happy, for they have been known to bark all night!

II. Agreement

Parallelism

Identifying Sentence Errors

1. New England Patriots coach Bill Belichick <u>is known as</u> a hard worker, <u>a disciplinarian</u> and
                                                     A   B
<u>to never</u> <u>take</u> a vacation.   <u>No error</u>
   C   D   E

2. <u>Truly</u>, madly, <u>and deep</u> is how one <u>should love</u>, <u>they say</u>. <u>No error</u>
  A   B   C   D   E

3. The grassy fields, the <u>blooming flowers</u>, the <u>trees on the hillside</u>, <u>all</u> <u>appear</u> as characters in
                            A   B   C   D
nature's splendid autobiography.   <u>No error</u>
                           E

4. This Presidential campaign <u>is going to be mean</u> and <u>hard-fought</u>
                                  A   B
<u>through the streets</u> of Boston and <u>beyond</u>.   <u>No error</u>
      C   D   E

5. The great saint gave money <u>to the poor</u> in <u>their hovels</u>, clothing <u>to unwed mothers</u>, and
                               A   B   C
<u>gave presents</u> to the elderly. <u>No error</u>
   D   E

II. Agreement

Parallelism

Improving Sentences

1. The engineers have designed a computerized robot that <u>cooks, cleans, and will shovel the snow.</u>
    A. cooks, cleans, and will shovel the snow.
    B. cooks, cleans, and is shoveling the show.
    C. cooks, cleans, and shovels the snow.
    D. cooks, will clean, and will shovel the snow.
    E. will cook, will clean, and shovels the snow.

2. Most audience members do not understand the necessary combination of actors' <u>cooperating, stamina, and talent.</u>
    A. cooperating, stamina, and talent.
    B. cooperating, having stamina, and being talented.
    C. cooperating, being strong and talented.
    D. cooperation, stamina, and talent.
    E. cooperation, being strong and talented.

3. All race car drivers should strive to drive <u>carefully, fearlessly, and speedy.</u>
    A. carefully, fearlessly, and speedy.
    B. carefully, fearlessly, and speedily.
    C. with care, without fear, and quickly.
    D. with care, speed, and no fear.
    E. carefully, fearlessly, and with speed.

4. The seasoned architect not only designs the most utilitarian spaces, <u>the aesthetic aspects are of great concern to him also.</u>
    A. the aesthetic aspects are of great concern to him also.
    B. but he concerns himself with the aesthetic aspects also.
    C. although he concerns himself with the aesthetic aspects also.
    D. the aesthetic aspects concern him.
    E. along with the aesthetic aspects.

5. The graduating seniors sat quietly listening to the speakers and <u>will wait for their diplomas.</u>
    A. will wait for their diplomas.
    B. wait for their diplomas.
    C. will have waited for their diplomas.
    D. had waited for their diplomas.
    E. waiting for their diplomas.

II. Agreement

D. Subject/Object Pronoun

Rule: When using a pronoun in place of a noun, make sure you use an object pronoun to replace an object of a sentence and a subject pronoun to replace a subject.

Examples:

Each first sentence is incorrect. Each second sentence corrects the problem. Compare and contrast each set.

1.　　The people **who** I was working with last summer were extremely friendly.
　　　The people **with whom I was working** last summer were extremely friendly.

2.　　Jason and me are the best players on the team.
　　　Jason **and I** are the best players on the team.

3.　　While my mother and my younger sister spend hours shopping in the mall, **my older sister and me** sit in the car and talk.
　　　While my mother and my younger sister spend hours shopping in the mall, **my older sister and I** sit in the car and talk.

4.　　If it were up to **myself**, I would sleep until 10:00am every morning.
　　　If it were up **to me**, I would sleep until 10:00am every morning.

5.　　Finding summer jobs was not easy **for Kristen and I**.
　　　Finding summer jobs was not easy **for Kristen and me**.

6.　　My neighbor, **who** I have never even had lunch with, just invited me on a weeklong cruise!
　　　My neighbor, **with whom I have never even had lunch**, just invited me on a weeklong cruise!

7.　　For **Jim and I**, the best aspect of the course was the chance to meet with local politicians.
　　　For Jim and me, the best aspect of the course was the chance to meet with local politicians.

8.　　Who is at the door? It is **me.**
　　　Who is at the door? It is **I.**

9.　　It was necessary for **Sheila and I** to take the SSAT test to get into a private high school.
　　　It was necessary **for Sheila and me** to take the SSAT test to get into a private high school.

10.　　The man behind the counter in the video store looked rather suspicious; it was **him** who overcharged me.
　　　The man behind the counter in the video store looked rather suspicious; **it was he** who overcharged me.

II. Agreement

Subject/Object Pronoun

Identifying Sentence Errors

1. <u>In the novel</u> *The Secret Life of Bees*, Rosaleen and Lily, <u>who</u> have run away from <u>their</u>
    A   B   C
home town, are taken into the care of May, June, and August, <u>who they become friends with</u>
                                                                                         D
<u>No Error</u>
  E

2. <u>Both</u> <u>Ashley and me</u> are running for class president even though <u>we</u> are best friends
   A   B   C
and don't usually like to <u>compete with </u>each other. <u>No error</u>
                           D   E

3. That's the one! It was <u>her</u>, the girl with the red hair and the Gucci accessories,
                              A
<u>who</u> tried to grab my backpack when <u>I was</u> <u>exiting</u> the subway station. <u>No Error</u>
 B   C   D   E

4. For <u>Mario and me,</u> <u>there is nothing</u> <u>more exciting than</u> designing new computer
          A   B   C
software and then marketing it and trying to find companies <u>that</u> are interested in
                                                                 D
buying it. <u>No Error</u>
           E

5. Most small children have difficulty sitting still for long periods of time, but my five-

year old cousin Rosalie, <u>who I have a close bond with</u>, can sit <u>with me</u> without moving
                                     A   B
or fidgeting, <u>even if she</u> does not have any toys <u>with which to play</u>. <u>No error</u>
                 C   D   E

II. Agreement

Subject/Object Pronoun

Improving Sentences

1. <u>To attend baseball games, hiking, and shopping are</u> just a few of the many activities in which my mother and I like to engage.
A. To attend baseball games, hiking, and shopping are
B. Attending baseball games, hiking, and shopping they are
C. Attending baseball games, hiking, and shopping are
D. Attending baseball games, hiking, and shopping is
E. Attending baseball games, to go hiking and shopping are

2. As soon as <u>Lucas and I</u> got involved in Karate, we noticed that we became better friends.
A. Lucas and I
B. Lucas and me
C. Lucas and myself
D. I and Lucas
E. him, meaning Lucas, and I

3. <u>If Bruce Springsteen and me were to have our photograph taken together,</u> I would be thrilled but very nervous, since I am a very big fan.
A. If Bruce Springsteen and me were to have our photograph taken together,
B. If Bruce Springsteen and I were to have our photograph taken together,
C. If a photographer was taking a picture of Bruce Springsteen and me,
D. Being with Bruce Springsteen in a photograph taken together,
E. If I and Bruce Springsteen were to have our photograph taken together,

4. <u>Who are you going to the store with?</u>
A. Who are you going to the store with?
B. You are going to the store with who?
C. You are going to the store along with who?
D. With whom are you going to the store?
E.   The store, with whom are you going?

5. <u>Him and I recently went</u> to WWF Slamdown, but viewed in person, the wrestling appeared amazingly fake and contrived.
A. Him and I recently went
B. Recently, I along with he
C. Recently we went, him and I,
D. He and I recently went
E. Me and him recently went

II. Agreement

E. Unclear and Incorrect Pronouns

Rule: A pronoun is used to replace a noun. When a pronoun is used, a) it must be the correct pronoun and b) it must be clear and obvious which noun it is replacing.

Examples:

Each first sentence is incorrect. Each second sentence corrects the problem.
Compare and contrast each set.

1.   Ed gave the present to **Tim and I**, entrusting us to take it to the party for him.
    Ed gave the present to **Tim and me**, entrusting us to take it to the party for him.

2.   In the newspaper, **they** say that even moderate use of cell phones can cause brain tumors.
    In the newspaper, **an article states** that even moderate use of cell phones can cause brain tumors.

3.   Tom gave the briefcase to Dan, who gave it to Harry, and then **he** ran away.
    Tom gave the briefcase to Dan, who gave it to Harry, and then **Tom** ran away.

4.   When the explorers came to the islands of the Phoenicians, the world knew nothing about **them**.
    When the explorers came to the islands of the Phoenicians, the world knew nothing about **those islands**.

5.   The man smoking the cigarette said that **they** can give him headaches.
    The man smoking the cigarette said that **cigarettes** can give him headaches.

6.   The kids' backpacks are all packed, and **they** are ready to go.
    The kids' backpacks are all packed, and **the kids** are ready to go.

7.   In Alaska, one mountain range after another is very impressive. **It** is quite breathtaking!
    In Alaska, one mountain range after another is very impressive. **Alaska** is quite breathtaking!

8.   Gymnasts depend on great coaching and great choreography. Without **it**, success is virtually impossible.
    Gymnasts depend on great coaching and great choreography. Without **them**, success is virtually impossible.

9.   We took the clothes out of the trunks, then gave **them** a thorough cleaning.
    We took the clothes out of the trunks, then gave **the trunks** a thorough cleaning.

10.   In Australia **they** have interesting animals of all kinds.
    Australia has interesting animals of all kinds.

II. Agreement

Unclear and Incorrect Pronouns

Identifying Sentence Errors

1. <u>Those men</u> with goatees, the short <u>ones</u>, seem more normal to <u>us</u> than do the <u>others</u>.
   A   B   C   D
   <u>No error</u>
   E

2. Unfortunately, many former rock-and-roll <u>icons</u> find themselves rehashing old, tired classics
                                             A

   <u>in front of</u> fans <u>who</u> would much rather hear them play <u>some of their</u> newer favorites.
        B   C   D
   <u>No error</u>
   E

3. Martina <u>regularly</u> brings flavored coffee <u>to her mother</u> <u>in the morning,</u> <u>though she</u> prefers
               A   B   C   D

   decaf. <u>No error</u>
              E

4. Why play sports or go jogging when, <u>according to</u> many doctors, <u>you can be</u> <u>perfectly healthy</u>
                                             A   B   C

   <u>without it</u>. <u>No error</u>
        D   E

5. The FBI's various reports included an <u>enumeration</u> of Al Capone's <u>outlandish</u> expenditures,
                                              A   B

   and, in fact, that is how <u>they</u> caught <u>him.</u> <u>No error</u>
                                C   D   E

II. Agreement

Unclear and Incorrect Pronouns

Improving Sentences

1. <u>In my book they say that</u> caffeine is addictive and can lead to a host of ailments from ulcers to high blood pressure.
A. In my book they say that
B. In my book it says which
C. My book indicates that
D. In my book it says
E. My book says which

2. The emperor summoned before him a man traveling with his <u>son, who looked at him with suspicion</u>.
A. son, who looked at him with suspicion
B. son whom looked at him with suspicion
C. son; the man looked at the emperor with suspicion
D. son, whom he looked at with suspicion
E. son, whom looked at each other with suspicion

3. Automatic speed detection devices are mounted over Connecticut's highways, and if you speed by one <u>they will come after you</u>.
A. they will come after you
B. the police coming after you
C. they, being the police, will come after you.
D. then police responding to these signals will come after you
E. the police will come after you

4. Lanie responded to the question by swiftly raising her hand and responding, <u>"It was I!"</u>
A. "It was I!"
B. "It was me!"
C. "It was I who does!"
D. "It was myself!"
E. "I who does!"

5. The popular limericks "Jack and Jill" and "Humpty Dumpty" are just two of many that have violent conclusions; nonetheless <u>parents recite it</u> joyously as if they had happy endings.

A. parents recite it
B. parents recite these limericks
C. parents recite one
D. parents continually recite each
E. parents recite it

II. Agreement

F. Adverb/verb and adjective/noun agreement

Rule: Adverbs are used to modify verbs and adjectives, while adjectives are used to modify nouns. In both cases, the correct form of the word must be used. Adverbs usually end in "ly." Although not always the case, it often is so on the SAT.

Examples:

Each first sentence is incorrect. Each second sentence corrects the problem. Compare and contrast each set.

1. Moments of inspiration may disappear as **quick** as they appear.
   Moments of inspiration may disappear as **quickly** as they appear.

2. Alex, a former ice hockey player, moves more **graceful** than most athletes I know.
   Alex, a former ice hockey player, moves more **gracefully** than most athletes I know.

3. Sliding down a large water slide can be **dangerously**, especially if the water level is low.
   Sliding down a large water slide can be **dangerous**, especially if the water level is low.

4. In her waning days, she stared **cold** into space, while her eyes remained the color of liquid crystal.
   In her waning days, she stared **coldly** into space, while her eyes remained the color of liquid crystal.

5. Suzanne worked **diligent** on her science fair project.
   Suzanne worked **diligently** on her science fair project.

6. Johnny A, as local blues fans refer to him, plays his guitar **sweet** and **subtle**.
   Johnny A, as local blues fans refer to him, plays his guitar **sweetly** and **subtly**.

7. Even though the children singing in the choir were less than twelve years old, their voices were **unexpected** well-developed.
   Even though the children singing in the choir were less than twelve years old, their voices were **unexpectedly** well-developed.

8. People suffering from Tourette's syndrome often blurt out **surprising** shocking statements.
   People suffering from Tourette's syndrome often blurt out **surprisingly** shocking statements.

9. She explained herself quite **clear**.
   She explained it quite **clearly**.

10. Kate stared **inquisitive** at the bizarre paintings of Andy Warhol.
    Kate stared **inquisitively** at the bizarre paintings of Andy Warhol.

II. Agreement

Adverb to verb/Adjective to noun agreement

Identifying sentence errors

1. A cloud forest is <u>similar to</u> a rain forest <u>except that</u> the cloud forest is less <u>dense</u> and
                    A   B   C

    gets <u>less rain</u>. <u>No error</u>
          D   E

2. In Mexico city, cars <u>generally</u> do not stop for pedestrians, <u>so</u> people <u>have learned to</u>
                      A   B   C

    move out of the way <u>quick</u>. <u>No error</u>
                    D   E

3. Donna went on vacation <u>glad</u>, <u>even though</u> she had to leave her young,
                              A   B

    sometimes <u>rambunctious</u> children with <u>their</u> father for two weeks. <u>No error</u>
                C   D   E

4. When, in the middle of winter, Pauline asked if <u>she could</u> go to the movies, her mother
                                                   A

    <u>glanced at</u> the light clothing she <u>was wearing</u>, then looked at her <u>strange</u>. <u>No error</u>
      B   C   D   E

5. He expressed his view <u>adamant</u> that <u>those</u> who express radical opinions <u>are rarely</u> open to
                           A   B   C

    <u>counter</u> persuasion. <u>No error</u>
      D   E

II. Agreement

Adverb to verb/Adjective to noun agreement

Improving Sentences

1. I like talking to my sister on the way to school, <u>but she is an extreme slow walker.</u>
A. but she is an extreme slow walker.
B. but she walks extremely slowly.
C. but she is walking extremely slow.
D. but she is someone who walks slow.
E. but she a person that is such a slow walker.

2. The success that the twins, Angela and Carla, have had in fooling people regarding their identities, <u>attests to how close the twins resemble one another.</u>
A. attests to how close the twins resemble one another.
B. attest to how closely the twins resemble one another.
C. is attesting to just how closely resembled the twins are.
D. attests to how closely the twins resemble one another.
E. attests to the twins resembling one another very close.

3. Even <u>students who perform strong on the SATs</u> may have a better chance of being accepted into competitive colleges if their grades are high and if they can demonstrate a particular interest, hobby or activity that makes them stand out to admissions committees.
A. students who perform strong on the SATs
B. students who are performing strong on the SATs
C. students who perform strongly on the SATs
D. students whose SAT performance is stronger than those whose scores are low
E. students who are strong in SATs

4. On her trip into the jungle, Marta <u>saw a sloth that was moving so slow that she could barely tell it was alive.</u>
A. saw a sloth that was moving so slow that she could barely tell it was alive.
B. saw a sloth that moved so slow, she could barely tell whether it was alive.
C. saw a sloth that was moving so slowly that she could barely tell that it was alive.
D. saw a slow-moving sloth that moved so slow, she could barely tell it was alive.
E. was seen by a sloth that moved so slowly that it seemed barely alive, but it could still be seen by Marta.

5. When a bus full of tourists pulled into town, <u>the thieves moved in quick, taking advantage of the chaotic moment</u> when the tourists descended from the bus, to steal several backpacks
A. the thieves moved in quick, taking advantage of the chaotic moment
B. the thieves quickly were taking advantage of the chaotic moment
C. the they moved in quick, and took advantage of the chaotic moment
D. taking advantage of the chaotic moment, the quick thieves moved in
E. the thieves moved in quickly, taking advantage of the chaotic moment

II. Agreement

G. Pronoun/noun-verb agreement

Rule: The form of the verb must match the person, place or thing performing the action.

Examples:

Each first sentence is incorrect. Each second sentence corrects the problem. Compare and contrast each set.

1. When **they arrives** in the morning, they can not find their luggage.
   When **they arrive** in the morning, they can not find their luggage.

2. **Rachael and James swims** gracefully, even though neither has taken a lesson.
   Rachael and James swim gracefully, even though neither has taken a lesson.

3. The **group** of tourists **wave** frantically, trying to warn a fellow tourist get on board.
   The **group** of tourists **waves** frantically, trying to tell a fellow tourist to get on board.

4. The university parachute **team** often **jump** from as high as 10,000 feet!
   The university parachute **team** often **jumps** from as high as 10,000 feet!

5. **Derrick and Matthew enjoys** reading as much as any kids I have ever seen.
   Derrick and Matthew enjoy reading as much as any kids I have ever seen.

6. Some tall **trees** are notorious for **its** ability to bend, but not break.
   Some tall **trees** are notorious for **their** ability to bend, but not break.

7. **Tanner** was seven when he started Breeding Orchids; **he have** so far named more than 200 new   varieties.
   Tanner was seven when he started Breeding Orchids; **he has** so far named more than 200 new varieties.

8. The faster **bicycles** become, the more sophisticated derailleurs **it** requires.
   The faster **bicycles** become, the more sophisticated derailleurs **they** require.

9. The boxes are stacked one on top of another forming a **pile** so high that many boxes **sags**.
   The boxes are stacked one on top of another forming a **pile** so high that many boxes **sag**.

10. **Diving**, like swimming, **are activities** that require great strength and conditioning.
    Diving, like swimming, **is an activity** that requires great strength and conditioning.

II. Agreement

Pronoun/noun-verb agreement

Identifying Sentence Errors

1. If those trucks are <u>on the highway</u>, <u>my brother and I</u> <u>will</u> spot <u>it</u> immediately.   <u>No error</u>
                      A   B   C   D   E

2. <u>In</u> a complex democratic society, each <u>of the</u> citizens <u>have</u> to share the <u>responsibilities</u>.
   A   B   C   D
   <u>No error</u>
   E

3. The jury could not <u>easily agree</u> on an appropriate punishment, so <u>each member</u> had to follow
                     A   B
   <u>their own</u> instincts <u>to decide</u> the fate of the convicted criminal.   <u>No error</u>
     C   D   E

4. Unfortunately, the school newspaper's staff was <u>writing and editing</u> <u>their</u> <u>timely</u> articles
                                               A   B   C
   <u>until</u> 2 A.M.   <u>No error</u>
   D   E

5. Cloud seeding was a popular technique <u>in the 1950s</u>, because <u>they</u> thought that pumping
                                         A   B
   clouds <u>with</u> chemicals would cause them <u>to release</u> water in the form of rain.   <u>No error</u>.
         C   D   E

II. Agreement

Pronoun/noun-verb agreement

Improving Sentences

1. Bailey lashed out at his captors, <u>berating them as hypocrites which used the cause</u> as an excuse to wage a war of aggression.
A. berating them as hypocrites which used the cause
B. berating them as hypocrites that used the cause
C. berating them as hypocrites who used the cause
D. berating themselves as hypocrites which used the cause
E. berating them as hypocrites and using the cause

2. We are not perfect. Indeed, <u>few of us can even claim to be close</u> to any moral standard of excellence.
A. few of us can even claim to be close
B. few of ourselves can even claim to be close
C. fewer than we can even claim to be close
D. fewer than us can even claim to be close
E. we being fewer can even claim to be close

3. "Life, liberty and the pursuit of happiness" <u>are statements that expresses a dream,</u> not so much a reality.
A. are statements that expresses a dream,
B. are a statement that expresses a dream,
C. is statements that expresses a dream,
D. is a statement that express a dream,
E. is a statement that expresses a dream,

4. <u>Venus Williams' fame preceded those of her sister Serena</u>. Nonetheless, the Williams sisters together deserve a great deal of credit for having done for women's tennis what Tiger Woods did for golf.
A. Venus Williams' fame preceded those of her sister Serena
B. Venus Williams' fame preceded that of her sister Serena
C. Venus Williams' fame preceded her sister Serena
D. Venus Williams'fame preceded that of Serena's
E. Venus Williams' fame preceded by that of her sister Serena

5. If Albert Einstein may be considered the father of modern physics, then surely the brilliant physicist <u>Stephen Hawking could at least be considered his grandson.</u>
A. Stephen Hawking could at least be considered his grandson.
B. Stephen Hawking could at least be considered its grandson.
C. Stephen Hawking could at least be considered Einstein's grandson.
D. Stephen Hawking could at least be considered as a grandson.
E. Stephen Hawking could at least be considered grandson.

II. Agreement

Subject/verb agreement

Rule: The form of the verb must match the person, place or thing performing the action.

Identifying Sentence Errors

1. The discovery of cavities <u>in the ruins</u> of Pompeii, <u>apparently</u> depicting Vesuvius' victims <u>in their</u>
A B C
last moments, are a sobering reminder of the human tragedy behind the archeological treasure
D
trove. <u>No error</u>.
E

2. <u>According to</u> reliable sources, neither Gomez <u>nor</u> Stanton are expected to <u>forego</u> free agency.
A B C D
<u>No error</u>.
E

3. <u>It seems that</u> the <u>profligate</u> use of chemical fertilizers and insect repellents <u>have</u> been <u>both</u> a
A B C D
curse and a blessing to modern agriculture. <u>No error</u>.
E

4. <u>Also</u> enthusiastically recommended by the committee <u>was</u> a <u>moratorium on</u> tax increases and a
A B C
<u>long-delayed</u> resumption of debate on gun control. <u>No error</u>.
D E

5. <u>Either</u> your unqualified support or your sincere opposition are acceptable; <u>damnation with faint</u>
A B C
praise <u>is not</u>. <u>No error</u>.
D E

121

II. Agreement

Subject/verb agreement

Improving Sentences

1. The strangely hypnotic music of Jim Morrison, Robby Kreiger and Ray Manzarek <u>leave fans wondering where music would be now,</u> had it not been for Morrison's untimely death in 1971.
A. leave fans wondering where music would be now
B. leave fans to wonder where music would be now
C. leaves fans wondering where music would be now
D. leaves fans to wonder about music nowadays
E. leaving fans to wonder where music would be today

2. Shorelines like this one are endangered all around the globe; <u>the one-two punch of oil spills and acid rain threaten</u> their future well being.
A. the one-two punch of oil spills and acid rain threaten
B. the one-two punch of oil spills and acid rain threatens
C. the one-two punch of oil spills and acid rain will be threatening
D. the one-two punch of oil spills and acid rain, they threaten
E. threatening them are the one-two punch of oil spills and acid rain

3. Volcanic force, not tectonic plate shifts, <u>create mountain ranges such as those</u> in the Hawaiian Archipelago.
A. create mountain ranges such as those
B. create mountain ranges as those we see
C. creates the mountain ranges like
D. can create the mountain ranges
E. creates mountain ranges such as those

4. Generally speaking, <u>a person who prefers dogs to cats tend to be</u> more group oriented and socially adaptive.
A. a person who prefers dogs to cats tend to be
B. a person who prefers a dog to cats tend to be
C. people who prefers dogs to cats tends to be
D. a person who prefers dogs to cats tends to be
E. people who prefers dogs over cats tend to be

5. <u>The ultraviolet rays emanating from the sun has been known to cause</u> major damage to cement surfaces, especially in inland cities not cooled by ocean breezes.
A. The ultraviolet rays emanating from the sun has been known to cause
B. The ultraviolet rays emanating from the sun have been known to cause
C. The ultraviolet rays of the sun has been known to cause
D. The ultraviolet rays which are emanated from the sun has been known to cause
E. The ultraviolet rays of the sun causing

III. Verb Tense

Verb Tense is used to express when events occur, or when they occur in relation to other events. In all cases, verb tense must match the intentional meaning (in relation to time) of the writer or speaker

A. Past, Present and Future Tenses
B. Perfect Tense
C. Subjunctive Tense (Mood)
D. Time sequences

III. Verb Tense

A. Past, Present and Future

Rule: The decision as to which tense to use to express an action is determined by the time at which that action occurs. The past, present and future tenses are used to express a simple, single event or period of time.

Examples:

Each first sentence is incorrect.   Each second sentence corrects the problem. Compare and contrast each set.

1. **Yesterday,** Johnny **is going** to the store.
    Yesterday, Johnny **went** to the store.

2. Is he coming or **was** he staying home?
    Is he coming or **is** he staying home?

3. The convention **was** coming to Boston **next month.**
    The convention **is** coming to Boston **next month.**

4. Awesome dude, you **hitting** the jackpot.
    Awesome dude, you **hit** the jackpot

5. **Right now,** I **saw** James building with his Lego set
    Right now, I **see** James building with his Lego set

6. Systems like this **have been** important for our **future business**
    Systems like this **will be (or are)** important for our **future business**

7. Before he left, the painter is **rising** his ladder to its greatest height.
    Before he left, the painter **raised** his ladder to its greatest height.

8. **Tomorrow,** I hope that the Clydesdales **showed up** for the parade.
    Tomorrow, I hope that the Clydesdales **will show up** for the parade.

9. What **is** Manny thinking when he swung at that pitch?
    What **was** Manny thinking when he swung at that pitch?

10. If all you **do** is criticize, then I **did not** listen.
    If all you **do** is criticize, then I **will not** listen.

III. Verb Tense

Past, Present and Future

Identifying Sentence Errors

1. Wise use of games in schools is effective because it encouraged students to think socially and
   A   B   C   D
   creatively. No error
                E

2. To the coaching staff during the first half season, it seems that whenever the team's offensive
                                                         A
   line was missing a person, though there were many excellent substitutes on the bench, invariably
        B   C
   they lost. No error
        D   E

3. Constantinople, formerly Byzantium, was sacked several times in its long history, most
                    A   B   C
   recently by the Turks: as a result, the city would now be called Istanbul. No error
                                                 D   E

4. It was the best of times and the worst of times, a time of great suffering and great
      A   B
   opportunity, and there will be no reason to hope for any immediate change. No error
                    C   D   E

5. Certain members of the delegation were tending their harvests many miles
                                      A
   distant from the convention held last December, and were therefore absent; so they were playing
                                                         B   C
   no role in the shaping of events. No error
           D   E

III. Verb Tense

Past, Present and Future

Improving Sentences

1. When asked if his lyrics were <u>intended to be critical of the administration, Henley simply replies</u>, "Yup!"
   A. intended to be critical of the administration, Henley simply replies
   B. intended as being critical of the administration, Henley simply replies
   C. intended critically of the administration, Henley simply replied
   D. intended to be critical of the administration, Henley simply replied
   E. intended to be critical of the administration, Henley simply is replying

2. The apparently destitute man had a kind face, <u>so I could not help but listening to his story</u>.
   A. so I could not help but listening to his story
   B. so I could not help but listen to his story
   C. so I could not help but to be listening to his story
   D. so I could not stop and listened to his story
   E. so I could not help listen to his story

3. The King said he would give his kingdom for a horse, <u>but there is not any horse to be found</u>.
   A. but there is not any horse to be found
   B. but there is not any horse to have been found
   C. but there is not any horse to find
   D. but there was no horse not to be found
   E. but there was not any horse to be found

4. A thousand years ago Druids stood on this mound and perhaps <u>participated in mystical rituals and sung ancient songs</u>.
   A. participated in mystical rituals and sung ancient songs
   B. participate in mystical rituals and sung ancient songs
   C. participated and sung in mystical rituals and ancient songs
   D. participated in mystical rituals and sang ancient songs
   E. had participated in mystical rituals and sung ancient songs

5. <u>When Englishmen leave their homeland to establish colonies in the New World</u>, they brought with them charters guaranteeing that they and their heirs would "have and enjoy all liberties and immunities of free and natural subjects."
   A. When Englishmen leave their homeland to establish colonies in the New World
   B. When Englishmen would leave their homeland to establish colonies in the New World
   C. When Englishmen leaving their homeland to establish colonies in the New World
   D. When Englishmen are leaving their homeland to establish colonies in the New World
   E. When Englishmen left their homeland in order to establish colonies in the New World

III. Verb Tense

B. Perfect Tenses

Rule: The perfect tenses are used to describe actions that occur prior to some understood or specified time. The present perfect is used to describe an action that occurred prior to the present. (Note: this event can be continuing in the present) The past perfect is used to describe an action that occurred prior to an understood or specified time in the past. The future perfect is used to describe an action that will occur prior to an understood or specified time in the future.

Examples:

Each first sentence is incorrect. Each second sentence corrects the problem. Compare and contrast each set.

1. If the U. S. women's soccer team **won** in the 2002 World Championship, the professional league would not have collapsed.
   If the U. S. women's soccer team **had won** in the 2002 World Championship, the professional league would not have collapsed.

2. The family **intended** to scout out Yellowstone park in two days, a task they later found impossible.
   The family **had intended** to scout out Yellowstone park in two days, a task they later found impossible.

3. **Since I had it** myself, I was not too concerned when my children showed signs of Chicken Pox.

   Since I **have had** it myself, I'm not too concerned that my children may have Chicken Pox.

4. If the weather **cleared** before lunch, we might still have gone hiking in Vermont.

   If the weather **had cleared** before lunch, we might still have gone hiking in Vermont.

5. The hostess wanted to know whether all the guests **arrived** yet.
   The hostess wanted to know whether all the guests **had arrived** yet.

6. Before the car accident occurred, they **were** drinking
   Before the car accident occurred, they **had been** drinking.

7. Before he packed for the canoe trip, Tim **worked out** at the gym.
   Before he packed for the canoe trip, Tim **had worked out** at the gym.

8. Before the Linkin Park show began, I **made it** all the way to the mosh pit.
   Before the Linkin Park show began, I **had made it** all the way to the mosh pit.

9. By the time the show was over, I **sustained** several minor injuries.

   By the time the show was over, I **had sustained** several minor injuries.

10. Since there was no radio or television, people living in ancient Italy may not have heard right away that Mt. Vesuvius **erupted and destroyed** the town Pompeii.
    Since there was no radio or television, people living in ancient Italy may not have heard right away that Mt. Vesuvius **had erupted and destroyed** the town Pompeii.

III. Verb Tense

Perfect Tenses

Identifying Sentence Errors

1. Ever since the internet boom <u>began</u> in the late 1990's, entrepreneurs
                                  A
    <u>have been endeavoring</u> <u>to use</u> it <u>to make money</u>. <u>No error</u>
                B   C   D   E

2. Now that you <u>ran</u> a mile, you <u>will</u> <u>have</u> <u>to consider</u> other fitness goals. <u>No error</u>
                  A   B   C   D   E

3. Whenever I <u>reach</u> for the ceiling, I <u>feel</u> a sharp pain in my left shoulder and
               A   B
    <u>there has been</u> a <u>tingling sensation</u> in my left hand. <u>No error</u>
          C   D   E

4. <u>He rescued</u> the man <u>just in time</u>; <u>moments later,</u> <u>there had been</u> a large explosion
         A   B   C   D
    <u>No error</u>
        E

5. He <u>would have had</u> time <u>to fill</u> the gas tank if he <u>had not gone</u> <u>to the store first</u>. <u>No error</u>
            A   B   C   D   E

III. Verb Tense

Perfect Tenses

Improving Sentences

1. By next year, <u>we have overcome</u> the obstacles that stand between freedom and us.

   A. we have overcome
   B. we had overcome
   C. we will overcome
   D. we will have overcome
   E. we would have overcome

2. Who ever said, "It is better to have loved and lost than <u>never to love</u> at all," never had his heart broken.

   A. never to love
   B. never to have loved
   C. never to be loved
   D. never to have been loved
   E. never love

3. Before the session has ended, the negotiators <u>will be placing</u> their cards on the table.

   A. will be placing
   B. placed
   C. placing
   D. would have placed
   E. will have placed

4. <u>Being a straggler myself</u> on the bike trip last year, I know how lonely it is at the back of the pack.

   A. Being a straggler myself
   B. To be a straggler myself
   C. To have been a straggler myself
   D. Having been a straggler myself
   E. To have been a straggler myself

5. When the storming of the Bastille took place in 1789, many French aristocrats <u>had already took flight</u>.

   A. had already took flight
   B. already took flight
   C. had already taken flight
   D. are already taking flight
   E. have already been taking flight

III. Verb Tense

C. Subjunctive

The subjunctive expresses a wish, a command, or a condition contrary to fact. These are rare on the SAT, though one should recognize them. Even grammarians have a hard time defining subjunctive.

Examples:

Each first sentence is incorrect. Each second sentence corrects the problem. Compare and contrast each set.

1. It's always the same with this team: '**would of, could of, should of**'!
    It's always the same with this team: '**would have, could have, should have**'!

2. If I **was** you, I would let sleeping dogs lie.
    If I **were** you, I would let sleeping dogs lie.

3. My little sister acts as if she **was** my mother.
    My little sister acts as if she **were** my mother.

4. What if the new kid **is** to play the saxophone
    What if the new kid **were** to play the saxophone?

5. He would be more popular if he **was** more punctual.
    He would be more popular if he **were** more punctual.

6. Though his passport said he was American, he spoke as though he **was** British.
    Though his passport said he was American, he spoke as though he **were** British.

7. I wish I **was** from Venus, not Earth.
    I wish I **were** from Venus, not Earth.

8. If only I **was** taller, I could ride the roller coaster.
    If only I **were** taller, I could ride the roller coaster.

9. Abraham Lincoln, who later **was** president, started out as an eloquent lawyer.
    Abraham Lincoln, who later **would become** president, started out as an eloquent lawyer.

10. If I **was** rich, I would book a flight on that zero gravity plane.
    If I **were** rich, I would book a flight on that zero gravity plane.

III. Verb Tense

Subjunctive

Identifying Sentence Errors

1. The determined lawyer <u>expressed</u> her wish <u>to the judge</u> that the <u>recalcitrant</u> witness <u>is</u>
                                 A   B   C   D

    cross-examined. <u>No error</u>
                   E

2. A thousand miles <u>from nowhere,</u> <u>I wished I</u> <u>was home</u> <u>instead</u>. <u>No error</u>
                            A   B   C   D   E

3. The board of directors <u>prefers</u> <u>that</u> the <u>secretive</u> new person <u>is</u> in charge. <u>No error</u>
                              A B   C   D   E

4. If it <u>were</u> true as you say that the sun <u>revolves</u> around the earth, and if the idea that the
            A   B

    earth <u>revolves</u> around the sun be in fact a government conspiracy, I <u>am</u> surprised. <u>No error</u>
           C   D   E

5. <u>Suppose</u> Ralph Nader <u>were elected</u>: what <u>might</u> he <u>accomplish</u>? <u>No error</u>
         A   B   C   D   E

III. Verb Tense

Subjunctive

Improving Sentences

1. <u>Even if the whole world was against him, Davy Crockett would stay and fight</u>.
A. Even if the whole world was against him, Davy Crockett would stay and fight.
B. Even if the whole world was against him, Davy Crockett will stay and fight.
C. Even if the whole world were against him, Davy Crockett would stay and fight.
D. Even if the whole world were against him, Davy Crockett stayed and fought.
E. Even when the whole world was against him, Davy Crockett stays and fights.

2. When the children told their mother they had cheated, <u>she looked as if she was ill</u>.
A she looked as if she was ill
B. she looked as if she would be ill
C. she looked as though she would be ill
D. she looked as though she was ill
E. ill is how she looked

3. Juliet's love for Romeo was so great, that <u>she swore she would wait for him in eternity even if he were to lose</u> his life
A. she swore she would wait for him in eternity even if he were to lose
B. she would wait for him, she swore in eternity even if he were to lose
C. she swore waiting in eternity for him would be what she would do even if he were to lose
D. she swore she would wait for him in eternity even if he was to lose
E. she swore she would wait for him in eternity even if he would lose his life

4. What if schools <u>were granted unlimited funds</u>, and teachers were paid what they deserve? What then?
A were granted unlimited funds
B. would be granted unlimited funds
C. was granted unlimited funds
D. would have been granted unlimited funds
E. be granted unlimited funds

5. The newly discovered world, with its hot surface, <u>is not the sort of place biologists can be expecting to find life as we know it.</u>
A. is not the sort of place biologists can be expecting to find life as we know it.
B. is not the sort of place biologists can be expecting life as we know it.
C. is not the sort of place biologists and life find each other as we know it.
D. is not the sort of place biologists expected to be finding life as we know it.
E is not the sort of place biologists would expect to find life as we know it.

III. Verb Tense

D. Time Sequences

Rule: Actions occurring at different times (different tenses) can be contained within a single sentence. You must understand the relationship among the times when actions occur in order to recognize errors in tense.

Examples:

Each first sentence is incorrect. Each second sentence corrects the problem. Compare and contrast each set.

1. John **is** under great pressure at work and so **missed** his son's game tomorrow
   John **is** under great pressure at work and so **will miss** his son's game tomorrow

2. I **ate** at a Greek restaurant last night and the atmosphere **is** lively.

   I **ate** at a Greek restaurant last night and the atmosphere **was** lively.

3. Yesterday, Daphne **met** with her co-star, whom she **knew** as a kid.
   Yesterday, Daphne **met** with her co-star, whom **she had known** as a kid.

4. **During Plato's time** people believed that atoms **are** the smallest particle in nature.
   During Plato's time people believed that atoms **were** the smallest particle in nature

5. **They did not believe** that one day man **can fly** to the planets.
   They did not believe that one day man **would fly** to the planets.

6. The Park Service **can** run on a lower budget if people **did** not litter.

   The Park Service **would be able** to run on a lower budget if people **would** not litter.

7. I am disappointed that I **played** that game and **will miss** the test.

   I am disappointed that by **having played that game, I missed** the test.

8. You would think he **would have learned by** now not to **have driven** into a closed garage door.
   You would think he **would have learned** by now not to **drive** into a closed garage door.

9. Before that race, Tommy **ran** a mile in four minutes flat and **planned** to do it again.
   Before that race, Tommy **had run** a mile in four minutes flat and was **planning** to do it again.

10. The 2006 Winter Olympics should be great, since controversy in the 2004 Summer Games is **creating** new, powerful rivalries.
    The 2006 Winter Olympics should be great, since controversy in the 2004 Summer Games **has created** new, powerful rivalries.

III. Verb Tense

Time Sequences

Identifying Sentence Errors

1. In December of 1991, <u>as</u> the world watched <u>in amazement</u>, the Soviet Union
                  A   B
    <u>had disintegrated</u> into fifteen separate countries, ending an aggressive expansion that <u>had</u>
       C   D
    spanned centuries. <u>No error</u>
                     E

2. There <u>was</u> <u>absolutely</u> no room <u>for improvisation</u> in last week's meeting, but Jane still <u>will try</u> it.
             A   B   C   D
    <u>No error</u>
      E

3. Not only <u>did</u> "Hammerin'" Hank Aaron <u>raise the bar</u> for home runs, <u>but he also</u> <u>established</u>
             A   B   C   D
    twelve other major league career records, including most games, at-bats, total bases and

    RBI. <u>No error</u>
           E

4. Teeth <u>were</u> very important <u>in determining</u> evolutionary <u>similarities among</u> species <u>such as</u>
           A   B   C   D
    modern elephants and extinct mastodons and mammoths. <u>No error</u>
                                                    E

5. Lafayette <u>was one of</u> the first <u>having advocated</u> a National Assembly, and <u>work toward</u> the
                A   B   C
   establishment of a constitutional monarchy during the <u>years leading up</u> to the French
                                                              D
   Revolution of 1791. <u>No error</u>
                       E

III. Verb Tense

Time Sequences

Improving Sentences

1. <u>Ernest Rutherford was the first to establish the theory</u> of the nuclear atom and, in 1919, actually carried out a transmutation reaction, which is the formation of hydrogen and oxygen isotopes by bombardment of nitrogen with alpha particles.
A. Ernest Rutherford was the first to establish the theory
B. Ernest Rutherford would be the first to have established the theory
C. Ernest Rutherford, the first to establish the theory
D. Ernest Rutherford was the first to be establishing a theory
E. Ernest Rutherford could be as the first to establish the theory

2. The many-faceted career of cellist Yo-Yo Ma is a testament to his continual search for new ways <u>to have communicated with audiences, and to his personal desire to have established</u> artistic growth and renewal.
A. to have communicated with audiences, and to his personal desire to have established
B. to communicate with audiences, and to his personal desire to establish
C. to have communicated with audiences, and to his personal desire to established
D. to communicate with audiences, and to his personal desire to established
E. to communicated with audiences, and to his personal desire to establish

3. Jenny certainly knew what she was up against. She <u>had seen her mother had given her that look before</u> and could predict with exactitude what was going to transpire.
A. She had seen her mother had given her that look before
B. She had seen her mother give her that look before
C. She had seen her mother gave her that look before
D. She saw her mother had given her that look before
E. She had been seen with her mother who had had given her that look before

4. If an atomic clock, taken into outer space and returned, shows an earlier time than an identical clock left behind on Earth, then that would prove that time itself <u>will have been progressing more slowly</u> in the space occupied by that clock
A. will have been progressing more slowly
B. was progressing more slowly
C. will be progressing more slowly
D. would be progressing more slowly
E. progressed more slowly

5. If the archaeologists of the last century had found that the mummy was older than the tomb in which it is still buried, they must have wondered <u>whether the mummy was moved there</u> at some earlier time, and why.
A. whether the mummy was moved there
B. whether the mummy would have been moved there
C. whether the mummy would be moved there
D. whether the mummy were moved there
E. whether the mummy had been moved there

IV. Diction and Idioms
Expressions and misused words

A. Wrong word
B. Wrong expression
C. Double negatives

IV. Diction and Idioms

A. Wrong Words

> Rule: On average there are two "wrong word" questions per exam, They are words that sound like the correct words, but which do not carry the correct meaning.

Examples:

Each first sentence is incorrect.   Each second sentence corrects the problem. Compare and contrast each set.

1. **Accept** for one bad test, your grades for the semester are quite impressive.
   Except for one bad test, your grades for the semester are quite impressive.

2. **Irregardless** of whether we win or lose, let's enjoy the campaign.
   Regardless of whether we win or lose, let's enjoy the campaign.

3. The fact that he never cleans his room **aggravates** me to no end.
   The fact that he never cleans his room **annoys** me to no end.

4. Most **importantly,** you must study very hard
   Most **important,** you must study very hard

5. The explorers in the old photo are Sir Edmund Hillary and Reginald Winterbottom, **irrespectively.**
   The explorers in the old photo are Sir Edmund Hillary and Reginald Winterbottom, **respectively.**

6. A best-selling book or major film release may **effect** the results of a presidential election.
   A best-selling book or major film release may **affect** the results of a presidential election.

7. The student was **uninterested;** she was unbiased, (uninterested means not caring)
   The student was **disinterested;** she was unbiased (disinterested means objective)

8. The teacher **talked** with a strong accent, so many students dropped out of her class.
   The teacher **spoke** with a strong accent, so many students dropped out of her class.

9. She **implicated** that she had merely been in the right place at the right time.
   She **implied** that she had merely been in the right place at the right time

10. He was **underneath** the misconception that all species of bats navigated by sonar.
    He was **under** the misconception that all species of bats navigated by sonar.

IV. Diction and Idioms

Wrong Words

Identifying Sentence Errors

1. When I called the box office, the man <u>who answered the phone</u> wouldn't be pinned

                                       A

   down but <u>implicated</u> that the show <u>would probably be</u> <u>sold out</u>. <u>No error</u>

       B   C   D   E

2. The violent hurricane <u>wrecked</u> <u>havoc</u> on the <u>normally</u> <u>tranquil</u> harbor. <u>No error</u>

                            A   B   C   D   E

3. <u>Mythology</u> has it that when Pandora's Box was <u>unlatched,</u> <u>misery</u> and evil were

   A   B   C

   <u>resolved</u> on the world, but hope, also. <u>No error</u>

  D   E

4. Given the risks of <u>hang-gliding</u> and <u>skydiving</u>, I'm <u>reticent</u> to try <u>either</u>. <u>No error</u>

                          A   B   C   D   E

5. When asked again <u>whether</u> she hoped to be married one day, the <u>shy</u>

                         A   B

   girl <u>repented</u> , 'kind of." <u>No error</u>

      C   D   E

IV. Diction and Idioms

Wrong Words

Improving Sentences

1. The politically charged documentary promises to be <u>highly relative</u> to the upcoming election.
A. highly relative
B. remunerative
C. related in a high degree
D. highly relegated
E. highly relevant

2. Mimeograph machines <u>have been largely relegated by more</u> sophisticated technology, but many are still being used.
A. have been largely relegated by more
B. have been largely replaced by more
C. have been largely relegated to more
D. relegated is how they have been made
E. to have been made by more

3. Illuminated by his radiant personality and propelled by his zest for life, Luciano Pavarotti, the man with the golden voice, <u>transposes the walls of the opera house to reach</u> inside every human heart and mind.

A. transposes the walls of the opera house to reach
B. transnavigates the walls of the opera house to reach
C. transports the walls of the opera house to reach
D. transfers opera house's walls to reach
E. transcends the walls of the opera house to reach

4. The hail storm had <u>a deleterious effect</u> on the delicate orchid gardens.
A. a deleterious effect
B. a dilatory effect
C. a dichotomous effect
D. a nugatory effect
E. a didactic effect

5. The counselor realized that the student's difficulty with a certain teacher stemmed from her relationship with her mother, <u>an astute observance</u> on her part.
A. an astute observance
B. an astringent observance
C. an abstruse observance
D. an astute observation
E. an abstruse observation

IV. Diction and Idioms

Prepositions

Pg. 164 memorize

> **Rule:** Idioms are expressions that have come to be accepted as proper grammar. Often, these idioms contain a preposition - which often times is incorrect.

Examples:

Each first sentence is incorrect.   Each second sentence corrects the problem. Compare and contrast each set.

1. His comments **in regards of** the play in the question-and-answer session afterwards were insulting.
    His comments in **regard to** the play in the question-and-answer session afterwards were insulting.

2. Her **perspective about** the punk music scene made her the best person to interview The Ramones.
    Her **perspective on** the punk music scene made her the best person to interview The Ramones.

3. His **ability for creating** Lego sculptures impressed his first grade teacher.
    His **ability to** create Lego sculptures impressed his first grade teacher.

4. No demagogue will ever **persuade** me **for becoming** a radical.
    No demagogue will ever **persuade** me **to become** a radical.

5. Recent climate changes on Wall Street may be **indicative to** a period of economic torpor.
    Recent climate changes on Wall Street may be **indicative of** a period of economic torpor.

6. I am **open for** any suggestions you might care to offer
    I am **open to** any suggestions you might care to offer.

7. The Big Dig construction crews had **myriads of** tasks to complete in order to make the new highway operational.
    The Big Dig construction crews had **myriad** tasks to complete in order to make the new highway operational.

8. The **reason** for the last-minute delay **is because** one of the actors is stuck in traffic.
    The **reason** for the last-minute delay **is that** one of the actors is stuck in traffic.

9. Let's just record today's game **under the category** "bad luck" and forget about it.
    Let's just record today's game **in the category** "bad luck" and forget about it.
    ("Under the heading" or "in the category", but not "under the category".)

10. The a cappella singers sang well but **should of** used more harmony.
    The a cappella singers sang well but **should have** used more harmony.

IV. Diction and Idioms

Wrong Expressions

Identifying Sentence Errors

1. Jane Austen's themes <u>include both</u> relations among families <u>as well as</u> the importance of
                A   B   C
   marriage <u>in the social class</u> known as the Gentry.   <u>No error</u>
                D   E

2. <u>Parents</u>, the responsibility of <u>talking</u> for your kids <u>about drugs</u> is <u>up to you</u>.   <u>No error</u>
     A   B   C   D   E

3. <u>Any reader</u> of *A Tale of Two Cities* <u>would of known something</u> about the <u>atrocities</u> of
        A   B   C
   the French Revolution.   <u>No error</u>
                         E

4. <u>Add</u> up the numbers <u>together to compile</u> the <u>final score</u>.   <u>No error</u>
     A   B   C   D   E

5. I <u>prefer being</u> a borrower <u>than being</u> a lender.   <u>No error</u>
      A   B   C   D   E

IV. Diction and Idioms

Wrong Expressions

Improving Sentences

1. In regards to your question about general amnesty, the library will indeed welcome overdue returns in July without levying any fee.
   A. In regards to
   B. Regarding
   C. With regards to
   D. While regarding
   E. With regards about

2. Winston Churchill praised his countrymen about their courage and perseverance.
   A. praised his countrymen about
   B. praised his countrymen over
   C. praised his countrymen concerning
   D. praised his countrymen for
   E. praised his countrymen with regard to

3. Widely and perhaps inconclusively studied, the fall of Rome was caused due to numerous factors.
   A. was caused due to
   B. was caused from
   C. was caused because of
   D. was caused by
   E. was caused of

4. The loud volume of the music at the graduation party prompted a visit by the local police.
   A. The loud volume of the music
   B. The high volume of the music
   C. The loud music
   D. The music's high volume
   E. The highness of the volume of the music

5. In the political environment of the modern high school, it is necessary to be aware about the diversity of viewpoints that may be encountered.
   A. to be aware about
   B. to be wary about
   C. to be aware of
   D. to be aware concerning
   E. to be wary concerning

IV. Diction and Idioms

C. Double negatives

Rule: A double negative results when one uses more than one negative word or construction to express a single negative thought. In reality, a double negative creates a positive, but in a practical sense, double negatives are just wrong!

Examples

Each first sentence is incorrect. Each second sentence corrects the problem. Compare and contrast each set.

1. Not only were no policemen there, but **no discovery had not yet** been made of the robbery.
   Not only were no policemen there, but **no discovery had yet** been made of the robbery.

2. Some became Crusaders for the love of change; some, in the hope of plunder; some, because they **did not have nothing** to do at home.
   Some became Crusaders for the love of change; some, in the hope of plunder; some, because they **had nothing** to do at home.

3. The pilot could **not** find **nowhere** to land.
   The pilot could **not** find **anywhere** to land.

4. What the letters truly contained is **not scarcely** known at all.
   What the letters truly contained is **scarcely** known at all.

5. I fear that the new tax incentive plan will **not** last **barely** a month.
   I fear that the new tax incentive plan will **not** last a month.

6. He had heard several distant gunshots, but that sort of thing was not uncommon, and they had **not made no** impression upon him.
   He had heard several distant gunshots, but that sort of thing was not uncommon, and they had **not made any** impression upon him.

7. There is **hardly no** more compelling challenge than the one related to fostering the cause of peace.
   There is **no** more compelling challenge than the one related to fostering the cause of peace.

8. When nothing is ventured, **nor nothing** is gained.
   When nothing is ventured, **nothing** is gained.

9. The explorers discovered that the place where they landed **did not have none** of the minerals they wanted.
   The explorers discovered that the place where they landed **did not have any** of the minerals they wanted.

10. He **can't** convince **no one** to go with him.
    He **can't** convince **anyone** to go with him.

IV. Diction and Idioms

Double negatives

Identifying sentence errors

1. <u>Despite</u> his <u>lack of</u> flight experience, the pilot had <u>scarcely no</u> doubt about his
   A   B   C
   <u>ability to</u> land the plane safely. <u>No error</u>
   D   E

2. <u>Though</u> Janice enjoys painting, <u>her work</u> is <u>hardly</u> considered <u>as good as</u>
   A   B   C   D
   her colleagues'. <u>No error</u>
                     E

3. With all the mosquitoes <u>on</u> the island, there <u>was</u> <u>hardly no</u> <u>unbitten</u> skin on my
                          A   B   C   D
   body. <u>No error</u>
          E

4. I <u>do</u> believe <u>that</u> there <u>aren't hardly</u> any superheroes <u>stronger than</u> Superman.
   A   B   C   D
   <u>No error</u>
   E

5. <u>Though</u> he <u>makes a living</u> as a fashion designer <u>to the</u> stars, Clyde is scarcely <u>never</u> seen
   A   B   C   D
   wearing matching socks. <u>No error</u>
                            E

IV. Diction and Idioms

Double negatives

Improving Sentences

1. <u>I don't want to work on Maggie's farm no more.</u>
A. I don't want to work on Maggie's farm no more.
B. I do not desire to work on Maggie's farm no more.
C. I can't work on Maggie's farm no more
D. I don't want to work on Maggie's farm any more
E. Maggie, I ain't not being working on your farm no way

2. <u>There weren't hardly any reasons for the team members to renegotiate their contracts.</u>
A. There weren't hardly any reasons for the team members to renegotiate their contracts.
B. The team members hadn't hardly any reasons for renegotiating their contracts.
C. There aren't hardly any reasons for the team members to renegotiate their contracts.
D. The team members had hardly any reason to renegotiate their contracts.
E. The team members' reasons to renegotiate were hardly any.

3. It is natural for those of us who live in freedom to desire to help those <u>who don't have scarcely any power</u>.
A. who don't have scarcely any power.
B. who don't have any power, scarcely.
C. who have not scarcely any power.
D. who have scarcely no power.
E. who have scarcely any power.

4. <u>There are hardly no boats in the harbor this morning.</u>
A. There are hardly no boats in the harbor this morning.
B. There are hardly any boats in the harbor this morning.
C. There are hardly none boats in the harbor this morning.
D. There are scarcely no boats in the harbor this morning.
E. In the harbor are hardly no boats this morning.

5. <u>Every pen I tried had scarcely not enough ink.</u>
A. Every pen I tried had scarcely not enough ink.
B. Every pen I tried had scarcely no ink.
C. No pen I tried had scarcely enough ink.
D. No pen I tried had enough ink.
E. No pen I tried had scarcely no ink.

V. Word Order and Sentence Structure

The basic structure of a sentence must be correct

A. Misplaced modifiers
B. Run-ons and fragments
C. Redundant or extraneous words
D. Punctuation
E. Prepositional and other phrases

V. Word Order and Sentence Structure

A. Misplaced Modifiers

Rule: When we begin a sentence with a modifying word, phrase, or clause, we must make sure the next thing that comes along can, in fact, be modified by that modifier. When a modifier improperly modifies something, it is called a "dangling modifier" or "misplaced modifier."

Examples:

Each first sentence is incorrect. Each second sentence corrects the problem. Compare and contrast each set.

1. **Gleaming** silver and black, **I** climbed into the new truck.
    I climbed into the new **truck, which was gleaming silver and black**.

2. With his radiant personality and zest for life, **Luciano Pavarotti's voice** transcends the walls of the opera house to touch every human heart and mind.
    With his radiant personality and zest for life, **Luciano Pavarotti** seems to transcend the walls of the opera house to touch every human heart and mind.

3. Having just returned from the stadium, **the Patriots' performance** seemed lackluster.
    Having just returned from the stadium, **we** felt the Patriots' performance was lackluster.

4. Always ready with a wag of his tail, **I** could always count on my dog to greet me at the door after I had had a long, trying day.
    Always ready with a wag of his tail, **my dog** would always greet me at the door after I had had a long, trying day.

5. The only person on stage, seeming larger than life, **a lion** couldn't have roared more forcefully than the actor playing King Lear.
    Alone on stage, seeming larger than life, **the actor** playing King Lear roared as forcefully as a lion.

6. Eager to escape the storm, **lightning** struck the cat just as he raced to find shelter in a tree.
    Eager to escape the storm, **the cat** raced to find shelter just as lightning struck the tree.

7. During his Presidency, **Nixon's controversial policies** succeeded in ending American fighting in Viet Nam and improving relations with the U.S.S.R. and China.
    During his Presidency, **Nixon**, though with controversial policies, succeeded in ending American fighting in Viet Nam and improving relations with the U.S.S.R. and China.

8. Though it is often misunderstood, **scholars** know that anarchy does not mean "lack of order."
    Though it is often misunderstood, **anarchy**, as is known by political scholars, does not mean "lack of order."

9. In order to understand what constitutes flawless style in soccer, **a thorough study** would include an analysis of each goal.
    In order to understand what constitutes flawless style in soccer, **one** should make a thorough analysis of each goal.

10. As he implies in his autobiography, **Steinbeck's "weapon of choice"** was a pencil.
    As he implies in his autobiography, **Steinbeck** chose a pencil as his "weapon of choice."

V. Word Order and Sentence Structure

Misplaced Modifiers

Improving Sentences

(All ten exercises here on misplaced modifiers are in the "Improving Sentences" variety.)

1. <u>Trying to be funny, "Crime doesn't pay, but at least the hours are flexible" is what Woody Allen once said</u>.
A. Trying to be funny, "Crime doesn't pay, but at least the hours are flexible" is what Woody Allen once said.
B. Being funny, "Crime doesn't pay, but at least the hours are flexible", Woody Allen once said.
C. To try to be funny, "Crime doesn't pay, but at least the hours are flexible" is what Woody Allen once said.
D. Trying to be funny, Woody Allen once said, "Crime doesn't pay, but at least the hours are flexible".
E. To try to be funny, it was Woody Allen who once said, "Crime doesn't pay, but at least the hours are flexible".

2. A classic in the field, <u>the fall of Rome is vividly narrated in the Englishman Edward Gibbon's *Decline and Fall of the Roman Empire*</u>.
A. the fall of Rome is vividly narrated in the Englishman Edward Gibbon's *Decline and Fall of the Roman Empire*
B. the vivid narration of the fall of Rome appears in the Englishman Edward Gibbon's *Decline and Fall of the Roman Empire*
C. the Englishman Edward Gibbon vividly narrated the fall of Rome in *Decline and Fall of the Roman Empire*
D. *Decline and Fall of the Roman Empire* by the Englishman Edward Gibbon is a vivid narration of the fall of Rome
E. the fall of Rome, in the Englishman Edward Gibbon's *Decline and Fall of the Roman Empire,* is vividly narrated.

3. Another classic in English historical scholarship, <u>Macauley wrote his five-volume *History of England* during the Eighteenth Century</u>.
A. Macauley wrote his five-volume *History of England* during the Eighteenth Century
B. Macauley was writing his five-volume *History of England* during the Eighteenth Century
C. Macauley's five-volume *History of England* was written during the Eighteenth Century
D. the Eighteenth Century was the time when Macauley wrote his five-volume *History of England*
E. the writing of Macauley's five-volume *History of England* took place in the Eighteenth Century

4. Having lived in a small, Midwestern town, <u>New York City was completely overwhelming</u>.
A. New York City was completely overwhelming
B. the overwhelmingness of New York City to me can hardly be overstated
C. you can imagine how overwhelming New York City was to me
D. nothing could have prepared me for New York City
E. I was completely overwhelmed by New York City

5. Heated naturally by thermal hot springs, <u>one could make this grotto a prime attraction as a place for swimming and bathing</u>.
A. one could make this grotto a prime attraction as a place for swimming and bathing
B. this grotto could be made into a prime attraction as a place for swimming and bathing
C. you could make this grotto a prime attraction as a place for swimming and bathing
D. a prime attraction as a place for swimming and bathing is what this grotto should be made into.
E. a place for swimming and bathing would make this grotto a prime attraction

V. Word Order and Sentence Structure

Misplaced Modifiers

Improving Sentences, cont.

6. <u>Seeing Mick Jagger ride his bicycle along the Esplanade, the surprise was overwhelming</u>.

A. Seeing Mick Jagger ride his bicycle along the Esplanade, the surprise was overwhelming
B. Seeing Mick Jagger ride his bicycle along the Esplanade, you could say we were overwhelmed
C. When we saw Mick Jagger ride his bicycle along the Esplanade, the surprise was overwhelming
D. Seeing Mick Jagger ride his bicycle along the Esplanade, overwhelming was the surprise
E. The surprise was overwhelming, seeing Mick Jagger ride his bicycle along the Esplanade

7. Confronted with the evidence, undeniable and incontrovertible, <u>a full confession was finally obtained from the accused</u>.
A. a full confession was finally obtained from the accused
B. we finally obtained a full confession from the accused
C. the obtaining of a full confession from the accused was finally done
D. the fullness of the confession was finally obtained from the accused
E. the accused woman finally made a full confession

8. High in the Crow's Nest, unwatched and alone, above the sea's vastness below me, <u>I clung to the ropes lest I should grow dizzy from the solitude and grandeur</u>.
A. I clung to the ropes lest I should grow dizzy from the solitude and grandeur
B. the ropes were my anchor lest I should grow dizzy from the solitude and grandeur
C. dizziness was a danger, from the solitude and grandeur
D. solitude and grandeur threatened to make me dizzy if I didn't hold fast to the ropes
E. clinging to the ropes was my anchor lest I should grow dizzy from the solitude and grandeur

9. The umbrella left behind on the subway <u>must have been Thomas's, who leaves a trail of umbrellas when it rains</u>.
A. must have been Thomas's, who leaves a trail of umbrellas when it rains
B. must have been Thomas's, umbrellas being something he tends to leave behind when it rains
C. must be Thomas's, who leaves a trail of umbrellas when it rains
D. must have belonged to Thomas, who leaves a trail of umbrellas when it rains
E. must be Thomas's, umbrellas being something he tends to leave behind when it rains

10. With their seemingly tireless rise and fall, <u>we seem to take the ocean's tides</u> for granted.
A. we seem to take the ocean's tides
B. the ocean's tides can easily be taken
C. we seem be taking the ocean's tides
D. we are taking the ocean's tides
E. one can take the ocean's tides

V. Word Order and Sentence Structure

B. Run-ons and incomplete sentences (fragments)

Rule: A sentence should be complete, containing a subject and a verb, but should not contain too many clauses so as to make its meaning unclear or convoluted, Since the only punctuation on this test is comma, colon and semicolon use, run-ons and sentence fragments usually occur in improving sentences and improving paragraphs sections.

Examples:

Each first sentence is incorrect.   Each second sentence corrects the problem. Compare and contrast each set.

1.   Pizza Pie. That is my favorite!
       Pizza pie is my favorite.

2.   The man, riding a bicycle. He was scary indeed!
       The man riding a bike was scary indeed!

3.   Though the path before us is long, and we may encounter obstacles, and we must finish.
       Though the path before us is long, and we may encounter obstacles, we must finish.

4.   In densely populated areas where the poor were often hidden from public view, driven to begging and tempted to crime.
       In densely populated areas, the poor were often hidden from public view, driven to begging and tempted to crime.

5.   Along the side of the road, asleep.
       He **was** along the side of the road, asleep.

6.   The man running after a bus having missed the train.
       The man was running after a bus, having missed the train

7.   My favorite animals? Dogs, cats, pelicans and flamingos.
       My favorite animals are dogs, cats, pelicans and flamingos

8.   That to secure these rights, governments are instituted among men, deriving their just powers from the consent of the governed.
       To secure these rights, governments are instituted among men, deriving their just powers from the consent of the governed.

9.   I could only hope, as many might, as many have, to have become one with my thoughts and feelings so as best to create a careful state of bliss and happiness and grandeur, I have hoped for this throughout my life, from the age of seven and beyond
       I could only hope, as many might, as many have, to have become one with my thoughts and feelings. In this way I could create a careful state of bliss and happiness and grandeur. I have hoped for this throughout my life, from the age of seven and beyond.

10.   Feelings of pain. Feelings of joy. These are common symptoms of love.
       Feelings of pain and joy are common symptoms of love.

V. Word Order and Sentence Structure

Run-ons and incomplete sentences (fragments)

Improving Sentences

1. From a front row bleacher <u>seat, the family watching the Red Sox in Fenway Park.</u>
A. seat, the family watching the Red Sox in Fenway Park.
B. seat, the family are watching the Red Sox in Fenway Park.
C. seat, the Red Sox are watched by the family in Fenway Park.
D. seat in Fenway Park, the family watching the Red Sox.
E. seat in Fenway Park, the family watches the Red Sox.

2. <u>Bob and Jay are promising students. One at Cornell and the other at Skidmore.</u>
A. Bob and Jay are promising students. One at Cornell and the other at Skidmore.
B. Bob and Jay are promising students, the former is at Cornell and the latter is at Skidmore.
C. Bob and Jay are promising students, one at Cornell and the other at Skidmore.
D. Bob and Jay are promising students: one at Cornell and the other at Skidmore.
E. Bob and Jay are promising students; Bob being at Cornell, Jay at Skidmore.

3. <u>Taken from the novel *Gone with the Wind,* Tara remaining a popular name.</u>
A. Taken from the novel *Gone with the Wind*^ Tara remaining a popular name.
B. Taken from the novel *Gone with the Wind:* Tara was remaining a popular name.
C. Taken from the novel *Gone with the Wind,* Tara was remaining a popular name.
D. Taken from the novel *Gone with the Wind;* Tara remained a popular name.
E. Taken from the novel *Gone with the Wind,* Tara has remained a popular name.

4. <u>We were seeking help after the storm; running from house to house searching for water.</u>
A. We were seeking help after the storm; running from house to house searching for water.
B. We were seeking help after the storm: as we ran from house to house searching for water.
C. We were seeking help after the storm; as we ran from house to house searching for water.
D. When we were seeking help after the storm; we ran from house to house searching for water.
E. Seeking help after the storm, we ran from house to house searching for water.

5. <u>One of the most delicious desserts offered; tiramisu was chosen by half of the diners.</u>
A. One of the most delicious desserts offered; tiramisu was chosen by half of the diners.
B. One of the most delicious desserts offered, tiramisu was the choice of half of the diners.
C. One of the most delicious desserts offered. Tiramisu was chosen by half of the diners.
D. One of the most delicious desserts offered was tiramisu, it was chosen by half of the diners.
E. One of the most delicious desserts offered: tiramisu was chosen by half of the diners.

V. Word Order and Sentence Structure

C. Redundant or unneeded words or phrases

Rule: A sentence should be clear and precise, without awkwardness or ambiguity.

Examples

Each first sentence is incorrect.   Each second sentence corrects the problem.
Compare and contrast each set.

1.   The **reason** for the delay **is because** the runway became icy.
     The reason for the delay **is that** the runway became icy.

2.   Members of **today's contemporary society** may enjoy material prosperity but face a degree
     of emotional isolation.
     Members of **contemporary society** may enjoy material prosperity but face a degree of
     emotional isolation.

3.   There is no cause for alarm **now, at this point in time.**
     There is no cause for alarm now (or at this point in time).

4.   There is a **complete dearth** of food on this rocky island.
     There is a **dearth** of food on this rocky island.

5.   **Surrounded on all sides,** the rebels were forced to surrender.
     Surrounded, the rebels were forced to surrender.

6.   You will need to **merge together** the two sets of documents **on a daily basis.**
     You will need to **merge** the two sets of documents daily.

7.   As I passed the **golf course where people golf,** I found myself **thinking thoughts** of being
     Tiger Woods.
     As I passed the **golf course,** I found myself with thoughts of being Tiger Woods.

8.   In *My life as a Dog,* **the main character in the leading role** is a radio talk show host.
     In *My life as a Dog,* **the main character** is a radio talk show host.

9.   The two warring factions sought to draw up a treaty that would address **the mutual
     concerns of both sides.**
     The two warring factions sought to draw up a treaty that would address their **mutual
     concerns.**

10. **My fellow colleagues** and I are in agreement that we must uphold the standard of
     excellence.
     My colleagues and I agree that we must uphold the standard of excellence.

V. Word Order and Sentence Structure

Redundant or unneeded words or phrases

Identifying Sentence Errors

1. The detective <u>ingeniously</u> <u>connected together</u> the dots and <u>correctly identified</u> the
                        A   B   C
<u>guilty party.</u>   <u>No error</u>
        D   E

2. The Red Army <u>advanced forward</u> along the river in a <u>bitterly cold</u> <u>forced march</u> that
                      A   B   C
left hundreds of soldiers frostbitten or <u>suffering from hypothermia</u>, or both.   <u>No error</u>
                                                        D   E

3. Despite the <u>many advances</u> in <u>weather-related technology</u> and storm-detection
                      A   B
in particular, the United States Weather Service was unable to <u>anticipate in advance</u> the
                                                                              C
tornadoes <u>that ravaged the Midwest</u>.   <u>No error</u>
                    D   E

4. The <u>important essentials</u> of molecular biology <u>are not limited to</u> the structures of DNA
                  A   B
and RNA, <u>but include</u> protein structure, enzyme chemistry, <u>and various metabolic</u>
                  C   D
pathways, among other things.   <u>No error</u>
                                          E

5. <u>In order to understand</u> <u>what constitutes</u> the best strategy for a soccer team, a coach
              A   B
<u>who has access</u> to videotapes of past games should analyze <u>each separate goal</u>.   <u>No error</u>
        C   D   E

V. Word Order and Sentence Structure

Redundant or unneeded words or phrases

Improving Sentences

1. Together, the bride and groom <u>descended down the spiral staircase to the grand ballroom below</u>, only to find that their guests had already been seated.
   A. descended down the spiral staircase to the grand ballroom below
   B. had been descending down the spiral staircase to the grand ballroom below
   C. descended the spiral staircase to the grand ballroom below
   D. were descending through the spiral staircase to the grand ballroom below
   E. down the spiral staircase to the grand ballroom below

2. Einstein theorized, then proved, that time and space are not unrelated, but rather <u>that these two concepts are inextricably tied together</u>.
   A. that these two concepts are inextricably tied together
   B. that two concepts inextricably tied together these are
   C. that two concepts may be tied together inextricably
   D. two concepts tied together are inextricable
   E. that these concepts, the two of them, are inextricably tied

3. An emotionally charged person will often use the downward overhead strike with a fist, knife, bottle or club <u>to lash out, hurt or injure you</u>.
   A. to lash out, hurt or injure you.
   B. lash out or to hurt or to injure you
   C. to lash out and injure or hurt you
   D. to lash out, then to hurt then injure you
   E. lashing out and injuring or hurting you

4. Some spiritual healers believe that amethyst <u>aids and helps in achieving spiritual quests and that wearing it helps promote meditation, peace, tranquility and oneness with spiritual goals.</u>
   A. aids and helps in achieving spiritual quests and that wearing it helps promote meditation, peace, tranquility and oneness with spiritual goals.
   B. aids in achieving spiritual quests and that wearing it helps promote meditation, peace, tranquility and oneness with spiritual goals.
   C. aids and helps in achieving spiritual quests and wearing it helps promote meditation, peace, tranquility and oneness with spiritual goals.
   D. aids and helps in achieving spiritual quests though wearing it helps promote meditation, peace, tranquility and oneness with spiritual goals.
   E. aids in achieving spiritual quests, wearing it helps promote meditation, peace, tranquility and oneness with spiritual goals.

5. Traditionally, <u>the curdling agent used to make or produce tofu is nigari</u>, a compound found in natural ocean water, or calcium sulfate, a naturally occurring mineral
   A. the curdling agent used to make or produce tofu is nigari
   B. the curdling agents used to make or produce tofu is nigari
   C. the agents that curdle tofu is nigari
   D. the curdling agent that is used to make or produce tofu is nigari
   E. the curdling agent used to produce tofu is nigari

V. Word Order and Sentence Structure

D. Punctuation: Commas, Semicolons and Colons

Rule: When joining two complete sentences, a comma cannot be used. Use a semicolon or colon when the sentences are understood to be directly connected to each other. (Note: You will not be tested on the differences between a semicolon and a colon on this exam.)

Examples:

Each first sentence is incorrect. Each second sentence corrects the problem. Compare and contrast each set.

1. When a heat wave strikes and humidity skyrockets, normal services like transportation, hospitals, and schools may break **down, also** chaos may ensue and people may be injured as a result.
When a heat wave strikes and humidity skyrockets, normal services like transportation, hospitals, and schools may break **down; as a result**, chaos may ensue and injuries may occur.

2. The young lady called the office looking for an editor for her article, but she was calling the wrong **office, she** had thought she was calling the office of the magazine Vogue.
The young lady called the office looking for an editor for her article, but she was calling the wrong **office; she** had thought she was calling the office of the magazine Vogue.

3. There was concern about ticket sales for her tour but fans packed the venue on Sunday to see the superstar unleash hit after **hit, many** of them came from early in her 20-year career.
There was concern about ticket sales for her tour but fans packed the venue on Sunday to see the superstar unleash hit after **hit; many** of them came from early in her 20-year career.

4. The storeowner collects unusual **items, ceramic** frogs, doilies, and lunchboxes.
The storeowner collects unusual **items; these** include ceramic frogs, doilies, and lunchboxes.

5. Digital cameras allow one to choose which photographs one wants to **develop however** the cost of developing the pictures may be higher than the cost of developing non-digital film.
Digital cameras allow one to choose which photographs one wants to **develop; however,** the cost of developing the pictures may be higher than the cost of developing non-digital film.

6. Human population is encroaching further and further into previously untouched woodland **areas, no** wonder reported wildcat attacks are on the rise.
Human population is encroaching further and further into previously untouched woodland **areas; no** wonder reported wildcat attacks are on the rise

7. The Boston Red Sox may never again win the World **Series; but** 2004 was a great thrill ride!
The Boston Red Sox may never again win the World **Series, but** 2004 was a great thrill ride!

8. That was one of the most exciting games of the **season, our** team caught up from behind in the final period, scoring two goals.
That was one of the most exciting games of the **season; our** team caught up from behind in the final period, scoring two goals.

9. Lois Greenfield has photographed dancers from many of the world's major dance **companies and her** photographs have been exhibited in museums and galleries worldwide.
Lois Greenfield has photographed dancers from many of the world's major dance **companies; her** photographs have been exhibited in museums and galleries worldwide.

10. The lightning flashed through the sky like a brilliant fireworks **display. Although** the sound of the thunder was not so dramatic.
The lightning flashed through the sky like a brilliant fireworks **display; the** sound of the thunder was not so dramatic.

V. Word Order and Sentence Structure

Punctuation: Commas, Semicolons and Colons

Identifying Sentence Errors

1. In an effort to curb obesity <u>among</u> teenagers, some high schools have

                                        A

removed sodas <u>that have</u> a high sugar <u>content; replacing</u> them <u>with</u> bottled water

                     B   C   D

and fruit juice. <u>No error</u>

                    E

2. Many young people <u>date and eventually</u> want to get <u>married, the</u> nation's

                           A   B

<u>high divorce rate</u> among those who marry young should be a <u>deterrent</u> for some. <u>No error</u>

     C   D   E

3. Big Sister is a non-profit <u>organization that</u> matches young girls with women

                                    A

<u>who serve as</u> <u>their</u> <u>mentors; the</u> mentor's role is to be a guide, a friend and a

    B   C   D

chaperone. <u>No error</u>

                E

4. <u>Even though</u> she <u>had never</u> skated <u>before, Johanna</u> was not afraid to learn to ice skate

      A   B   C

  <u>at the age of</u> 45. <u>No error</u>

     D   E

5. Many adults <u>who grew up in</u> New York City do not know how to <u>drive because</u>

                  A   B

the streets of New York are <u>so congested that</u> most people travel by <u>taxi they do not</u> drive

                                 C   D

their own cars. <u>No error</u>

                    E

V. Word Order and Sentence Structure

Punctuation: Commas, Semicolons and Colons

Improving Sentences

1. <u>House and Senate budget negotiators reached agreement on a budget plan for next year. The first in several years that does not include severe cuts in popular programs and services.</u>

A. House and Senate budget negotiators reached agreement on a budget plan for next year. The first in several years that does not include severe cuts in popular programs and services.
B. House and Senate budget negotiators reached agreement on a budget plan for next year and it is the first in several years that does not include severe cuts in popular programs and services.
C. The first in several years that does not include severe cuts in popular programs and services, House and Senate budget negotiators reached agreement on a budget plan for next year.
D. The budget plan that was reached by the House and Senate budget negotiators for next year is the first that does not include, in several years, severe cuts in popular programs and services.
E. House and Senate budget negotiators reached agreement on a budget plan for next year, the first in several years that does not include severe cuts in popular programs and services.

2. Several countries such as Poland and the Czech Republic<u> have recently joined the European Union and have not yet</u> started using the Euro as their currency.

A. have recently joined the European Union and have not yet
B. have recently joined the European Union, but have not yet
C. has not yet joined the European Union or
D. have recently joined the European Union while not having
E. has recently joined the European Union and

3. When traveling to Costa Rica, <u>one should bring mosquito repellent, layered clothing, bottled water, a hat, and walking shoes.</u>
A. one should bring mosquito repellent, layered clothing, bottled water, a hat, and walking shoes.
B. one should be bringing the following items: mosquito repellent, layered clothing, bottled water, a hat, and walking shoes.
C. one should bring the following items mosquito repellent, layered clothing, bottled water, a hat, and walking shoes.
D. one should bring the following items, mosquito repellent, layered clothing, bottled water, a hat, and walking shoes.
E. mosquito repellent, layered clothing, bottled water, a hat, and walking shoes should be brought.

4. With the current technology available, Mark, a musician, was able to make his own compact disc for relatively little <u>money, he was able to save a lot </u>and put that money into other things.
A. money, he was able to save a lot
B. money, he saved a lot
C. money; he saved a lot
D. money which he saved a lot
E. money, saving a lot

5. <u>The "Beats for Peace" program brings together youth and national musical celebrities to spread the message of peace through hip hop and it does a tour across New England.</u>
A. The "Beats for Peace" program brings together youth and national musical celebrities to spread the message of peace through hip hop and it does a tour across New England.
B. The message of peace gets spread through hip hop by the "Beats for Peace" program bringing together youth and national musical celebrities. They tour across New England.
C. The "Beats for Peace" program, which tours across New England, brings together youth and national musical celebrities to spread the message of peace through hip hop.
D. Youth and national musical celebrities are brought together by the "Beats for Peace" program to spread the message of peace through hip hop, doing a tour across New England.
E. Being all about peace, The "Beats for Peace" program brings together youth and national musical celebrities to spread the message of peace through hip hop and it does a tour across New England.

VI. Other Grammar Issues

A. Prepositions and Phrases
B. Passive and Active Voice
C. Being + ing
D. Assorted Exercises

VI. Other Grammar Issues

A. Prepositions and other expressions

Rule: A prepositional phrase consists of a preposition, a noun or pronoun that serves as the object of the preposition, and, more often than not, an adjective that modifies the object. Make sure you know the correct preposition to fit the phrase.

Examples:

Below are examples of common prepositional (and other) phrases, along with the common errant word or words.

1. Darwin's celebrated *Theory of the Evolution of Species* had its **origin in** laboratory observations of fruit flies.
(Not "... had its origin from...")

2. The students **protested against** plans for a new school without handicapped-accessible bathrooms.
(Not "protested over")

3. Only Superman was **capable of** saving the planet.
(Not "capable to")

4. Are you **able to** climb a rope?
(Not "able of ")

5. Utopian ideas pertain to a world **in which** everything is perfect.
(Not "where")

6. The ambassador's **insight into** the situation in the Middle East made him a foremost authority on the question of how to plan for peace.
(Not "insight about" or "insight on")

7. Most bicyclists **prefer** flat roads **to** hills.
(Not "prefer... over")

8. Jan was **preoccupied with** the upcoming cheerleading try-outs.
(Not "preoccupied about")

9. **Both** humanitarians **and** economists are critical of the penitentiary system.
(Not "both... and also" or "both... as well as")

10. **According to** the ancient rule, you, **together with** the other travelers, must choose **between** Door A **and** Door B, even if you're **indifferent to** the outcome.
(Not "according of"; "together to"; "between... or"; or "indifferent about")

VI. Other Grammar Issues

Prepositional and other phrases

Fill-in-the-blanks exercise

1. Old-fashioned remedies are not always the best **solution** _____ the common cold.

2. Listening to her great-grandmother, Sheila was able to gain some **insight** _____ the 1920's and the Jazz Age.

3. The children at the daycare wanted to visit **both** the circus _____ the ice cream shop.

4. Each of the news anchors made a personal **commentary** _____ Reagan's funeral.

5. At the United Nations, spontaneous translations are quite **helpful** _____ allowing the members to fully understand other delegates.

6. Many Massachusetts politicians do not seem to be **sensitive** _____ the concerns, ambitions and desires of the majority of their constituents.

7. Paul's ancestors and their customary traditions **originated** _____ either Ireland or Scotland.

8. When Marie enters the bakery, she often has difficulty choosing **between** the chocolate croissants _____ the almond macaroons.

9. Charles Dickens' *Oliver Twist* is an intricate **novel** _____ the poverty-stricken are portrayed as carefully as the well off. (Choose between 'where' & 'in which')

10. Smoking and asthma may **prevent** an aspiring athlete _____ competing seriously in cross-country meets.

VI. Other Grammar Issues

B. Passive and active voice

A general note: a passive voice is seldom incorrect, but one can often <u>improve</u> a sentence by making it more "active." Therefore, this guideline is usually relevant only in <u>improving sentences</u> sections.

Examples:

Each first sentence is incorrect. Each second sentence corrects the problem. Compare and contrast each set.

1. A light is being shined by the lighthouse.
The lighthouse beam is shining.

2. The meal was prepared by Julie.
Julie prepared the meal.

3. Julie painted the house, but the landscaping was done by her brother.
Julie painted the house, but her brother did the landscaping.

4. The conference will be attended by many delegates.
Many delegates will attend the conference.

5. In the novel *The DaVinci Code,* a cliffhanger is found at the end of each chapter.
In the novel *The DaVinci Code,* each chapter ends with a cliffhanger.

6. The experiment that is going to be conducted by the students is the first of its kind.
The students are going to conduct an experiment which is the first of its kind.

7. The songs are being sung loudly and clearly by the children.
The children are singing the songs loudly and clearly.

8. My face is being blown by the air coming from the fan.
The fan is blowing air into my face.

9. The photographs produced by my camera are grainy and pale.
My camera produced pale, grainy photographs.

10. Cars painted with unusual patterns by their owners are rare.
Car owners rarely paint their cars with unusual patterns.

VI. Other Grammar Issues

Passive and Active Voice

Improving Sentences

1. <u>Milk containing rBGH, a growth hormone given to cows, is permitted by the Department of Agriculture to be sold by farmers in the United States, although it is not allowed by many European nations to be sold by their farmers.</u>
A. Milk containing rBGH, a growth hormone given to cows, is permitted by the Department of Agriculture to be sold by farmers in the United States, although it is not allowed by many European nations to be sold by their farmers.
B. The cows given rBGH, which is a growth hormone, are allowed to have their milk sold by farmers, because the United States Department of Agriculture says they can, even though it is not allowed by many European nations to be sold by their farmers.
C. rBGH, which is contained in milk from the cows who were treated with it by the farmers, is permitted by the Department of Agriculture to be sold by farmers in the United States, although many European nations don't let their farmers sell it.
D. The United States Department of Agriculture allows farmers who treat their cows with the growth hormone rBGH to sell their milk, even though many European nations do not allow their farmers to do the same.
E. Being that many European nations don't allow their farmers to sell milk from cows who have been treated with rGBH, a growth hormone, in the United States where they are allowed.

2. Buddhism has become popular in the West, and, as a result, <u>sitting meditation is practiced by many people.</u>
A. sitting meditation is practiced by many people.
B. many people can be found practicing sitting meditation
C. many people practice sitting meditation.
D. sitting meditation, as practiced by many people, has also become popular.
E. with sitting meditation being practiced by many people.

3. <u>*Eats, Shoots & Leaves*, a humorous book about grammar, is being read by many people who have never before taken an interest in grammar.</u>
A. *Eats, Shoots & Leaves,* a humorous book about grammar, is being read by many people who have never before taken an interest in grammar.
B. Many people who previously have never taken an interest in grammar are reading *Eats, Shoots & Leaves,* a humorous book about grammar.
C. *Eats, Shoots & Leaves,* a humorous book about grammar, is being read by many people even though, in the past, grammar has not been liked by many of these people,
 D. Even though many people have never before taken an interest in grammar, *Eats, Shoots & Leaves,* a humorous book about grammar, is being read by them.
E. Grammar has not been liked by many people, but they are still reading *Eats, Shoots & Leaves,* a humorous book about grammar.

4. <u>While we were watching the volcano in Costa Rica, the fiery lava flowed down the mountain.</u>
A. While we were watching the volcano, the fiery lava flowed down the mountain.
B. While the volcano was being watched by us, the fiery lava flowed down the mountain.
C. While the volcano was being watched by us, the mountain was being covered by fiery lava.
D. While we were watching the volcano and fiery lava flowed down the mountain.
E. Being watchers of the volcano, we saw the fiery lava flow down the mountain.

5. My camera broke during my vacation, but fortunately <u>I was offered copies of the photographs which my friends who were traveling with me took.</u>
A. I was offered copies of the photographs which my friends who were traveling with me took.
B. there were pictures taken by my friends who offered copies of their photographs.
C. other photographs were offered to me by my friends who also took pictures.
D. the friends I was traveling with offered to make copies of their pictures for me.
E. I was traveling with friends who also took pictures and offered to make copies of their photographs for me.

VI. Other Grammar Issues

C. Being and other "ing" words

Note: "Being" or other such "ing" constructions are seldom wrong, but can generally be improved. Thus, you will almost never chose an "ing" construction in *Identifying Sentence Error questions,* but you may often need to select a choice other than an "ing" construction in *Improving Sentences* questions.

Examples:

1. <u>Being the fastest runner in the Boston Marathon</u>, Lee is expected to win the New York City Marathon.
   A. Being the fastest runner in the Boston Marathon
   B. Being the fastest runner for the Boston Marathon
   C. Being the most fast runner in the Boston Marathon
   D. By being the fastest runner in the Boston Marathon
   E. The fastest runner in the Boston Marathon

2. <u>Being her favorite jewel</u>, diamonds are all that Sally would wear.
   A. Being her favorite jewel
   B. Because they are her favorite jewel
   C. Because it is being her favorite jewel
   D. Her favoritest jewel
   E. By being her most favorite jewel

3. <u>Being an Oscar-winning film</u>, *Casablanca* is on many top ten lists.
   A. Being an Oscar-winning film
   B. As being as Oscar-winning film
   C. An Oscar-winning film
   D. Because of it being an Oscar-winning film
   E. By being an Oscar-winning film

4. <u>Being absent</u>, I missed the test.
   A. Being absent
   B. Because I was being absent
   C. Because I was absent
   D. Having been previously absent
   E. As being absent

5. <u>Having lost the starring role</u>, Charlotte was devastated and heartbroken.
   A. Having lost the starring role
   B. Being that she lost the starring role
   C. Having losing the starring role
   D. The role being lost
   E. Losing the role of the star

VI. Other Grammar Issues

Common prepositional phrases and expressions

Memorize these!

<u>Correct</u> <u>Common Error</u>

Origin	In	(not: from)
Sensitive	To	
Originate	In	(not: from)
Insensitive	To	(not: about)
Protest	Against	(not: over)
Helpful	In	(not: for)
Comment	On	(not: about)
Indifferent	To	(not: about)
Commentary	On	(not: about)
In order	To	(not: for)
Solution	To	(not: for)
According	To	
Capable	Of	(not: to)
Subsequent	To	
Able	To	(not: for)
Together	With	(not: along with)
Ability	To	(not: for)
Plan	In which	(not: where)
World	In which	(not: where)
Map	In which *	(not: where) * "on" may be becoming accepted as an idiom
Insight	Into	(not: about)
Caused	By	(not: from)
Prefer	To	(not: over)
Preoccupied	With	(not: about)
Preoccupation	With	(not: about)
Prevent	From	(not: to)
Both	And	(not: as well as)
Between	And	(not: or)
Along	With	
Aside	From	
Next	To	
Because	Of	
By means	Of	
In front	Of	
In spite	Of	
Out	Of	
Owing	To	

Three Practice Tests

SAT Writing Test I
Time -- 30 minutes
36 Questions

Directions: For each question in this section, select the best answer from among the choices given and fill in the corresponding oval on the answer sheet.

1. Since my colleagues are <u>often</u>
                           A
<u>unreasonably</u> preoccupied <u>by</u> their personal
      B   C
problems, I made a plan to <u>protest</u> against
                           D
their lack of contributions. (E) <u>No error</u>

2. Either the young man <u>or</u> his sister will
                        A
comment <u>on</u> this society's lack <u>of</u> freedom of
        B   C
speech which prevents citizens <u>from</u> playing
                               D
a role in the national government.

(E) <u>No error</u>

3. Often helpful <u>in</u> translating the news, our
                 A
multilingual friend <u>has</u> the <u>distinction of</u>
                    B   C
communicating <u>in</u> seven different languages.
              D
(E) <u>No error</u>

4. Sensitive <u>to</u> the problems of immigrants,
             A
our city has offered multicultural assistance

to those <u>who</u> do not have <u>any</u> insight <u>on</u>
         B   C   D
contemporary life. (E) <u>No error</u>

5. Yesterday morning, the President of the

United States fell <u>off</u> his dirt bike <u>when</u> he
                    A   B
was indifferent <u>about</u> the riding conditions
                C
near the <u>poorly</u> lit road. (E) <u>No error</u>
         D

6. <u>However</u> many times I ask her, Shelby
   A
refuses <u>to entertain</u> the notion that cleaning
        B
her room <u>would make</u> it <u>easier</u> to find her
         C   D
schoolwork. (E) <u>No error</u>

7. When her doctor <u>handed</u> her a
                   A
prescription, Jacqui <u>saw</u> that the medication
                     B
<u>was</u> the same as <u>her sister</u>. (E) <u>No error</u>
C   D

8. <u>Despite</u> his <u>degree in</u> Art History, my
   A   B
grandfather can identify <u>scarcely no</u>
                         C
<u>famous paintings</u>
D
(E) <u>No error</u>

9. As an <u>employee of</u> the Do-It-Yourself
         A
publishing company, the editor <u>specializes</u> in
                                B
books <u>about</u> yard work, <u>how to cook</u>, and
       C   D
home improvement. (E) <u>No error</u>

10. Neither of my brothers <u>understand</u> that
                           A
in order to <u>lower</u> one's weight, <u>one</u> must
            B   C
exercise more consistently and eat

<u>more healthily</u>. (E) <u>No error</u>
D

11. Along the east <u>side of</u> the beach <u>blooms</u>
                   A   B
the wild flowers <u>that</u> make the scenic area
                 C
<u>so colorful</u> during the summer. (E) <u>No error</u>
D

12. <u>All of the players</u> except Frances and <u>I</u>
    A   B
<u>have agreed</u> to sign next year's contract to
C
increase the <u>number</u> of the basketball games.
             D
(E) <u>No error</u>

13. Each critic observed that the

fundamental ideas <u>seem</u> both
                    A
<u>profound and common</u> because of
       B
Shakespeare's <u>ability toward</u> presenting his
                    C
<u>weighty themes</u> along with human frailties.
       D
(E) <u>No error</u>

14. The narrative described the eerie tale

<u>where</u> witches, together <u>with</u> goblins, <u>predict</u>
   A   B   C
the future as well as <u>influence</u> the present.
                           D

(E) <u>No error</u>

15. One way in which my brothers'

experience <u>differs from</u> yours <u>is that</u> our
               A   B
family is <u>subject to</u> the wishes of neither a
               C
mother <u>nor</u> a father. (E) <u>No error</u>
           D

16. After the initial success of the Beatles,

hundreds of teenagers <u>who wanted</u> <u>to be</u>
                            A   B
<u>a rock musician</u> decided to sign up <u>for</u> music
       C   D
lessons. (E) <u>No error</u>

17. <u>Fewer and fewer</u> attorneys now practice
           A
in the city; <u>they</u> prefer the suburban
B   C
neighborhoods <u>to</u> the metropolitan
                    D
environment. (E) <u>No error</u>

Directions: Choose the answer that best expresses the meaning of the original sentence. If you think the original is better than any of the alternatives, choose it; otherwise choose one of the others. Your choice should produce the most effective sentence — clear and precise, without awkwardness or ambiguity.

18. Julia failed to appear at work this <u>morning, without even calling in sick.</u>
(A) morning, without even calling in sick.
(B) morning, without having called in sick.
(C) morning; and without calling in sick.
(D) morning and did not even call in sick.
(E) morning, did not even call in sick.

19. The rare piece of artwork sold <u>for beyond above its asking price of one million dollars.</u>
(A) for beyond above its asking price of one million dollars.
(B) for above it's asking price, one million dollars.
(C) for more than the asked one million dollars' price.
(D) for well above its one million dollar asking price.
(E) for well above it is one million dollar asking price.

20. When the protestors began their sit-in, <u>so the police yelled over their megaphones for the crowd to disperse.</u>
(A) so the police yelled over their megaphones for the crowd to disperse.
(B) they heard the police yell over their megaphones for the crowd to disperse.
(C) they heard the police yelled
(D) over their megaphones for the crowd to disperse.
(E) the police yell that the crowd should disperse over their megaphones.
(F) the police yelled that, over their megaphones, the crowd should disperse.

21. Despite their fear of heights, <u>the parachutes in the jumpers' packs opened without difficulty.</u>
(A) the parachutes in the jumpers' packs opened without difficulty.
(B) the parachutes opened without difficulty in the jumpers' packs.
(C) the jumpers' packs opened the parachutes without difficulty.
(D) the jumpers opened the parachutes from their packs without difficulty.
(E) the jumpers opened their packs' parachutes without difficulty.

22. There are seven stars in that <u>constellation, only however four are visible without a telescope.</u>
(A) constellation, only however four are visible without a telescope.
(B) constellation, however, four are visible without a telescope only.
(C) constellation, without a telescope however only four are visible.
(D) constellation; however, only four are visible without a telescope.
(E) constellation; however, only four are visible avoiding a telescope.

23. It is hard for many Americans to <u>believe, other countries where death is celebrated</u> as the next step of a journey.
(A) believe, other countries where death is celebrated
(B) believe that other countries where death is celebrated
(C) believe that other countries' death is celebrated
(D) believe, but other countries where death is celebrated
(E) believe that there are countries where death is celebrated

24. <u>Whenever a singer has the hiccups, they are detrimental to the performance.</u>
(A) Whenever a singer has the hiccups, they are detrimental to the performance.
(B) Whenever a singer has the hiccups, the performance is detrimental.
(C) The hiccups are always detrimental to a singer's performance.
(D) Always the hiccups are detrimental to a singer's performance.
(E) Whenever the performance of a singer has the hiccups, it is detrimental.

25. The rainstorm not only forced the beachgoers inside, <u>but also caused</u> the temperature to rapidly drop ten degrees.
(A) but also caused
(B) but it caused
(C) it caused
(D) and additionally caused
(E) as well as caused

26. By attracting a higher caliber of employees, <u>the company's future was ensured.</u>
(A) the company's future was ensured.
(B) the company's future became ensured.
(C) the company ensured its future.
(D) the company future was ensured.
(E) the future of the company was ensured.

27. The subway map caused more confusion than <u>understanding, it contained a misprint.</u>
(A) understanding, it contained a misprint.
(B) understanding; it contained a misprint.
(C) understanding because of the misprint contained on it.
(D) understanding because of its contained misprint.
(E) understanding; its contained misprint.

28. The doctor was completely <u>insensitive about Seth's fear of needles.</u>
(A) insensitive about Seth's fear of needles.
(B) insensitive for Seth's fear of needles.
(C) insensitive to Seth's fear of needles.
(D) insensitive due to Seth's fear of needles.
(E) insensitive with Seth's fear of needles.

29. Some say that money is the root of all <u>evil; but evil predates money.</u>
(A) evil; though evil predates money.
(B) evil; but it predates it.
(C) evil, but, it predates it.
(D) evil, but money predates evil.
(E) evil, but evil predates money.

30. In a nationwide poll about the color preferences of ten thousand volunteers, <u>seventy-four percent of men prefer blue over pink.</u>
(A) seventy-four percent of men prefer blue over pink.
(B) seventy-four percent of men prefer blue more than pink.
(C) seventy-four percent of the men in the poll prefer blue to pink.
(D) seventy-four percent of men prefer blue against pink.
(E) seventy-four percent of men prefer blue to pink.

Directions: The following passage is an early draft of an essay. Some parts of the passage need to be rewritten.

(1) Nearly everyone is troubled by the annoyance of a cough often enough that it affects his or her life adversely. (2) More than drug store medicines and lozenges. (3) There are quite a few remedies one can implement at home to help lessen the burden of this oft-spread illness. (4) For those who want to avoid just popping pills, here are some proven methods to ease that cough.

(5) If your cough seems to emanate primarily from your lungs, try steam. (6) If possible, take several long, hot showers a day, focusing on letting the water pound your chest to loosen congestion and breathe deeply as your cough allows. (7) Another option, more appropriate for someone who has responsibilities (such as watching the children at home) from which they cannot take a shower break, is to place a large pot of water on the stove and, with a towel over one's head, lean over the pot and breathe the steam directly. (8) Use caution if there are young people around the hot stove and never use this method on children. (9) There are small, portable machines that can be bought which serve this function as well; again, keep them away from children not old enough to understand that they get extremely hot and involve boiling water.

(10) If the pain is really bad and a home remedy is required, maybe something to numb the throat. (11) Some store-bought lozenges will do the trick, but if these are in short supply, try a Popsicle or some fresh-out-of-the-freezer ice cream. (12) These will provide some time away from the pain and are especially good for children. (13) Remember to be careful of hot liquids and foods while your throat is numb.

31. The writer's main purpose in the essay is to
(A) advise how to best deal with a specific situation
(B) suggest that children are hindrances
(C) point out the uselessness of modern medical practices
(D) ask for aid in getting well
(E) document a humorous story

32. Which of the following is the best way to combine sentences 2 and 3 (reproduced below)?

More than drug store medicines and lozenges. There are quite a few remedies one can implement at home to help lessen the burden of this oft-spread illness.

(A) (As it is now)
(B) More than drug store medicines and lozenges, there are quite a few
(C) In addition to drug store medicines and lozenges, there are quite a few
(D) In addition to drug store medicines and lozenges; there are quite a few
(E) Drug store medicines, lozenges, and quite a few

33. Which of the following is the best version of the underlined portion of sentence 6 (reproduced below)?

If possible, take several long, hot showers a day, focusing on letting the water pound your chest to loosen <u>congestion and breathe deeply as your cough allows</u>.

(A) (As it is now)
(B) congestion, and deeply breathe as your cough allows.
(C) congestion, and breathe as deep as your cough allows.
(D) congestion and breathing deep as your cough allows.
(E) congestion and breathing as deeply as your cough allows.

34. The writer's point would have been strengthened most by the inclusion of
(A) another home remedy suggestion
(B) information about the best brand of steam machine
(C) statistics about the ages at which children are most susceptible to coughs
(D) a list of cold foods
(E) experts' analysis of why health care is currently so expensive

35. Which of the following is the best version of the underlined portion of sentence 10 (reproduced below)?

If the pain is <u>really bad and a home remedy is required, something</u> to numb the throat.

(A) (As it is now)
(B) particularly strong and a home remedy is required, try something
(C) really strong and a home remedy is required, perhaps something
(D) really bad and a home remedy is required, try something
(E) particularly strong and a home remedy is required, something

36. In sentence 12, "some time away" is best replaced by
(A) a respite away
(B) some help
(C) temporary help
(D) temporary relief
(E) some escape time away

End of Test I
Answer key follows Test III

SAT Writing Test II
Time -- 30 minutes
36 Questions

Directions: For each question in this section, select the best answer from among the choices given and fill in the corresponding oval on the answer sheet.

1. This interior decorator <u>completely</u>
                              A
    transformed the <u>traditional</u> dining room
                       B
    <u>and they</u> had been used by other
       C
    decorators simply <u>to furnish</u> a place to
                          D
    eat. (E) <u>No error</u>

2. His thirst for knowledge led Hutton

    <u>to have studied</u> more than a hundred
          A
    theories <u>a year</u>; <u>still</u> he
               B   C
    <u>considered himself</u> lazy. (E) <u>No error</u>
       D

3. Betty Friedan, who <u>helped to launch</u>
                            A
    the feminist movement, <u>is</u> not only a
                             B
    superb organizer <u>while she is</u> also an
                        C
    <u>impressive</u> public speaker. (E) <u>No error</u>
       D

4. Fossils <u>found in</u> the region extending
                A
    from the river to the ocean's shore <u>attests</u>
                                           B
    to the <u>presence of</u> dinosaurs there
              C
    <u>as long ago as</u> one million years.
       D
    (E) <u>No error</u>

5. <u>As</u> the film industry grew in the
       A
    United States, the audiences began to

    <u>flock to</u> the local movie theaters;
       B
    <u>formally</u> they <u>had attended</u> the Vaudeville
       C   D
    theaters with more frequency.

    (E) <u>No error</u>

6. <u>Having received</u> an endorsement from
          A
    the Governor <u>so powerful that</u> it
                     B
    <u>could not hardly</u> be disregarded, Senator
       C
    Billingsworth was determined <u>to keep</u> his
                                     D
    campaign promises. (E) <u>No error</u>

7. Her younger sister assumes that

    everyone <u>is</u> as friendly <u>as her</u> and that
              A   B
    <u>nobody would</u> <u>deliberately be</u> mean.
       C   D
    (E) <u>No error</u>

8. Cher, who originally was

    <u>regarded by some</u> as <u>no more than</u> a
       A   B
    pop singer, has <u>recently received</u>
                       C
    widespread <u>critical acclaim</u> as an actress.
                  D
    (E) <u>No error</u>

9. <u>Although</u> the new jungle gym was
       A
    the <u>most clever</u> designed one that Paula
           B
    had <u>ever owned</u>, it could not prevent the
          C
    children <u>from</u> scratching the painted metal.
               D
    (E) <u>No error</u>

10. Lung cancer caused by excessive

    smoking <u>has been studied</u> for years, <u>but</u>
               A   B
    only recently <u>has</u> the truly harmful effects
                     C
    of cigarette smoking <u>become</u> known.
                            D
    (E) <u>No error</u>

172

11. <u>Until they</u> can be replaced by a crew of
     A

talented and creative actors, the theater

company <u>will not receive</u> <u>most of its</u>
         B   C

funding <u>from the public or private</u> sector.
            D

(E) <u>No error</u>

12. <u>Closely associated</u> with the rise of
      A

nationalism in Germany <u>was</u> an insistence
               B

on the part of many politicians that their

country <u>declare itself</u> naturally <u>superior to</u>
       C   D

the neighboring Western European

countries. (E) <u>No error</u>

13. Her love for children <u>led</u> <u>her</u> to enjoy
                 A B

watching Sesame Street on television

<u>as well</u> as <u>a career</u> at a community
  C   D

daycare center. (E) <u>No error</u>

14. Since <u>there is</u> a chair, two tables and a
       A

a bed in the apartment, Betty's roommate

<u>does not have</u> <u>to bring</u> <u>her own</u> furniture.
    B   C   D

(E) <u>No error</u>

15. The <u>breakdown</u> in communication
      A

between my cousin and his boss <u>was</u>
                    B

more a <u>result of</u> Kevin's stubbornness
       C

<u>rather than</u> of Mr. Hardy's strict dress
  D

code. (E) <u>No error</u>

16. All courts <u>impose</u> severe <u>penalties on</u>
        A   B

drivers who do not stop when <u>he or she is</u>
                    C

<u>followed by</u> police cars with sirens
  D

blaring. (E) <u>No error</u>

17. <u>Obviously,</u> Gauguin's paintings,
    A

<u>unlike Renoir</u>, are <u>unusual in</u> <u>their</u>
     B   C   D

South Pacific settings. (E) <u>No error</u>

Directions: Choose the answer that best expresses the meaning of the original sentence. If you think the original is better than any of the alternatives, choose it; otherwise choose one of the others. Your choice should produce the most effective sentence -- clear and precise, without awkwardness or ambiguity.

18. While working as an attorney in Manhattan, <u>that was when Martha developed a deep affinity for the Broadway stage</u>.
(A) that was when Martha developed a deep affinity for the Broadway stage.
(B) Martha developed a deep affinity for the Broadway stage.
(C) then the development of Martha's deep affinity for the Broadway stage took place.
(D) Martha's deep affinity for the Broadway stage developed.
(E) a deep affinity for the Broadway stage developed in Martha.

19. In 1990, consumers believed that non-smoking hotel rooms were <u>rare, it was estimated</u> that these designated rooms composed only a small proportion of the total number.
(A) rare, it was estimated
(B) rare, however it was estimated
(C) rare; they estimated
(D) rare; with estimates
(E) rare; estimates being

20. After soaking for twenty minutes in the hot tub, the swimmers were as relaxed as <u>if sleeping</u> on a cloud.
(A) if sleeping
(B) having slept
(C) if from sleeping
(D) if they had slept
(E) if they would have slept

21. Citizens are often capable of adopting a favorite politician's initiatives long before <u>any of the implications of the plans have been understood by them.</u>
(A) any of the implications of the plans have been understood by them.
(B) any implications for the politician's initiatives are understood by them.
(C) some of the implications for the politician's initiatives have been understood by them.
(D) they are understanding any of the implications of the politician's initiatives.
(E) they understand the implications of the politician's initiatives.

22. Barry liked to watch television <u>documentaries, of which he found the historical programming especially fascinating.</u>
(A) documentaries, of which he found the historical programming especially fascinating.
(B) documentaries; he found the historical programming especially fascinating.
(C) documentaries, and it was especially the historical programming that were of fascination.
(D) documentaries; the fascination of the historical programming especially.
(E) documentaries, especially fascinating to him were the historical programs.

23. Civil rights leader Martin Luther King was interested in non-violence because he believed that <u>if you protested peacefully it could</u> have a greater, more lasting effect than any violent demonstration.
(A) if you protested peacefully it could
(B) with the peaceful protests it could
(C) protests which were peacefully done could
(D) by doing peaceful protests it could
(E) protesting peacefully could

24. No factor was more instrumental <u>in bringing Pavarotti's tenor voice to the attention of a large, non-classical audience than</u> his appearance with the Three Tenors.
(A) in bringing Pavarotti's tenor voice to the attention of a large, non-classical audience than
(B) to bring Pavarotti's tenor voice to the attention of a large, non-classical audience than
(C) in bringing Pavarotti's tenor voice toward the attention of a large, non-classical audience than
(D) in bringing Pavarotti's tenor voice to the large, non-classical audience's attention than
(E) in the bringing of Pavarotti's tenor voice to the attention of a large, non-classical audience than

25. Strolling on the wooden boardwalk above the lake, <u>right beneath her a large spotted fish surfaced.</u>
(A) right beneath her a large spotted fish surfaced.
(B) there was a large spotted fish surfacing right beneath her.
(C) a large spotted fish surfaced right beneath her.
(D) she saw a large spotted fish surface right beneath her.
(E) she saw right beneath her a large spotted fish surfaced.

26. In the early and mid 20th century, before the invention of the computer, manuscripts were typed out on <u>a manual typewriter so it was difficult to correct any errors.</u>
(A) a manual typewriter so it was difficult to correct any errors.
(B) a manual typewriter, therefore it was difficult to correct any errors.
(C) a manual typewriter; that is why it was difficult to correct any errors.
(D) a manual typewriter, the reason being that it was difficult to correct any errors.
(E) a manual typewriter; as a result, it was difficult to correct any errors.

27. The ballet last Sunday evening was even better than any of the dancers could have <u>imagined, having received</u> a standing ovation from the enthusiastic audience.
(A) imagined, having received
(B) imagined; they had to receive
(C) imagined; they received
(D) imagined: including the reception of
(E) imagined and so they received

28. Feeding your infant too much food is as unhealthy <u>than if you feed</u> the baby too little.
(A) than if you feed
(B) as feeding
(C) as if one feed
(D) than it could be by feeding
(E) as for feeding

29. Though all of the artists had submitted extraordinary paintings on the same theme, <u>each painting had its own personality.</u>
(A) each painting had its own personality.
(B) each painting had their own personalities.
(C) with each there was their own personality.
(D) which had his own personality.
(E) they each had personalities of their own.

30. Sheldon was nervous about the song he had to sing, <u>this</u> nervousness helped to make him perform even better than he had expected.
(A) this
(B) furthermore
(C) but this
(D) for which
(E) that

Directions: The following passage is an early draft of an essay. Some parts of the passage need to be rewritten.

(1) It's your son's high school graduation and you know they've outgrown Big Bird and the Power Rangers. (2) Or perhaps it's your daughter's sweet sixteen party. (3) Don't know what to plan. (4) What to do for the big bash?

(5) Keep in mind that communication is key; while all the ideas below are hip and trendy, nothing is "right" unless it matches your teenager's interests. (6) Plan a time to sit down with him or her for fifteen minutes and seek ideas that work for both of you. (7) Again, no matter how great you think your plan is, it's sure to be a disaster without mutual approval.

(8) That said, here are numerous very cool and contemporary ideas for party themes. (9) Print them out, discuss them with your teen and expect a wonderful time!

THE MATRIX
(10) The key to this party is the color black: go with black invitations that ask guests to wear all black, with sunglasses, in their best Neo or Trinity imitations. (11) Use technology as your inspiration when planning decorations. (12) Not everyone in the world liked the film. (13) You might pass around red and blue tic tacs and be giving everyone a code name as they come in. (14) Remember, the goal is always to celebrate your teen's achievement, so perhaps the (computer-shaped) cake might read "Joey's out of the matrix!" for your graduating son.

31. What is the best way to improve sentence 1?
(A) replace "they've" with "he's"
(B) replace "son's" with "child's"
(C) replace "you know" with "one knows"
(D) delete "you know"
(E) delete "and the Power Rangers"

32. In context, what is the best way to improve sentences 2 and 3?
(A) party for her sweet sixteen. Don't know what to plan.
(B) sweet sixteen party; don't know what to plan.
(C) sweet sixteen party and don't know what to plan.
(D) sweet sixteen party and you don't know what to plan.
(E) sweet sixteen party, you don't know what to plan.

33. In context, where does sentence 6 best belong?
(A) where it is now
(B) after sentence 4
(C) after sentence 8
(D) after sentence 14
(E) deleted

34. In context, what is the best way to improve sentence 13?
(A) Be passing around red and blue tic tacs and be giving everyone a code name
(B) Pass around red and blue tic tacs, be giving everyone a code name
(C) Pass around red and blue tic tacs; giving everyone a code name
(D) Pass around red and blue tic tacs and give everyone a code name
(E) Passing around red and blue tic tacs and giving everyone a code name

35. What would best belong after the passage to continue its purpose?
(A) ideas about how to speak with teenagers
(B) ideas about how to print articles from the Internet
(C) ideas about why *The Matrix* is so popular with teenagers
(D) ideas about other themes for teen parties
(E) ideas about how to adapt Big Bird into a *Matrix*-themed party

36. The fourth paragraph would be strengthened by deleting which sentence?
(A) sentence 10
(B) sentence 11
(C) sentence 12
(D) sentence 13
(E) sentence 14

End of Test II
Answer key follows Test III

SAT Writing Test III
Time -- 30 minutes
36 Questions

Directions: For each question in this section, select the best answer from among the choices given and fill in the corresponding oval on the answer sheet.

1. <u>Despite</u> all the manned and unmanned
       A
space flights, <u>surprising</u> little is known
                    B
about the atmosphere of some planets <u>like</u>
                                          C
Pluto, which <u>lie</u> far from Earth.
              D
(E) <u>No error</u>

2. <u>Introducing</u> new advertising slogans
       A
or even revamping <u>old ones</u> <u>is</u> always a
                   B   C
highly delicate matter, <u>especially in</u> a
                          D
diverse and ever-changing consumer

market. (E) <u>No error</u>

3. Topaz, like <u>other</u> gemstones that chip
                 A
<u>easily</u>, <u>are</u> beautiful <u>in</u> necklaces.
  B   C   D
(E) <u>No error</u>

4. One way in which films <u>differ from</u>
                            A
novels <u>is that</u> the film characters <u>are seen</u>,
       B   C
not just imagined, by the audience

<u>members</u>. (E) <u>No error</u>
   D

5. Students who wish to be

<u>a licensed driver</u> should remember that
       A
driving <u>is not simply</u> a right, <u>but that</u> it is
        B   C
a privilege and responsibility <u>as well</u>.
                                  D

(E) <u>No error</u>

6. The endless quarreling between the

coach and <u>he</u> began as soon as the team
          A
captain <u>learned</u> that the coach insisted <u>on</u>
        B   C
<u>no days</u> off for the players this month.
   D
(E) <u>No error</u>

7. <u>No matter</u> where they came from
       A
<u>or what</u> their native <u>language is</u>, the music
   B   C
students were <u>grateful</u> for the
              D
complimentary concert tickets.

(E) <u>No error</u>

8. The jurors, <u>which ranged</u>
                  A
<u>from Dr. Jon Smyth</u> to the custodian
       B
Franklin Lowry, <u>heard little testimony</u>
                      C
<u>to give them</u> a clear understanding of
       D
the case. (E) <u>No error</u>

9. Only the <u>top two</u> candidates <u>had ran</u>
             A   B
a <u>clean</u> campaign before the <u>first primary</u>
  C   D
in Dixville Notch, New Hampshire.

(E) <u>No error</u>

10. The charm <u>of</u> that small inn lies in the
              A
simple comforts and <u>amenities</u>;
                      B
generally, <u>they competently</u> <u>take care of</u>
           C   D
weary travelers. (E) <u>No error</u>

11. The butterflies <u>drew</u> a crowd of
                    A
students, <u>for</u> <u>they</u> had <u>never</u> been seen on
         B   C   D
campus before. (E) <u>No error</u>

12. The new cell phone is more a high

tech toy <u>than like a</u> simple communication
         A
tool; <u>its</u> software <u>encourages</u> distractions
     B   C
and <u>less</u> focus on work. (E) <u>No error</u>
     D

13. If you <u>are interested</u> <u>in learning</u>
           A   B
<u>even more</u> about William Hearst, <u>one</u>
  C   D
should read his biography. (E) <u>No error</u>

14. Local shopping malls have discovered

that shopper turnout is diminished

<u>considerably</u> <u>whenever</u> the weatherman
     A   B
<u>projected</u> thunderstorms early <u>in the day</u>.
    C   D
(E) <u>No error</u>

15. Innovative use of computers in theater

<u>allows</u> musical directors <u>to undertake</u>
  A   B
projects that <u>encourages</u> them to <u>both</u>
           C   D
experiment and to diminish the number of

musicians hired. (E) <u>No error</u>

16. The reconstruction of Boston's Trinity

Church is based on a plan <u>where</u> <u>each</u> of
                      A   B
the interior walls <u>as well as</u> the stained
               C
glass windows will be <u>restored to</u> their
                     D
original beauty. (E) <u>No error</u>

17. <u>Despite</u> the child's emotional plea,
   A
his parents insisted <u>on</u> a 'time-out' alone
               B
<u>in</u> his bedroom for an <u>indecisive</u> period.
C   D
(E) <u>No error</u>

Directions: Choose the answer that best expresses the meaning of the original sentence. If you think the original is better than any of the alternatives, choose it; otherwise choose one of the others. Your choice should produce the most effective sentence -- clear and precise, without awkwardness or ambiguity.

18. Raised near the cornfields of Iowa, <u>it was only when I went away to college in New York that I learned how convenient public transportation could be</u>.
(A) it was only when I went away to college in New York that I learned how convenient public transportation could be.
(B) when I went to college in New York that I learned how convenient public transportation could be.
(C) going away to college in New York that I learned how convenient public transportation could be.
(D) I did not learn how convenient public transportation could be until I went away to college in New York.
(E) public transportation was unknown to me until I went away to college in New York.

19. If you wish to maintain an exercise regimen, <u>a person should avoid taking the elevator when the stairs are available.</u>
(A) a person should avoid taking the elevator when stairs are available.
(B) avoid the elevator when stairs are available.
(C) taking the elevator is to be avoided when stairs are available.
(D) avoiding taking the elevator when stairs are available.
(E) a person should avoid when there are available stairs, taking the elevator.

20. When played at top volume, <u>you can damage your eardrums with loud music.</u>
(A) you can damage your eardrums with loud music.
(B) loud music can damage your eardrums.
(C) you could be damaging your eardrums.
(D) loud music, it can damage your eardrums.
(E) then loud music could be damaging to your eardrums.

21. The war's perplexing difficulties, <u>already complicated by the intervening nations, threatens </u>to become even more severe as a result of the various internal factions looking to gain control.
A. already complicated by the intervening nations, threatens
B. already complicated by the intervening nations, threaten
C. already more complicated by the intervening nations, threatens
D. already becoming complicated by the intervening nations, threatens
E. after having been made complicated by the intervening nations, threaten

22. <u>Michael Jordan's influence has had a great impact on many more recent basketball players who followed him</u>, including Shaquille O'Neal.
(A) Michael Jordan's influence has had a great impact on many more recent basketball players who followed him,
(B) Michael Jordan's influence has impacted on many basketball players,
(C) Michael Jordan has influenced many more recent basketball players,
(D) The influence of Michael Jordan's was great on many basketball players,
(E) Many basketball players who followed him have felt the influence and impact after Michael Jordan,

23. Some doctors believe that the <u>problem of allergies in the spring and autumn are no different for women than for men.</u>
(A) problem of allergies in the spring and autumn are no different for women than for men.
(B) problem of allergies in the spring and autumn is no different for women or men.
(C) problem of allergies in the spring and autumn is no different for women than for men.
(D) problems in spring and autumn differ no more for men's allergies than women.
(E) problems of allergies are no different for women and men regarding the time of year.

24. <u>Because of his unhappy experience with nasty campers,</u> Robert always avoided summer camps.
(A) Because of his unhappy experience with nasty campers,
(B) His unhappy experience resulted from nasty campers, and
(C) Because he was unhappy resulting from his nasty campers,
(D) His unhappy experience with nasty campers is what accounts for why
(E) From having an unhappy experience with nasty campers,

25. The convenience and availability of the town lake <u>account for its popularity</u> with citizens of all ages.
(A) account for its popularity
(B) account for their popularity
(C) accounts for its popularity
(D) is why it is popular
(E) are a reason for its popularity

26. Many changes occurred while Mendes was president of this manufacturing <u>firm, and they included its complexity as well as effectiveness.</u>
(A) firm, and they included its complexity as well as effectiveness.
(B) firm, they both included the complexity and effectiveness of the firm.
(C) firm, which both added to its complexity as well as increased its effectiveness.
(D) firm, these changes included its complexity and effectiveness.
(E) firm, changes that added to the complexity of the firm while they increased its effectiveness.

27. Although now involved in marketing his new autobiography, <u>Clinton's next job will be to support fellow democrat John Kerry for President.</u>
(A) Clinton's next job will be to support fellow democrat John Kerry for President.
(B) the next job Clinton will do will be to support fellow democrat John Kerry for President.
(C) but Clinton will next support fellow democrat John Kerry for President.
(D) fellow democrat John Kerry will next be supported by Clinton for President.
(E) Clinton will next support fellow democrat John Kerry for President.

28. Our staff wanted to combine our monthly meeting and a summer <u>outing; staff members planned on munching barbecue treats while listening to the agenda.</u>
(A) outing; staff members planned on munching barbecue treats while listening to the agenda.
(B) outing, which meant that staff members planned on munching barbecue treats while listening to the agenda.
(C) outing; therefore, it meant that staff members would munch barbecue treats while listening to the agenda.
(D) outing and therefore the staff members would be munching barbecue treats while listening to the agenda.
(E) outing; staff members munching barbecue treats while listening to the agenda.

29. The Congressman has a dangerous perspective on the proposed highway; the drawbacks predicted by the councilmen <u>who oppose the measure far outweigh the supposed benefits.</u>
(A) who oppose the measure far outweigh the supposed benefits.
(B) that oppose the measure far outweigh the supposed benefits.
(C) opposing the measure far outweighing the supposed benefits.
(D) that had opposed the measure far outweigh the supposed benefits.
(E) who were opposing of the measure far outweigh the supposed benefits.

30. Determination, rather than sincerity or intelligence, <u>are the quality that a successful entrepreneur must convey</u> in order to beat out the competition and survive in a poor economy.
(A) are the quality that a successful entrepreneur must convey
(B) is the quality that a successful entrepreneur must convey
(C) are the qualities that a successful entrepreneur must convey
(D) the quality that a successful entrepreneur must convey
(E) the qualities which a successful entrepreneur must convey

Directions: The following passage is an early draft of an essay. Some parts of the passage need to be rewritten.

(1) The time is immediately before the start of the American civil rights movement. (2) The place is a Chicago apartment. (3) From amongst the ragged furniture and appliances of an appropriately drab brown set emerge four amazingly distinct characters to amuse, shock and tantalize in *The Sty of the Blind Pig*.

(4) The focus is on Alberta, being a thirty-something woman seeking a soul mate yet also attempting to convince herself that she is strong enough to remain on her own. (5) Actor Kana Shaw's portrayal is desperately real and spine tingling often. (6) She is trapped, still living with her mother, a tiny guilt-tripping whippersnapper played by seasoned performer Barbara Meek, in their South Street apartment.

(7) One is somewhat reminded of the lonely daughter Laura from Tennessee Williams' *The Glass Menagerie* when a gentleman caller arrives, the intriguing street singer Blind Jordan. (8) Arthur Price handles Jordan's slow "all I got is time" mentality well, his voice is suitably rich and haunting.

(9) As the quartet weaves in and out through playwright Philip Hayes Dean's intricate, realistic writing, the drama intensifies. (10) Aided by the beautiful and sometimes fierce window-themed lighting, the actors carry the piece through hatred, sorrow, love and even charming historical references such as "some young preacher" getting certain Southerners riled up (the Reverend Martin Luther King.) (11) Alberta's gambling uncle Doc completes the square of characters.

(12) This is a powerful production, filled with emotion and truth. (13) Director Frank Michael Orway has made beautiful use of some very talented designers and performers, creating a surprising, enjoyable experience.

31. The desired effect of the first paragraph is to
(A) critique the playwright's talent
(B) set the scene and give background
(C) explain why the play is set in Chicago
(D) describe the childhood of the lead actor
(E) suggest the show is too shocking

32. In context, which of the following changes should be made to sentence 4?
(A) change "the focus" to "focusing"
(B) change "yet also attempting" to "even as she attempts"
(C) change "attempting" to "attempts"
(D) delete "being"
(E) delete "the focus is on"

33. In context, which of the following endings best improves sentence 5?
(A) desperately real, spine tingling.
(B) desperately real, spine tingling often.
(C) desperately real and often spine tingling.
(D) desperate, real and spine tingling often.
(E) desperately really often spine tingling.

34. Which is the most effective way to deal with sentence 8?
(A) leave it as it is now
(B) combine it with sentence 7
(C) combine it with sentence 9
(D) delete it
(E) split it into two sentences

35. In context, where does sentence 11 best belong?
(A) where it is now
(B) after sentence 3
(C) after sentence 6
(D) after sentence 8
(E) after sentence 12

36. What would be the most appropriate title for this essay?
(A) *The Glass Menagerie* and Blindness
(B) Martin Luther King, Jr. and His Influence on Theater
(C) A Pleasing and Shocking Production of *The Sty of the Blind Pig*
(D) How to Act in a Four-Person Play
(E) Civil Rights and Playwrighting

End of Test III

Answer Key to Tests I , II, III

ANSWER KEY – GRAMMAR TEST I	ANSWER KEY – GRAMMAR TEST II	ANSWER KEY – GRAMMAR TEST III
1.C	1.C	1.B
2.E	2.A	2.E
3.E	3.C	3.C
4.D	4.B	4.E
5.C	5.C	5.A
6.E	6.C	6.A
7.D	7.B	7.C
8.C	8.E	8.A
9.D	9.B	9.B
10.A	10.C	10.C
11.B	11.A	11.C
12.B	12.E	12.A
13.C	13.D	13.D
14.A	14.A	14.C
15.E	15.D	15.C
16.C	16.C	16.A
17.E	17.B	17.D
18.D	18.B	18.D
19.D	19.C	19.B
20.B	20.D	20.B
21.D	21.E	21.B
22.D	22.B	22.C
23.E	23.E	23.C
24.C	24.A	24.A
25.A	25.D	25.A
26.C	26.E	26.E
27.B	27.C	27.E
28.C	28.B	28.A
29.E	29.A	29.A
30.E	30.C	30.B
31.A	31.A	31.B
32.C	32.D	32.D
33.E	33.A	33.C
34.A	34.D	34.E
35.B	35.D	35.D
36.D	36.C	36.C

Answer Keys to All Grammar Exercises

Pages 85, 86

Identifying Sentence Errors
1. C
2. D
3. C
4. A
5. C

Improving Sentences
1. B
2. B
3. D
4. C
5. A

Pages 88, 89

Identifying Sentence Errors
1. D
2. C
3. E
4. B
5. D

Improving Sentences
1. C
2. D
3. B
4. C
5. D

Pages 91, 92

Identifying Sentence Errors
1. E
2. D
3. B
4. D
5. B

Improving Sentences
1. B
2. B
3. A
4. C
5. D

Mastery Exercise Page 93

1. I enjoy the pizza at Santarpio's much more than the pizza at Pizza Regina.
2. Our teenage club members contribute fewer hours than your club's members.
3. The results of the research done in 2004 were better received than those of 2003 (or than the 2003 research).
4. Woodward's quiet influence and spirited energy encouraged as much quality and teamwork as did Johnson's brash verbal flogging.
5. Can you compare the Starbuck's coffee to the coffee at (or that of) Dunkin Donuts?

Pages 95, 96

Identifying Sentence Errors
1. D
2. D
3. D
4. D
5. A

Improving Sentences
1. D
2. C
3. A
4. A
5. B

Pages 97, 98

Identifying Sentence Errors
1. C
2. E
3. A
4. E
5. A

Improving Sentences
1. B
2. D
3. A
4. B
5. A

Pages 101, 102

Identifying Sentence Errors
1. A
2. A
3. D
4. D
5. C

Improving Sentences
1. D
2. C
3. D
4. C
5. C

Pages 104, 105

Identifying Sentence Errors:
1. C
2. C
3. A
4. B
5. C

Improving Sentences:
1. D
2. E
3. C
4. C
5. A

Pages 107 108

Identifying Sentence Errors:
1. C
2. B
3. E
4. E
5. D

Improving Sentences:
1. C
2. D
3. B
4. B
5. E

Pages 110, 111

Identifying Sentence Errors:
1. D
2. B
3. A
4. E
5. A

Improving Sentences:
1. C
2. A
3. B
4. D
5. D

Pages 113, 114

Identifying Sentence Errors
1. B
2. D
3. D
4. D
5. C

Improving Sentences
1. C
2. C
3. E
4. A
5. B

Pages 116, 117

Identifying Sentence Errors:
1. E
2. D
3. A
4. D
5. A

Improving Sentences:
1. B
2. D
3. C
4. C
5. E

Pages 119, 120

Identifying Sentence Errors
1. D
2. C
3. C
4. B
5. B

Improving Sentences
1. C
2. A
3. E
4. B
5. B

Pages 121, 122

Identifying Sentence Errors
1 D
2 C
3. C
4. B
5. B

Improving Sentences
1. C
2. B
3. E
4. D
5. B

Pages 125, 126

Identifying Sentence Errors:
1. C
2. A
3. D
4. C
5. C

Improving Sentences:
1. D
2. B
3. E
4. D
5. E

Pages 128 129

Identifying Sentence Errors:
1. E
2. A
3. C
4. D
5. E

Improving Sentences:
1. D
2. B
3. E
4. D
5. C

Pages 131, 132

Identifying Sentence Errors:
1. D
2. C
3. D
4. D
5. E

Improving Sentences:
1. C
2. C
3. A
4. A
5. E

Pages 134, 135

Identifying Sentence Errors:
1. C
2. D
3. E
4. A
5. B

Improving Sentences:
1. A
2. B
3. B
4. E
5. E

Pages 138, 139

Identifying Sentence Errors:
1. B
2. A
3. D
4. C
5. C

Improving Sentences:
6. E
7. B
8. E
9. A
10. D

Pages 141, 142

Identifying Sentence Errors
1. C
2. D
3. B
4. B
5. C

Improving Sentences
1. B
2. D
3. D
4. C
5. C

Pages 144, 145

Identifying Sentence Errors
1. C
2. E
3. C
4. C
5. D

Improving Sentences
1. D
2. D
3. E
4. B
5. D

Pages 148, 149

Improving Sentences
1. D
2. D
3. C
4. E
5. B
6. C
7. E
8. A
9. D
10. B

Page 151

Improving Sentences
1. E
2. C
3. E
4. E
5. B

Pages 153, 154

Identifying Sentence Errors:
1. B
2. A
3. C
4. A
5. D

Improving Sentences:
1. C
2. A
3. A
4. B
5. E

Pages 156, 157

Identifying Sentence Errors:
1. C
2. B
3. E
4. E
5. D

Improving Sentences:
1. E
2. B
3. A
4. C
5. C

Page 160

1. to
2. into
3. and
4. on
5. in
6. to
7. in
8. and
9. in which
10. from

Page 162

Improving Sentences:

1. D
2. C
3. B
4. A
5. E

Page 163

Being + ING

1.E
2.B
3.C
4.C
5.A

Mastering the SAT Essay

Introduction To Mastering the SAT Essay

Introduction to Adaptable Essay vs. Spontaneous Essay

In this book, you'll be learning about two different types of essays – The Adaptable Essay[sm] and the Spontaneous Essay. Which of these you'll write on test day will be your choice. Practice in order to become proficient at both, then write the one that works best with your test-day prompt. Of course, the choice is always yours. You can elect to not write an adaptable essay and to focus exclusively on learning how to write a well-constructed spontaneous essay.

The Problem with Holistic Scoring

The adaptable essay strategy was developed back by Chyten in 1996 when there was growing concern over the method of grading used by the College Board in scoring student essays. That method was, and still is, referred to as Holistic Scoring. Holistic Scoring is, at best, a subjective measure of a students writing ability, based on a narrow set of criteria and open to interpretation on the part of the reader.

Student Essay

> The more you know, the happier you are. This is definitely a valid statement in my opinion. I have been involved in various situations in which I have thanked God for making me the person that I am. Each day, I learn something new, and each day it seems that I am happier than the previous one.
>
> One example of why I agree with this statement involves my work in school. In my school, I am considered to be an intelligent and diligent person. I have never missed honor roll; I have always been a student who received A's and B's. I am even part of an organization at my school in which students strong in certain subjects assist those whom are not as strong. Each time my lesson with a student terminates, he or she is always grateful to me. The feeling that I received was that I helped another person. Knowing that you have helped someone is one of best ways to make you feel happy. Another example of why I agree with this statement involves baseball. Over the years, my knowledge for baseball has increased significantly. Now, baseball is the love of my life, both playing and observing. Whenever my dad and I attend the Red Sox games, he has to listen to my judgment on each play and situation. However, he never becomes irritated by it. He agrees with everything I say and says I have knowledge of true baseball coach, although he claims that I have more talent in the sport than knowledge. My dad is not the only person who has complimented me in baseball. People in my town have also, along with the teachers and students at my school. This is the best feeling that I know of, when somebody compliments you in what you do best.

Could you read and grade this student-written essay in two minutes or less?

The problem faced by the College Board was this:

***so many essays –
so little time.***

But, instead of training enough readers to accomplish the task of reading and grading essays, the College Board devised a plan that allowed essays to be graded in ninety seconds.

College Board euphemistically uses the term "Holistic Scoring" to describe its grading procedure. In actuality, it is just "fast scoring." Readers take an average of 90 seconds to score an essay. They are expected to score at least 30 per hour.

Take Me to Your *Reader*

Meet Roger Reader

"Hi, my name is Roger and I'll be your reader today - at least for the next 60 - 90 seconds! Could I interest you in a high score? Six perhaps? Oh, sorry, you forgot to vary your sentence structure.   Gotta go. I'll give your essay a.........................4.   NEXT ESSAY!

Essay Readers Needed
Flexible Hours
$.60 per essay

What is Roger Reading?

Roger Reader will eventually be reading <u>your</u> essay. But your essay is file # 320 in a zip file containing a seemingly endless number of essays that he needs to read this week.   So, Roger warmed up his computer and is reading essays and he is reading essays and he is reading essays and he is . . . . *getting just a bit crazy because it seems as though every essay is saying the same thing and Roger is thinking that if he reads one more essay about how a student must give up time with friends to earn good grades or how we won the big game against the school rival or how my soccer coach is a hero or how Martin Luther King "had a dream" or about the atrocities of Hitler or about "how sad I was when my dog died" then Roger thinks……he just might…………………………cry!*

After all, Roger took this assignment for the money! He was hired by the College Board for a week to read papers. He was given nine hundred student-written essays, and though he is used to grading papers, the task is starting to get to him. He had no idea that 90% of them would be so. . . . so. . . . so. . . . SIMILAR!

So. Will your essay serve as Roger's shining light, or will it be just another painful pebble on the beach for Roger to step on?

The 1-6 Grading Scale

Fact #1: 90% of all essays receive a score of 3 or 4!

Fact #2: the difference between an essay score of 3 and a score of 6 can register as a 100 point increase in your test score.

Essays are graded on a 1 - 6 scale by two readers. A third reader is appointed when the two scores are more than one point apart - a situation that rarely occurs. Nearly 90% of all essays receive at least one grade of three or four. It is quite easy to receive a grade of three. If you can put words on paper without too many mistakes and if you write a full-length essay, you will get at least a three. A grade of four reflects competent writing that contains no major grammatical mistakes and that follows a logical pattern. A grade of five reflects quality work. In order to attain a five, an essay must be well organized and well written. About 10% of all essays receive a five/five or a five/six. A grade of six reflects high-quality work. For an essay to receive a six, it must be well written, well organized and it must be interesting! Only about one out of 120 essays receives a double six. A grade of zero means you did not tie your essay to the prompt.

Another 3. Another 3. Another 4. Another. . . .

3-3-3-4-4-3-4-4-3-3-2-3-4-4-3 3-3-3-4-4-3-4-3-2-3-4-4-3-3-3 3-
4-4-3-4-4-3-3-2-3-4-4-3- 4   3-4-4-3-3-2-3-4 4-3-3-3-3 4-4-3-44
-3-3-2-3-4-4-3-3 3 3-4-4-3-4-4-3-3 2 3-4-4-3-3-3-3-4-4-3-4-
4-3-3-2-3-4-4-3-3 3 43-3-2-3-4-4-3-4-3-3-3-4-3-3 4 3 3-3-2-
3-3 3-3-2-4-3-4-4.

> Fact: 90% of all essays receive a score of 3 or 4. for a total score of 6 (below average) to 8 (average).

How You Can Help Roger to Raise Your Score

To receive a high grade you'll need to include some very specific elements in your essay. The grammar, style and structure of the essay will be discussed next. But there is more to receiving top scores than the College Board cares to admit. Evidence has shown that you'll need to engage the reader in order to make the reader want to give you a good grade. Also, you cannot offend the reader with negative allusions to children, teachers or schools. Most important, you cannot write the same paper everyone else is writing!

Make Roger Smile! When he reads the following opening to your essay, he will be eager to continue reading. Right from the start, he is thinking about giving you a higher grade!

When I first saw Van Gogh's "Self-Portrait", it seemed to stare at me, drenching me with its pungent colors, beckoning me to swim in its wild waves. Art has the power to transform madness into beauty and art into emotion. Like many impressionist painters of the era, Van Gogh had the gift to alter reality. For a moment, I thought. . .

Roger is ravished by the power of your writing and grateful to have been relieved of the terrible burden placed upon him, reading boring, predictable essay after boring predictable essay. He *will* reward your essay with a higher score.

193

College Board's <u>Official</u> 1-6 Scoring Guide

SCORE OF 6 - An essay in this category is outstanding, demonstrating clear and consistent mastery, although it may have a few minor errors. A typical essay

- effectively and insightfully develops a point of view on the issue and demonstrates outstanding critical thinking, using clearly appropriate examples, reasons, and other evidence to support its position
- is well organized and clearly focused, demonstrating clear coherence and smooth progression of ideas
- exhibits skillful use of language, using a varied, accurate, and apt vocabulary
- demonstrates meaningful variety in sentence structure
- is free of most errors in grammar, usage, and mechanics

SCORE OF 5 - An essay in this category is effective, demonstrating reasonably consistent mastery, although it will have occasional errors or lapses in quality. A typical essay

- effectively develops a point of view on the issue and demonstrates strong critical thinking, generally using appropriate examples, reasons, and other evidence to support its position
- is well organized and focused, demonstrating coherence and progression of ideas
- exhibits facility in the use of language, using appropriate vocabulary
- demonstrates variety in sentence structure
- is generally free of most errors in grammar, usage, and mechanics

SCORE OF 4 - An essay in this category is competent, demonstrating adequate mastery, although it has lapses in quality. A typical essay

- develops a point of view on the issue and demonstrates competent critical thinking, using adequate examples, reasons, and other evidence to support its position
- is generally organized and focused, demonstrating some coherence and progression of ideas
- exhibits adequate but inconsistent facility in the use of language, using generally appropriate vocabulary
- demonstrates some variety in sentence structure
- has some errors in grammar, usage, and mechanics

SCORE OF 3 - An essay in this category is inadequate, but demonstrates developing mastery, and is marked by one or more of the following weaknesses:

- develops a point of view on the issue, demonstrating some critical thinking, but may do so inconsistently or use inadequate examples, reasons, or other evidence to support its position
- is limited in its organization or focus, but may demonstrate some lapses in coherence or progression of ideas
- displays developing facility in the use of language, but sometimes uses weak vocabulary or inappropriate word choice
- lacks variety or demonstrates problems in sentence structure
- contains an accumulation of errors in grammar, usage, and mechanics

SCORE OF 2 - An essay in this category is seriously limited, and is flawed by one or more of the following:

- develops a point of view on the issue that is vague or seriously limited, demonstrating weak critical thinking, providing inappropriate or insufficient examples, reasons, or other evidence to support its position
- is poorly organized and/or focused, or demonstrates serious problems with coherence or progression of ideas
- displays very little facility in the use of language, using very limited vocabulary or incorrect word choice
- demonstrates frequent problems in sentence structure
- contains errors in grammar, usage, and mechanics so serious that meaning is somewhat obscured

SCORE OF 1 - An essay in this category is fundamentally lacking and severely flawed by one or more of the following:

- develops no viable point of view on the issue, or provides little or no evidence to support its position
- is disorganized or unfocused, resulting in a disjointed or incoherent essay
- displays fundamental errors in vocabulary
- demonstrates severe flaws in sentence structure
- contains pervasive errors in grammar, usage, or mechanics that persistently interfere with meaning

SCORE OF 0 - Essays not written on the essay assignment will <u>receive a score of zero.</u>

The Secret, <u>Unofficial</u> Scoring Technique

You will probably never read about this anywhere else, but the fact remains that this is true, and has been corroborated by real-life Roger Readers.

Many readers do not read their essays. Instead, they scan their essays. Since four is an average grade, (marked by few errors but few outstanding features), readers start by assuming an essay gets a 4. Errors make it a 3 (or even a 2 or 1 in extreme cases). Positive attributes push it to a 5 (or 6 in an extreme case, such as with the essay below)

Prompt: *"Once your mind has been stretched by a new concept or idea, it can never return to its previous shape."*

Roger notices the alliteration,

(Roger starts by assigning a value of 4, then. . . . .)

I can still see **his pale powdered** face, with its solemn, emotionless expression in my mind if I think about it. The bandage that **adorned** the back of his head from the autopsy **peeked out** from behind what was left of his **silvery** hair. His gray suit partially covered by the dark **mahogany** coffin and the bouquet of flowers that **cascaded** over the side and **seemed to stretch their vines nearly to the floor.**

likes the interesting verbs and adjectives,

The bright fluorescent lights illuminated the tears running down people's cheeks, and the cheap and tacky stained glass windows blocked the outside world. I wanted to leave, to turn my back to those who sought comfort in my arms, but instead I clutched the tissue that I held in my hands, slowly twisting the edges until they fell off. I buried my face in my father's chest, and then, I cried.

digs the personification,

(By now, Roger certainly knows this is at least a 5. If, at this point, nothing had stood out, Roger might have skipped to the end and assigned a grade of 4. If at this point there were a few errors in grammar and spelling, he could have easily assigned a 3. It takes many more errors to get down to a 2 or 1. Since the essay is clearly a 5 or 6, he must read to the end to make that determination).

is moved to tears by this amazing sentence.

I **cried** because I had never been to a funeral before. I **cried** because the first funeral I ever attended was that of my grandfather, and I **cried** because my grandfather was murdered. I **never thought that I would have to experience such pain.** I assumed hurt that severe would never affect me or my family. But I was wrong. Now that my mind has been stretched to these new thoughts and feelings, it can never return to its previous innocent state.

I returned home among a **sea of mourners.** I pressed my lips upon **ruddy** cheeks after ruddy cheek of semi-strangers and distant relatives. Finally, I found the courage to face my mother. In her **translucent, indigo** eyes I saw **enduring strength** that **belied** her inner pain. I wrapped around her as tightly as a quilt while she clung to me like a frightened puppy. At that very moment I learned that change, as hard as it may be, can be a unifying force in people's lives.

Wow! The accumulation of great stuff makes this a clear 6!

Wiping his eyes, Roger assigns this essay a 6, then quickly clicks his mouse to move to the next essay.

Mastering the Essay

Writing the essay is your first assignment on the SAT. That's right. the essay is always first. There are two elements to writing a successful SAT essay. They are

1) Content

2) Structure.

Essay Content

Good topics are those that are interesting, flexible and balanced

Interesting
A good writing subject is one that will interest both you and the reader. Moreover, a good subject is one in which you have a great deal of knowledge. While avoiding the cliché topics such as Martin Luther King, Mother Theresa and the current President of the United States, you should write about something you have studied, have experienced or have become acquainted with. A well-known person could work well. So could a group of people. Impressionist painters, for example, would work. Great explorers, researchers or activists might make worthy subjects. Even an infamous gangster who might have had redeeming qualities would make for an interesting subject. You could write about radio or a radio astronomer or even Sir Isaac Newton. You could also write about an interesting personal experience.

Flexible
Since you are not sure what your prompt will be, your chosen subject must be flexible enough to fit many different types of prompts. You must be able to pick one or two aspects of your subject to write about, while filling in the rest with background information about your subject. Clearly, you must know your subject very well in order to do this.

Balanced
Since your prompt can be either positive or negative, your subject must be balanced. For the same subject, you must be able to write about the negative and the positive. Once again, knowing your subject is key! Here are some things to think about.

- Could you write something bad about Albert Einstein?
- Could you write something good about Joseph Stalin?
- Could you write something bad about Abraham Lincoln?
- Could you write something good about Bonnie and Clyde?
- Could you write something bad about Michael Jordan?
- Could you write something good about the space shuttle disasters?
- Could you write something bad about children?
- Could you write something good about Charles Manson?
- Could you write something bad about Venus and Serena Williams?

If you answered yes to all of these, you are ready to write an adaptable essay.
If not, you need to keep thinking and practicing.

Examples of Good Topics

- The invention of the automobile (or the inventor of the automobile)
- Fire (Example: A forest fire recycles nature's elements, creating new life)
- Athletes (pick one)
- Technology (pick a product or products)
- Science (pick a branch)
- Actors (screen or stage - pick one or more)
- Famous musicians (Probably not Eminem or Britney Spears!)
- A favorite author
- Genius is often accompanied by madness (Van Gogh is one example)
- The Internet
- The invention of television
- A life-changing experience
- Radio or television
- Working for a charity
- Performers/Performance (stage fright?)
- Art - pick a flavor
- Astronomy - is the benefit worth the expense?
- Teachers - low pay, high importance
- Firefighters
- The Nobel Prize
- Freedom of Speech
- The Patriot Act
- Democracy

Think about how you could give these a positive spin or a negative spin. Pick a topic that is familiar to you, one that you enjoy writing about and one that will impress Roger.

Examples of Bad Topics

Why are these topics bad? The reasons vary. Some have been made trite by overuse, and others would make the reader feel uncomfortable. Still others make you appear not worthy of high grades, even though your intentions may be honorable. Avoid bragging while focusing on your good deeds. Avoid taking controversial positions on what may be considered taboo subjects. Finally, be crunchy! That means, be Earth friendly and respectful of all living creatures.

- Friends
- Parties
- Drinking
- Drugs
- Cigarettes
- School
- School cliques
- Jocks, geeks, dweebs, greasers, cool kids, nerds
- Teachers
- Coaches
- Most hometown issues
- Local sports
- Professional sports
- Dating
- Girlfriend
- Boyfriend
- Your job

- Martin Luther King
- Mother Theresa
- Sadaam Hussein
- Hitler
- Osama Bin Laden
- The Events of September 11
- Eminem - an American Icon
- Britney Spears- Pure Talent
- Most cartoons - Sorry Scooby!
- MTV's Real World
- Too strict parents
- Too much homework
- Not enough TV time
- The current President of the U.S.
- Summer Camp
- It rained all week on your vacation to Tortola
- Your maid didn't show and you had to clean your own room
- Your second home in the Catskills

Matching Your Essay to the Prompt: Exercise

Subject of your essay	Prompt
1. Venus and Serena Williams	A. "Style is more important than substance.
2. Medical researchers	B. "Novelty is too often mistaken for progress."
3. Ferdinand Magellan (explorer)	C. "Conscience motivates more than money power."
4. Scientists	D. "Censorship is sometimes necessary."
5. An author whose life/work you know well	E. "Nothing requires more discipline than Freedom"
6. A painter whose life/work you know well	F. "To move a mountain, one must start with the smallest rocks."
7. Michael Jordan	G. "Other people's expectations affect your behavior."
8. Athletes and steroids	H. "Often we find out what works by first discovering what does not work."
9. Illegal immigrants	
10. Survivors of domestic violence	
11. A particular person battling a disease	

Now, Mix and match numbers to columns. Pick a number and a letter. How would you adapt each subject to match each prompt?   Here are some examples

Example: 9/B

I agree with the statement: novelty is too often mistaken for progress. Nowhere is this more true than in the arena of illegal immigration. Though, new and novel technologies are applied to this problem, illegal immigration is a growing concern for our country. Though some progress has been made, that progress has been too slow and too sporadic to have stemmed the flow of illegal immigrants who continue to flood across the borders as easily as a river cuts through a canyon.

Example: 1/D

"I could not disagree any more with the statement: censorship is sometimes necessary. Without a free flow of information and points of view, our country and world would move toward a system more indicative of a totalitarian regime than a democracy. This is true in many facets of life. One of these facets would pertain to the right of public figures to speak their minds. Two examples that come instantly to mind are Venus and Serena Williams, whose outspoken manner often gets them into trouble, while their unparalleled abilities on the tennis court continue to inspire. Should athlete's controversial words be censored? Of course not. Though the Williams sisters have skills unmatched by any women's tennis players in the history of the sport, they are often criticized for their outspoken comments about minorities in sport. In my opinion, not only should these comments not be censored, they should be encouraged."

Now you try. Match any/all numbers and letters. See if you can do it. If so, then you can write an adaptable essay. Recently, scoring criteria have changed to include relevance to prompt as a grading factor. In other words, how well you relate your topic to the question (or failure to do so) could have consequences on your score. Additionally, it seems that recently the College Board has been experimenting with less general topics. Look for trigger words to help you write an acceptable essay.

Trigger Words

"The more things <u>change</u>, the more they <u>stay the same</u>." Agree or disagree.

"<u>Style</u> is more important than <u>substance</u>." Respond.

Note the trigger words, <u>change</u>, <u>stay the same</u>, <u>style and substance</u>. These words make it very easy for a reader to distinguish between an extemporaneous (standard) essay and an adaptable essay. When adapting your essay, use trigger words early, then repeat them at least a couple of times in the body of your essay.

The SAT Essay's Dual Purpose

The SAT essay will be made available to admissions officers at the colleges and universities to which you apply. So make sure your essay is factually sound (unless you intend for it to unmistakably fictional like, for example, writing a first person narrative from Benjamin Franklin) and well researched, while not sounding too over-the-top or contrived.

When polled, Admissions Officers said they might use the SAT essay in admissions. . . .	
A. To provide additional information about a candidate's writing skills	78%
B. To compare and verify an application essay	46%
C. To use as an additional placement essay	32%
D. To replace an application essay	19%
E. To replace an essay currently used for placement	16%
F. Other	7%

As you can see, the SAT essay has implications that extend far beyond your SAT score!

Essay Structure

A Smooth Essay is a Good Essay. Use Connectors!

How your essay sounds is as important as what it says. Try reading your essay out loud.

Many students write essays that read and sound like a series of disconnected sentences.

Connectors

Connectors indicating contrast or agreement:

Indeed	Furthermore
However	But
In fact	As a result
Nonetheless	On the contrary
Moreover	And
Conversely	Even so
Consequently	Similarly
Despite this	Quite the opposite
	Still

Without Connectors

In World War Two, we dropped the atom bomb on Japan. We won the war. Many innocent people died. We should think before we act. The gains do not justify the consequences.

With Connectors

In World War Two, we dropped the atom bomb on Japan. Indeed as a result of this action, we won the war. Sadly, however, many innocent people died. This hard lesson should have taught us one thing: we should think before we act, because sometimes the gains do not justify the *consequences of our actions.*

Use the Multiple-Sentence Technique

When you make a point with one sentence, it often reads as a series of disconnected fragments. Try introducing a detail with a lead sentence, then follow it with a descriptive sentence and a summary sentence.

Here are two examples.

Example 1:

It has been proven that flowers can have a healing effect on patients who must endure long stays in the hospital. Perhaps this healing effect is a result of the effect flowers have on the brain. I think this effect comes about because people who receive flowers know they are still connected to the "real world" outside the hospital.

Example 2:

It seems that many successful people care only about themselves. Yet there are others who use their lofty positions to help others. Cellist Yo Yo Ma is such a person. He often volunteers his time to perform at charitable functions, hospitals and universities.

Be interesting and original. Don't use clichés.

Create word pictures similar to the images in a film.   If Roger Reader sees one more cliché, he will *"blow a fuse."*

Examples of clichés:

- The world in which we live
- In today's society
- I am pleased to report
- Live and let live
- Leave well enough alone
- The events of September Eleventh
- He had reached a point of no return
- I couldn't believe my eyes
- I saw with my own two eyes
- Battle-tested
- I owe it all to. . .
- Rise to the occasion
- Take it one game at a time
- Keep your head above water
- He wouldn't take no for an answer
- She got a raw deal
- Not playing with a full deck
- Throw in the towel
- Pop the question
- Move heaven and earth
- Labor of love
- Give credit where credit is due

Can you think of any others. Check your school work. Have you used any clichés lately?

Use Interesting Images and Fresh Expressions

Examples:

- He stood like a three-legged chair
- He forced his will on others, like a pushy salesman
- She learned to hide her inner pain with empty smiles
- An uphill climb on a downhill road
- I had to pause for a moment to remember who and where I was
- My fears battered against my ribs like caged birds
- Microscopes reveal an invisible world of microbes and amoeba
- He cloaked himself in his work
- Laughter is a panacea
- Sorrow is a gift; happiness a curse
- Music is a bonding force

Use Literary Devices,

Roger enjoys a good oxymoron. Who doesn't?

Metaphor

- Sometimes, he was a tiger; other times he was a kitten.
- The elderly are the cement that holds our society together

Simile

- I woke up feeling like a pair of old socks.
- To me, nature is like a baby brother that needs to be protected from the neighborhood bullies.

Alliteration

- All day long he silently stared at reams and reams of reports.
- The three necessities of life are sun, sand and surf.

Examples of Personification

- The river spoke softly, as if it were afraid of being overheard.
- The cool breeze touched my face as I stared into the eyes of the tallest mountain
  I had ever seen.

Examples of Oxymoron

- A dark light entered the hallway.
- A deafening silence pierced the night air.
- He was offensively inoffensive, never stirred to action by even the most violent acts committed against him.

Examples of Repetition

- Somehow, I knew what he was thinking. I knew because I had seen that look before, and I knew because he was my brother.
- Singing can be very therapeutic. Personally, I sing when I am sad. I sing when I am alone. Most often, I sing when I am angry.

SAT Writing Vocabulary

Since use of vocabulary words is one of the factors that gets high scores – indeed you essay should include as many as ten great, well-placed, smooth-sounding vocabulary words - we have dedicated several pages to vocabulary. In these pages, a variety of high-scoring words are presented in a number of formats.   From the vocabulary pages located in the SAT Reading section, come up with a list of words to include in your essay.   Or use your own carefully constructed list of top SAT words!

Use Several Interesting Verbs and Adjectives.

All too often, students settle for dull, generic verbs that minimize the impact of your message.

Why would you "walk" when you could. . . .
trot, gallop, meander, stroll, skip, amble, bounce, hike, march, or maneuver?

Why be happy when you could be. . . .
mirthful, genial, sparkling, blissful, sunny, congenial.

Colors Are a Unique Way to Get Vocabulary Words Into Your Essay.

Here are some examples:

Trade the word red for. . . .
scarlet, vermilion, crimson, magenta, ruddy, fuchsia (watch the spelling!) or cerise.

Trade the word yellow for. . . .
flaxen, saffron, jasmine, tawny or sallow

Trade the word blue for. . . .
azure, indigo, sapphire (watch the spelling!) turquoise or aqua

Trade the word green for. . . .
emerald, jade, chartreuse (watch the spelling!), sage

Trade the word purple for. . . .
lilac, mauve, heliotrope, magenta, plum or lavender

Trade the word black for. . . .
ebony, somber, raven

Trade the word grey for. . . .
ashen, grizzled, dusty or smoky
By using more descriptive interesting verbs, your message tends to attract the attention of Roger.

Alliterating Vocabulary Words.

This clever little device has seemed to work very well for Chyten students over the years. The alliterated pair must sound good – not tacky or forced

Here are some examples of tacky, forced alliterated pairs:

Tricky transient
Dastardly Despot
Pungent pundit
Silly Sybarite
Cacophonous cat
Very good virtuoso
Mean malefactor

Here are some unforced and fluid-sounding examples:

Cantankerous curmudgeon
Mellifluous melody
Raucous reaction
Meddling malefactor
Translucent tunnel
Desperate detractor
Malicious meddler
Prowling prankster
Cryptic code
(He was at once) revered and reviled
Fecund fields

Try creating awesome alliteration
(Then, have some ready to include in your essay!)

_____ sycophant
_____ pedagogue
_____ proponent
euphonious _____
strident _____
_____ martinet
listless _____
_____ pariah

_____ figurehead
_____ benefactor
_____ pariah
soporific _____
pedantic _____
supercilious _____
_____ mercenary
_____ polyglot

Uncommon Writing

Common everyday writing gets common everyday scores!
Uncommon grades are reserved for uncommon writing.

So, be poetic, metaphoric and interesting.   Focus on the sound of your sentences as much as the on the content.

Common Writing – Score: 4

When I was seven, I went on weekly trips with my mother to a nursing home to visit my grandmother. I didn't know it was a nursing home, though. I always looked forward to seeing her. Then one day, I was told that Gramma had passed away. I didn't really know what that meant, only that we would not be going to see her anymore.

Uncommon Writing – Score: 6

Every Saturday, I bounced out of my bed early to get ready for our trek to "Gramma's apartment", as I called it. I never believed it to be a nursing home, a place where the elderly are tenderly tossed into symmetrical cubes, conveniently located in rural settings, or down obscure side streets, well out of the way. The last time I saw her, she appeared so frail that my eyes seemed to pierce her. I sensed that something was wrong. A few days later, my best friend vanished from my life, forever. To a child, death is never simple.

Multiple-Paragraph Format

You WILL NOT get a high grade if your essay has fewer than four well-organized paragraphs. An essay containing four or five paragraphs is preferable. Be sure to clearly indent your paragraphs!!

A good essay will look like this:

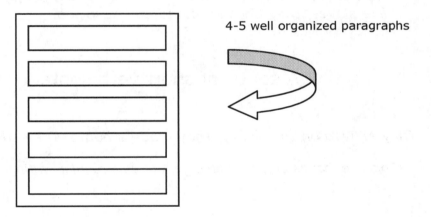

4-5 well organized paragraphs

Vary your Sentence Structure

Roger has been instructed by the College Board to look for different kinds of sentences in your essay. This is one of the standard grading factors used by all readers in evaluating essays.

Examples:

Long descriptive sentence followed by a short accentuating sentence.

Many people believe that it was actually considered wrong in the roaring twenties for a woman to smoke a cigarette. This is entirely incorrect.

A question followed by an answer.

How could this have occurred? Simple. When people treat others like slaves, they become hated and despised.

A series of short verb sentences.

They arrived on the island. They made a home. They survived.

(This is effective only as a change, not as a regular writing style).

Don't overdo it.

Each of these techniques should be done subtly and tastefully. Don't try to be overly fancy. Use these techniques to enhance your essay; don't smother a good essay with overly ornate language.

Here's an example that incorporates many of the techniques just discussed.

When we look out of our windows on a clear summer day, we think we are seeing a beautiful, pristine sky. Yet that beautiful sky is merely the illusion. In reality, our atmosphere is killing us, causing cancer and other deleterious diseases. Although we are the main source of this atmospheric adulteration (alliteration), it is our children and their children who will suffer the consequences of our poor environmental decisions.

Starting Your Essay

Perhaps the hardest thing about writing an essay is starting out. You will not have a second chance to begin, so make sure your first step out of the gate is in the right direction.

Thesis Essay

Give multiple examples and weave them together, comparing and contrasting

The Marx Brothers were comedy's first family. Their slapstick form of humor was later echoed (compare) by such comedic teams as The Three Stooges and Laurel and Hardy, and in the films of Mel Brooks. Other, more subtle forms of humor were soon to follow (contrast) exemplified by The Smothers Brothers and Sonny and Cher, and in television shows such as Laugh-In and Saturday Night Live.

Personal Anecdote Essay

Keep it real and interesting

Our last meal in Ecuador had the feel of a last supper. We knew once we left that we would return to our mundane existence, the day-to-day grind of school and homework. Yet we also knew that we had made a difference in the lives of the people we were leaving. A school playground stood as a tribute to our work. We knew even as we were leaving, that behind us children would be playing. That sense of satisfaction was far greater than any remorse we might have been feeling.

You may use either of these techniques – or others. But you should always keep in mind that you have two audiences:

- Roger Reader
- College Admission Department

Actual College Board Writing Prompts

Writing topics usually include a statement followed by instructions which direct you to comment using appropriate examples from History, Literature, art, personal experience, etc. In most cases, we have removed the initial statement, since it is usually unnecessary when considering writing your essay. When you take the SAT, you should read the opening statement briefly, but then quickly get to the prompt and answer it directly. The categories below were determined by Chyten, not by the College Board.

NEGATIVE/POSITIVE

- Explain the importance of knowing what is right and wrong. (Oct 12, 2002)

- There is always a however. (June 1, 2002)

- Any advance involves some loss (Agree/Disagree)

- Sometimes a negative experience can lead to positive results.

- Some things that seem unsuccessful actually turn out to be worthwhile in the end.

- A student saw an aquatic insect drying out on a rock. Saddened by the prospect of the insect's death, the student nevertheless watched the process and to her surprise observed the emergence of a brilliantly colored dragonfly. She noted the following in her journal: "A change that at first appears to lead to destruction may instead lead to unexpected and dramatic results."

- Often we find out what works by discovering first what does not work.

- To move a mountain, one must start with the smallest rocks.

- The more you know the happier you are. (Agree/Disagree)

- Censorship is sometimes necessary. Agree/Disagree*

*Note: The Censorship prompt has appeared multiple times (at least 4-5 times of which we are aware) for students taking extended time testing.

CHANGE

- "Novelty is too often mistaken for progress."
  Your Assignment: The statement above suggests that what is new and different is often confused with progress. Write an essay in which you challenge, defend, or qualify this statement, using an example or examples from history, politics, science and technology, literature, the arts, current events, or your experience or observation.

- I have experienced various things that have made me feel worthwhile, but I have never felt better than when

- "And things changed significantly afterward."
  Choose an event or a development that had a profound impact on history, on an individual, or on a group of people.

- Once a person's mind has been stretched by a new idea, it will never return to its original shape. Explain how a book, an idea you have discovered, or a specific experience has had a lasting effect on you.

- For many reasons, _____ had a big impact on me.
- Strength of character reveals itself in _____.

- Sometimes it is necessary to adapt in order to survive. Agree or Disagree. Explain your answer. . .

INFLUENTIAL FACTORS / MOTIVATION

- Conscience motivates more than money, fame or power. (Oct 23, 2002)

- A challenge teaches a person what his or her strengths and weakness are. The situation is the same when a group, an organization, or a nation is challenged. One such challenge occurred when_____.

- Other people's expectations affect your behavior. Choose an event or a specific experience that illustrates the impact of such expectations.

- There has always been great passion to keep things as they are. OR There has always been great passion to bring about change. Choose ONE and discuss.

- Some people and places have reputations that are greater than they deserve OR less than they deserve. Choose one person or place that would illustrate one of these two statements.

- If we have seen further, it is because we have stood on the shoulders of giants. Your Assignment: What person or group would you identify as a "giant who has made it possible for others to progress?"

MORE RECENT EXAMPLES OF COLLEGE BOARD ESSAY PROMPTS

- Is persistence more important than ability in determining a person's success? (2008)

- Does planning interfere with creativity? (2009)

- Do highly accomplished people achieve more than others mainly because they expect more of themselves? (2009)

- Should people change their decisions when circumstances change, or is it best to stick with their original decisions? (2009)

- Is striving to achieve a goal always the best course of action, or should people give up if they are not making progress? (2009)

- Is it easier to work under pressure from others when you have a deadline? (2010)

Examples of Adaptable Essays Written by Chyten Students

All of the essays that follow were written by Chyten students as adaptable essays. Each was later adapted to the prompt and received the grade that you see next to the title. These were written back when relating your essay to a particular prompt was not important and did not affect one's grade. Today, several ties to the prompt are necessary. These are presented for writing style, not for how to relate an essay to a particular prompt.

See if you can identify the point-enhancing techniques and devices included in each of these essays.

Special thanks to our students for allowing us to use their
essays as examples for other Chyten students to follow

SKI ESSAY 6-6

<u>Contains a bit of everything. Lots of alliteration. Great description.</u>

There is nothing quite like the feel of stepping into skis, lifting up ones heels, and speeding down the slope. There is nothing quite like the feel of freshly waxed skis slipping silently through freshly fallen powder. Until recently however, these blissful clashes against pristine nature were reserved only for the rich. However, I have recently become involved in a program that teaches inner city youths how to ski.

The kids arrive early in the morning. As they march nearly single-file from the parking lot to the triple-decker lodge, the bright sun begins to slowly rise over the pointy tops of the pine trees. Tired from the bus ride up to the picturesque White Mountains of New Hampshire, the children appear to be walking in their sleep.

Once inside the lodge, several of the kids ask various teachers if they "really have to learn to ski." Skiing is clearly is as foreign to these youngsters as the wide-open areas of land. I leave the lodge and all its wonderful smells of cafeteria food. As I start toward the slope, I can't help but remember my first day on skis. It was a majestic morning, not unlike this one. The temperature was hovering around 30 degrees, and a few snowflakes were barely visible in their heavenly descent.

Suddenly I noticed the young students walking toward me. I turned for one last look at the mountain. There was a single streak of sunlight slashing across the glittering snow. It was as if somebody had dislodged a single slat of a boarded up window, and this was the only light coming through. My students approached me and we began our lesson. Although these youth began the day with animosity and dislike, they soon grew more enthused and anxious for more runs. By the end of the day I was ready to go to sleep on the chairlift ride, and they were begging me for "just one more run" before we all had to return to the lodge for the day.

The kids realized once they arrived that there was no way out, and that they should make the best of it. All the students and instructors eventually returned to the big blue lodge. The students packed up, and left with smiles on their faces. After that, the instructors had a meeting and then were dismissed. As everybody left the building, I sat and reflected on the day. These children came all the way from an urban environment, were thrust into a situation as well as surroundings that were completely foreign to them, and they adapted to have a great time. At that point I realized that I had not been the teacher, but rather the student, all along.

POETRY CLUB ESSAY 6-6

<u>Great use of verbs. Good metaphors and similes. Great variation of sentence structure. Too short for an SAT essay (written for SAT-II Writing).</u>

I was curled up in my feather blanket, crouching over a book of poetry by Pablo Neruda. His words, sharp and vibrant, held my attention like a child about to be served an ice cream sundae. I anticipated his fluid language and honesty before I read each line. Yet, even though I was engrossed in the poetry, I felt a hollowness creep up on me like a jaguar in a hazy jungle. I had no one with whom to share my interest.

I decided to change my life. Within a week, I had developed a plan to start a poetry organization at my school. After a plethora of different announcements to grab the attention of the students, I was ready to have the first Poetry Club meeting. Six people showed up. Together we devoured a poem by Emily Dickinson, analyzing word for word the symbolism and metaphors embedded in the piece. Was I ready to take my interest in poetry to the next level?

After two months of weekly meetings, I, with the help of members from the poetry club, decided to have an open-mike night at my school. I was incredibly nervous the night of the reading. What if people would not show up? How will students react when I read my own poem? My fears battered against my ribs like caged birds.

I was exuberant when I saw forty students and teachers sprawled on the pillow facing the stage we had set up. For two hours, people read their own work or poems that they admired. Before I began to read my own poem, I looked out from the podium into a sea of support. I was no longer alone. My sense of isolation evaporated and contentment washed over my body like a cleansing wave.

PERFORMANCE ESSAY 6-6

<u>Good repetition of short verb sentences. Good variation of sentence structure</u>

"Places." The command came from stage left, followed by a scurry of activity. Orlando rushed left, hiding behind the proscenium. Rosalind went right to find her place among the other "ladies." I dashed off to take my place backstage left. The theater darkened. The murmur faded. The curtains rose.

Performance can be very fickle. You never know quite how you'll react until the curtain is fully drawn. My heart, at first fluttering like a caged bird, relaxed as I delivered the opening lines of my first number. The words of William Shakespeare to the tune of Bob Dylan flooded through me like a cooling rainstorm in the heat of the summer. I knew early on that I was hopelessly hooked.

Perhaps the most difficult aspect of live performance is the darkness out beyond the stage. You can feel the people there. You sense that they are watching you. You wonder what they are thinking. When my first number concluded, I was welcomed by warm applause. With this applause, the darkness lifted. By applauding, the audience members had revealed themselves to me. They were no longer to be feared. There was nothing more to overcome.

The play proceeded "uneventfully". Though a few lines were missed, a few cues were ignored and an occasional spotlight missed its mark. The audience seemed to enjoy its moment away from reality. People in the audience have a responsibility to suspend belief and a responsibility to enjoy. My first live performance opened my eyes to a totally new side of life that I had never before been a part of. I love the theater, but it makes me sad to think of its future.

Our world is constantly changing around us, but change has two faces. On one hand, change brings about new and wonderful things, like technological advances or the way that humans see one another. This type of change is beneficial and necessary. * Although, on the other hand, change is threatening aspects of our culture that are very important. The modern theater is being challenged by change in the form of cheaper, more convenient forms of entertainment, like motion pictures or television. Theater should not be allowed to die out. Cultural change is one thing that should not happen. Culture is very important to a society, without it that society means nothing.

RADIO ESSAY 6-6

<u>Great vocabulary. Terrific topic. Overall great writing.</u>

There is an entire invisible world, thousands of voices, passing through my body on radio waves. At this moment, I play host to tumultuous talk shows, shallow cellular phone calls, and frantic emergency broadcasts. The air that fills my lungs is replete with unwavering walls of information. At any moment I am unwillingly subjected to a barrage of top-secret military transmissions or the discordant demands and resonant proclamations emanating from baby monitors. I ease into my bed every night, the unsuspecting antenna of televisions sitcoms and spy codes. Radio is never static. Twenty-four hours a day radio is a tonic or a tumult of infinite ideas and images.

Haven to firebrands and pacifists, radio is home to all types of people. In the nether regions of the dial I've found charlatans and idealists alike. The radio possesses the powerful ability to connect individuals as if they are branches of a burgeoning oak As effortlessly as radio creates images of glee and merriment with baseball commentaries and the latest pop tunes, radio also caters to propaganda and lies. During World War II, radio was the medium of choice for the Nazi Party's
demonic messages. Ironically, it also served as the bellwether of liberty for occupied nations. The unrelenting magnetism of radio can be used for good or evil with equal effectiveness.

My fervor for radio began when I was ten years old. Tuning up and down the dial, I spent my nights like a miner panning for auditory gold in rivers of silty static. I felt an awesome admiration for the far-reaching power of radio when I would chance upon faint signals from hundreds of miles away. At age thirteen I bought my first scanning radio from a local electronics store. As it allowed me to receive signals beyond the standard AM/FM bands, my understanding of the invisible worlds in which I live grew considerably. I began to listen to emergency broadcasts
from the local fire and police departments. My radio now told of robberies, fires, and loss that I could not fathom.

Emergency broadcasts became a spark of excitement in my otherwise mundane life of recreational soccer and fresh baked cookies. Every night I fell asleep listening to vibrant, emotional stories of crime and tragedy on my radio. With radio as my constant companion, my understanding of the world evolved greatly.

It is hard to believe that Guillermo Marconi could have envisioned the world to which he gave birth when he invented the long distance radio transmitter over one hundred years ago. Radio has since become a lucid beacon of provocative thought and information. Even as I write these words, radio waves float like feathers to an awaiting world.. Even as I sit in class, radio continues to educate the world. Even as I lie in bed falling asleep to the soporific sounds of classical music and exigent
events, radio awakens a sleeping public with its ability to rise above the landscape with the ease of a soaring eagle through the undulating air of a country canyon.

VIOLENCE ESSAY 6-6

<u>Great writing. Great vocabulary. Great sentence variation. Too long.</u>

As if the savage wails of the winds outside weren't frightening enough, the airwaves emanating from the television set caused me to embrace my knees like they were my protectors. The tumultuous tempest radiating from the cathode ray tube was more impactful than any storm. It is often said that television can ravage one's mind and dull one's senses. But today, with the suddenness of a jaguar pouncing upon its ignorant prey, the television set caused me to become acutely aware of a major problem occurring in our society: media-induced violence.

With the sudden speed of a bullet, an eleven year old boy had become an eleven-year-old murderer. Influenced by the violent media that permeates our culture, the boy's anger exhibited itself as a heinous crime. I know this incident was part of the pervasive problem of media violence. At that moment I had an epiphany: I realized I could no longer be still. Something had to be done. I dashed from the room. I picked up the phone. I made a call.

With that call, my life was to change forever. I was no longer the passive child, barred from making a difference in society by my own ignorance. Now, like a determined young bird emerging expeditiously from its familiar nest into a world of reality, I was determined to take my own stand within society. I decided to begin a movement in my school to increase people's awareness of the negative influences of media violence on children. At our first meeting, only two people came. Then with the unexpectedness of an arrow, something incomprehensibly dreadful happened, (something that both stunned our country and taught us an invaluable lesson.) The Columbine School shooting had occurred.

The next day, the head of my school called me and asked our group to enlighten the student body as to the dark influences of media violence on children. I agreed, knowing that the students yearned for a sense of guidance and a platform on which they could rest their questions, fears and uncertainties about the influences of media violence. I was determined that we, like a sole star poised in an eternity of darkness, would be that platform, that bright oasis of comfort.

In doing research for our presentation, I learned that media violence could create the image that the world is a dark place, full of violence and hatred. Consequently, a child may fear being a victim of violence, which can lead to a strong mistrust of others. I found that the media glamorizes violence, and in this idealistic mode, violence has a strangely compelling mien, which further intensifies the strength of its impact. Despite the negative effects of media violence on children, the entertainment industry advertises its violent product to kids. The Federal Trade Commission found that 80% of the 44 best selling movies rated R for violence were targeted at children.

Continued on next page

Yet the media is more than violence. It offers so much promise and so much genuine truth. Despite the harmful influences of media violence on children, the media can also affect our country in positive ways. For example, the media encourages us to search for the truth. It presents us with current global information that helps to bind us together as one human race. Media can be a valuable tool, or it can be a dangerous weapon.

Then the night of the presentation came. To my surprise, as I stepped into the school auditorium, I saw an incredible number of individuals. These were individuals who held within them the burning desire to improve our community. They were individuals who wanted to shelter and chains of media violence that bound our student body, our country. I then stepped onto the podium. I took a deep breath. I slowly smiled. I am making a difference, I thought. A sense of inspiration seeped like warm maple syrup through my whole body. Slowly I pushed the words out of my mouth and I gently opened my eyes. "We are all making a difference," I said.

FREEDOM ESSAY 6-6

<u>This is, perhaps, the perfect essay. Great metaphors and similes. Several great lines. Good alliteration. Written for SAT II Writing. May be a bit too short for SAT.</u>

The hours prior to inspection passed like water through a canyon. After infinite moments of torturous travel, the last thing I sought to do was convince soldiers of my identity. I took my place among the other weary and disenfranchised people in a monotonous line of exhaustion waiting to board the ship that would take us to freedom. The line shortened. The murmur faded. The soldiers grew near. The moment for which I had trained was finally before me.

I kept my gaze low so as to avoid eye contact. I fought back the tumultuous trembling emanating deep within my soul and radiating out through my body. I recited the lines I had been memorizing with the cool clarity of an accomplished actor. As the faceless soldier scanned a myriad of documents, I bit my lip and tried to act nonchalant, though inside I felt like cattle heading into slaughter. Finally, the soldier signaled for me to pass. For the first time in hours, my lungs filled with air. For the first time in years, my lungs filled with the air of freedom.

With the deliberate gate of a cougar, I strode upon the stairway toward the upper-deck. I was immediately confronted by a wave of blue and white shirts. Across the sea of itinerant travelers, I located my friends and fought my way through the moribund masses to reach them. Our mouths moved with the pretense of communication but the real message came across like a silent storm. We were free.

I never realized how much more quickly the hours of a free man pass compared to those of a prisoner. After what seemed like only a few moments, we were abruptly interrupted by a cacophonous rumble of human thunder. The deck had exploded. I stretched my head over the field of heads and could distinguish, through faintly, a shadowy outline of land separating the turquoise sea and azure sky. Israel! I stood in silent wonder, allowing myself to become satiated with the magnificent sight. Filled with pure joy, we danced without any inhibition as if we had already landed on the sacred soil.

DINNER AT THE WARD ESSAY 5-5

<u>Great story, but lacks vocabulary words and other devices. Also, a bit too short</u>

"God only made so many perfect heads, the rest are covered with hair." I had never met the boy in the poster, but it didn't matter. I knew him. I had seen him over a hundred times within the first few weeks. His name was Franky. Her name was Meghan. Her name was Julia. They were all the boy in the poster. And the more I got to know him, the more I learned about myself. Together, we
were able to change each other's lives.

My job was rather menial. I made and served dinner to the patients in the pediatric ward. But it didn't matter to them; to them I was the older sister many of them so desperately needed. They often asked me about myself, who I was, what my interests were, and most of all why I was there. They couldn't understand why anyone would come here voluntarily. They, after all, had no choice.

Dinner at my home was always a special time, a time when my family would come together and reflect on the events of the day. Dinner, therefore, had always had an important significance to me. In bringing the children dinner, it was almost as if they were becoming a part of my family. At least that's what it felt like to me. It's amazing how a basic need, such as eating, can make people feel so connected to each other. It's also amazing what a little boy inflicted with cancer, can mean to a
normal, healthy girl such as myself. It's funny where life's lessons come from. Sometimes they come from a poster hanging on a wall.

When it came time for my service to end, I had to say goodbye to the children in the ward. Franky, Julia and Meghan, one by one, gave me hugs and thanked me for bringing them dinner and for being there to talk to. I approached the exit. The door opened automatically as it had at the end of each night of my service. Though as it closed behind me this time, I knew I was leaving a changed person. My experience at the ward had opened a door within me that I never knew existed.

SNOW ESSAY 6-6

<u>Good verbs. Good vocabulary. Good variation of sentences</u>

Most people find snow sparkling and magical, yet I find it smothering. Dark, dreary winter days manage to depress even the cheeriest people. I dread the five months of winter that plague the North East yearly. Long nights follow short days without pause, leaving me to hibernate in my room letting the cold slide by.

One afternoon during the winter, I was awoken from a deep slumber by the boisterous ringing of the phone. The chattering voice on the other end reminded me that I was expected at the local soup kitchen that night. Sloth-like, I forced myself to move. Neither fully awake nor completely conscious, I left my warm cocoon to greet the cold with a grimace.

As I entered the dilapidated dining hall, a variety of pungent odors filled my nostrils. I was standing alone, surrounded by people. Before I managed to find a quiet corner in the bustling room, a swarm of volunteers circled me and swept me into the main kitchen. The orange light glared at me while the coral green walls simply ignored my existence. Before I grew accustomed to my new surrounding, my hair was tied back, my hands scrubbed and a bolt of vigor struck my body.

Courageously, I would begin by peeling pyramids of potatoes. On most nights, just as my wrists would begin to begin to ache, I would have to tackle the carrots. Everywhere I looked vegetables dangled in front of my eyes, entreating me to continue my perfunctory task. On unlucky nights, I was chosen to serve the soup.

As I would cheerfully slop this sticky substance into hundreds of bowls, I would wait apprehensively to clean the enormous vat. Have you ever come across a bathtub of soup? Unlike me, you surely have never swam in one in order to empty it of every last drop when the ruckus in the dining room would subside, troops of volunteers would march into the battlefield of upturned chairs, scattered food and mysterious splatters on the walls. We would bare our arms and begin to scrub until our hands were raw. Late at night I would return home physically exhausted yet emotionally ecstatic.

Soon, I began volunteering more often. My long busy days were protracted into the nights. Wiping tables and folding up chairs replaced my once torpid evenings. Caring for others and their well being replaced constant preoccupation with myself. I could no longer meander through such a meaningless life. When I left a faceless and transparent culture, I embraced a new era of care and self-fulfillment.

GRANDFATHER ESSAY 6-6

<u>Good vocabulary. Good metaphors and similes. Great topic</u>

The trip to Vermont was only a few hours long, though it felt like a trip to another country. The leaves danced and dangled past our windshield while those of us inside shared silent remembrances of past years. The alien landscape outside beckoned us, yet we remained firmly flashing toward our inevitable destination. But what we did not know was that the innermost thoughts of my grandmother were churning like an angry sea. Inside her pale and placid exterior was a maelstrom that would send her swirling and spiraling downwards.

What made this trip different was not that we had gained a year, but that we had lost a family member. I couldn't help but wonder as I stared at my grandmother as she scrutinized the leaves floating past if she weren't, in fact, looking right through them. After all, it was she who had lost her husband and life-long companion. It was becoming abundantly clear that, although we could sense her pain, we could do little to ameliorate it.

My grandfather died a little over a year ago. Unknown to us, he had developed pancreatic cancer that had spread through him with the speed of an oncoming train. Before any of us could say goodbye, he had already departed. It was the very suddenness of this disease that had caused my grandmother to feel a great hollowness within her. This hollowness, I came to understand, would leave her only after she allowed herself to fully believe that my grandfather was gone. Her silence belied her inner pain and the more silent she became, the more I understood her anguish. My grandmother looked away from the bleakness outside. Occasionally, our eyes met. When they did, we shared a sullen smile.

The car continued on its inexorable journey carrying us along. I paused for a moment to reflect on the meaning of our trip, a tradition that dated back to days long before my memory begins. Though this trip was intended to be a simple sojourn to the country, it had become so much more. The life that my grandmother had known had come to an end. She, like the leaved falling outside, was now at the mercy of the wind. Her roots had been cut out from under her and it was up to those around her to provide support. Who better to provide this support than those who had relied upon her for support over the many decades gone by?

This short, uneventful trip to the country has changed me in many ways. In a sense, it has shown me that (left blank for the purpose of adapting later)_____.
It was, in some ways, an epiphany, in that it has made me understand the importance of supporting one's family members in times of turmoil and despair. It has also taught me to understand the finite relationships that we form in life and that once the coldness of winter had passed, there would once again be life upon this lifeless landscape.

ROSE ESSAY 6-6

<u>Great topic. Great description. Good Vocabulary. A bit long</u>.

As I approached, the sun shone brilliantly on my shoulders, yet the house was engulfed in a black, shadowy veil. My arms grew steadily more tired from the bundles I carried, bundles that seemed to grow heavier with every step toward the home. This was a ritual I had performed many times before but today seemed particularly different.

For a moment, I was once again an eight-year-old boy going to my grandfather's house. I still vividly recall the day; it was a day much like today with the sun shining through thick, white clouds. The leaves lashed at my face as I, with great anticipation, sped toward the door. The beauty of the day instantly vanished when I was greeted by my grandmother's solemn face.

I meandered down the straight road, dawdling the whole time. I kicked carelessly through piles of leaves, stopped to stare into open windows, and carefully studied two graceful birds, in flight, weaving in and out of each other. The world, I noticed, was effervescent; life seemed abundant even in this small urban neighborhood. My task seemed infinitesimal in the whole scheme of things, but to one old woman it would mean the world.

I had first signed up for community service merely to gain credit for school. Each Sunday I would visit an elderly lady named Rose, bringing her groceries. It seemed to me that she would prepare all week for my arrival. My long awaited advent would be accompanied by an effusive greeting complete with cookies and an occasional present. Through the months that I shopped for her, we grew closer, and we often engaged in topics far more interesting than shopping lists and coupons. Soon I began to consider her a friend.

Only a week earlier I had been told that Rose was ill, and would not be needing my services that week. I was scared that I was going to lose another friend, and the thought of her dying brought back memories of my grandfather. That is why today seemed different. That is why the house was so somber. That is why I walked with such trepidation. That is why I appreciated a world teeming with life. I didn't want her to die. I couldn't go through that again.

She wasn't like the other old people I would always see loitering around McDonald's or Dunkin Donuts - or perhaps she was. After my first few visits I began to wonder: if I were to sit down with anyone of them, would we develop the same bond that I had with my friend Rose? I realized that we would. Until recently, I saw the elderly as cantankerous curmudgeons, ill tempered, and querulous. However, now I have learned that couldn't be farther from the truth. I suddenly saw the elderly in a new way. They shouldn't be scorned or shunned by younger generations, but should rather be listened to. We can learn a lot from their wisdom, a special wisdom that can only be acquired with time.

I arrived at her doorway but was hesitant to ring the bell. I didn't want to be greeted by another solemn face at the door. I couldn't feel the grief as I had before. As I reached out to ring the bell, the door swung open as if some mystical force had anticipated my approach. To my delight it was Rose wearing a huge grin, and carrying a platter of freshly baked cookies.

Mastering SAT Math

SAT Math Skills and Strategies

Statistical Ranking of Math Question Types
From College Board's Official SAT Study Guide

Question Type	Total # in 8 tests	as % total	Av. of questions per test	Rank
Solving Equations and Inequalities	46	10.6%	5.8	1
Functions: Evaluating, solving	17	3.9%	2.1	2
Functions: Parabolas	9	2.1%	1.1	2
Functions: Symbols	8	1.9%	1.0	2
Functions: Qualitative	4	0.9%	0.5	2
Functions: Glide Translations	3	0.7%	0.4	2
Functions: Linear	3	0.7%	0.4	2
Triangles	31	7.2%	3.9	3
Word Problems	28	6.5%	3.5	4
Coordinate Geometry	25	5.8%	3.1	5
Lines and Angles	23	5.3%	2.9	6
Number Theory	23	5.3%	2.9	7
Data Interpretation	22	5.1%	2.8	8
Statistics (mean, median and mode)	19	4.4%	2.4	9
Arithmetic	15	3.5%	1.9	10
Ratio and Proportions	15	3.5%	1.9	11
Circles	14	3.2%	1.8	12
Evaluate Expressions and Equations	13	3.0%	1.6	13
Sequences and Series	13	3.0%	1.6	14
Sentence Translation	12	2.8%	1.5	15
Polygons	11	2.5%	1.4	16
Exponents	10	2.3%	1.3	17
Solids	10	2.3%	1.3	18
Probability	8	1.9%	1.0	19
Absolute Value	7	1.6%	0.9	20
Counting Techniques	7	1.6%	0.9	21
Percentages	7	1.6%	0.9	22
Direct and Inverse Variation	6	1.4%	0.8	23
Quadratics	6	1.4%	0.8	24
Logical Reasoning	6	1.4%	0.8	25
Other	5	1.2%	0.6	26
Sets	4	0.9%	0.5	27
Simplify Expressions	2	0.5%	0.3	28

Mastering SAT Math

Critical Reading Applies to Math Too

Many math problems you'll find on the SAT demand your best <u>reading skills</u> and familiarity with all mathematical terms and symbols used.

On multiple-choice problems, test makers often include one or more incorrect answers that represent the result obtained by making commons errors. These errors might include <u>misreading</u> or <u>not reading</u> key terms.

Careful!!!

Examples of words that cause common SAT Math reading errors:

could be/must be/could not be
greatest possible/least possible
integer (for example, x is an integer)

Also: know the set of numbers that is relevant to each question.

For example:
   "x > 0" (means positive number)
   "x < 0" (means negative number)
   "x is an integer (means whole number, positive, negative or zero)
   1 > x > 0 (means positive fraction)

Math Traps

What are "math traps" and why are they in SAT Math questions?

Math traps are wrong answers that seem *to be correct* when one makes *common mathematical errors or incorrect assumptions.*

SAT test makers design math problems with math traps in order to catch the time-pressed or unwary student. A <u>time-pressed student</u> may feel anxious (from either anxiety or losing too much time on other problems within the section) going from problem to problem, and so may read complicated questions with less care while the unwary does this from bad habit. An <u>unwary</u> student will often find the math sections easy, all the while blissfully unaware of test makers' traps. This leads to the apparent irony that many students who feel the test was easy, actually do poorly relative to their potentials.

Math Trap Example 1

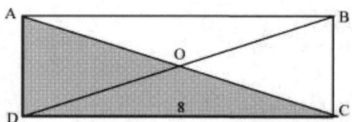

Q. In rectangle ABCD above, △ADC has an area of 12 cm². What is the

ratio $\dfrac{\triangle AOB}{\triangle BOC}$?

You can see how one could easily get caught up in all the letters and solve for the wrong thing! Read carefully and make sure you are solving for the right thing!

Math Trap Example 2

Q. For integers x and y, x>y. What is the least possible non-negative integer value of x/y?

A. ½
B. ¾
C. 0
D. 1
E. it cannot be determined

The answer to example 1 is 1:1. Each has an area of 6cm²
The answer to example 2 is C. A and B are out, because the answer must be an integer. C works, because x could be 0 and y could be negative. E (cannot be determined) is usually just an easy out, and usually incorrect, when offered as a solution to a hard question.

SAT Math Strategies

Quick Estimation and Mental Math

<u>Estimation</u> serves three important functions on the SAT:

(1) it quickly and easily rules out obviously-wrong answers
(2) it double checks an answer found
(3) it verifies or discredits a series of calculator keystrokes that could lead to an answer that is magnitudes off.

<u>Example of Estimation</u>:

"A rectangular plot of land is 208 ft. x 292 ft...."

If the area is needed to arrive at the answer, then you can estimate the area of the plot must be near 60,000 sq. ft. (i.e., round 208 down to 200 and 292 up to 300, making the estimate 200 x 300, or 60,000).

Also, you can rule out those answers whose last digit is not "6" since the last digits of the two factors will multiply together to arrive at the last digit of the product, i.e., two numbers that end in 8 and 2 will produce a product that ends in a six.

Quick <u>mental math</u> vs calculators: calculators are useful during the test for certain types of problems or to minimize time taken on more involved calculations. For those comfortable with the concept of mental math, however, a calculator may often be unnecessary. For those of you who use mental math regularly, you may merely ask yourself "does this answer make sense?"

<u>Example of Mental Math</u>

76 x 84 can be estimated like above, 80x80, which in turn can be computed in two mental short cut steps:
(1) Multiply the two numbers without the ending zeroes, or 8x8, first, or 64.
(2) To this result, replace the ending zeroes that had been removed (this technique works when multiplying numbers with ending zeroes, or those estimated to have ending zeroes), or 6,400, an example of applying mental math to estimation.

Grid-In Key Points

Important points about student-produced responses

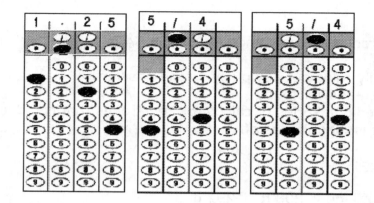

This is what the grid-boxes look like. See tips below for maximizing scores on these questions, otherwise referred to as student-produced response questions

(A) You don't have to reduce fractions to lowest terms unless your answer won't fit in the grid.

(B) Mixed numbers <u>MUST</u> be expressed as improper fractions or decimals. For example, to grid $1\frac{1}{6}$, you must express it as 7/6, 1.17 or 1.16.

(C) Grid as much of the repeating decimal as will fit in the grid. For example, grid $\frac{2}{3}$ as 2/3 or .666 or .667, and <u>NOT</u> .66 or .67

(D) To grid an answer zero, just enter 0 in a single column where 0 appears

(E) There are no negative answers to grid-in questions.

(F) There are no variables in answers to grid-in questions

(G) You may use any part of the grid, but we suggest you always start from the left-most column.

(H) Wrong answers to grid-ins do not subtract points from your test score.

(I) You are not graded on what you write in the spaced above the grid. That space is merely a convenient place for you to write your answers before actually placing the numbers into the grid.

(J) Since grid-ins do not have multiple-choice answers, indirect strategies such as plugging in answers cannot be employed.

Know the Terminology of the Test

Integers: {-4, -1, 0, 1, 100}	All whole numbers. The set of all integers contains positive whole numbers, negative whole numbers, and zero. It is important to remember that a number referred to as an integer could be negative or it could be zero.
Real Numbers:	All numbers, whole, fractions, negative, positive, zero, etc.(-3/8, -12,1,20). On the SAT, all numbers are members of the set of real numbers.
Rational Numbers $\left\{-\dfrac{3}{2}, 2\dfrac{1}{3}, 0, -18, 0.75, .\overline{34}\right\}$	All integers and fractions, including terminating decimals, and repeating decimals.
Irrational Numbers $\left\{3\pi, \dfrac{2}{\pi}, \sqrt{2}, -\sqrt{3}, \sqrt{42}, \sqrt[3]{4}\right\}$	All numbers that CANNOT be expressed as an integer or ratio of two integers, such as π. The most commonly found irrational numbers on the SAT are $\sqrt{\ }$ numbers, or square roots, as long as the square root is of a number that is NOT a perfect square, e.g., $\sqrt{2}, \sqrt{3}$ and $\sqrt{6}$, but NOT $\sqrt{4} = \sqrt{2^2} = 2$
Positive Numbers: $\left\{\dfrac{1}{2}, 1, 30, 25/4\right\}$	All non-zero, non-negative numbers. Could be whole numbers, fractions, irrational numbers, etc.
Negative Numbers: $\left\{-\dfrac{1}{2}, -1, -30, -25/4\right\}$	All non-zero, non-positive numbers. Could be integers, fractions, irrational numbers, etc.
Non-negative Numbers: $\left\{\dfrac{1}{2}, 1, 30, 25/4, 0\right\}$	All non-negative numbers, INCLUDING zero. Could be integers, fractions, irrational numbers, etc.
Prime Numbers: The first eight prime numbers are: 2,3,5,7,11,13,17,19...	A number evenly divisible by itself and 1.(i.e. with no remainder). The set of prime numbers begins with the number 2. Neither 0 nor 1 are prime numbers.
Consecutive Integers: 1, 2, 3, 4,... Or -4, -3, -2, -1, 0, 1...	A set of integer numbers that follow each other in their natural order (i.e., like on the number line).

Terminology, cont.

Distinct, Different	Important words used to clarify that repeated numbers, values, expressions, or figures are to be counted only once. For example, 72 has only 2 <u>distinct</u> prime factors, 2 and 3, even though a prime factorization of 72 shows it equal to 2•2•2•3•3.
Digit	A whole number 0-9 that can exist alone or as part of a multi-digit. For example, the "4" in 9,473 is the *hundreds* digit. It identifies how many hundreds are included in the number. "3" is the *units* digit. It identifies that there are three "ones."
Set	Unless referring to data (in which observations can repeat), it is a collection of distinct numbers, objects, or figures.
Member, Element	Individuals units that are part of a defined set.
Intersection; given set A and set B, the intersection is known as A $\cap$ B	The set defined by all elements that belong to all sets of the intersection. For example, if A = {all odd integers} and B = {all positive integers less than 11}, then A $\cap$ B= {1,3,5,7,9}.
Union; given set A and set B, the intersection is known as A $\cup$ B	The set defined by all elements that belong to at least one set of the union. For example, if A = {all positive integer powers of 2 less than 100} and B = {all positive integers between 49 and 51, inclusive}, then A $\cup$ B = {2, 4, 8, 16, 32, 49, 50, 51, 64}.
Algebraic Expression, or simply Expression $\{3, -12, 4x^{-1}, 2x -3xy, \sqrt{12}\pi r^3\}$	A combination of numbers and variables. Commonly, numbers are substituted for unknowns to determine a value, in a process known as "plugging in."
Equation $2x + 3y = 9x + 4y$	When two expressions are set equal. Equations are fundamental to the idea of isolating an algebraic quantity, or "solving" for unknowns.
Direct Variation or Direct Proportion; also, quantity 1 "directly varies with" or "is directly proportional to" quantity 2	A situation in which two (or more) quantities increase or decrease at the same rate, or are in constant proportion. For example, as one quantity doubles, the other quantity doubles.
Inverse Variation or Inverse Proportion; also quantity 1 "inversely varies with" or "is inversely proportional to" quantity 2	A situation in which one quantity increases as another quantity decreases, while the product of the quantities remains constant. For example, as one quantity doubles, the other quantity is cut in half.
Domain and Range (of a function)	<u>Domain</u>: the set of all values for which the function is defined. <u>Range</u>: the set of all values that are the output, or result, of applying a function.

Arithmetic and Algebraic Terms and Operations

Sum (addition) 2+3 = 5 (5 is the sum) 2x + 4x = 6x (6x is the sum)	The result you arrive at when two or more quantities or expressions are added together.
Difference (subtraction) 5 - 3 = 2 (2 is the difference) 3x - 2x = x (x is the difference)	The result you arrive at when subtracting one quantity or expression from another.
Product (multiplication) 9 • 4 = 36 (36 is the product) 2x • 10x = 20x² (20x² is the product)	The result you arrive at when multiplying two or more quantities or expressions together.
Quotient (division) 10 ÷ 4 = 2.5 (2.5 is the quotient)	The result you arrive at when dividing one quantity or expressions by another.
Remainder (division) 9 ÷ 4 leaves Remainder of 1	The quantity left over after one number or expression has been divided by another.
Divisor (division) The even divisors of 10 are 2 and 10. The odd divisors of 10 are 1 and 5.	A number that divides evenly into another without leaving a remainder.
Multiple Multiples of 2 include 2, 4, 6, 8, 10.... Multiples of 5 include 5, 10, 15, 20, etc. (multiples can also be negative, e.g., multiples of 3 INCLUDE ...-9, -6, -3, 0, 3, 6, etc.—negative multiples are not usually found on the SAT)	A specified number or expression multiplied by any integer (see examples).

Common Algebraic and Arithmetic Operations and Formulas, cont

Percentage A number expressed as part of 100	A percentage is a part of 100. For example, 40% = $\frac{40}{100}$ or 0.40. Percentages are usually used to express a quantity less than 1. For example 50% = $\frac{50}{100}$ or $\frac{1}{2}$. However a percentage can also express a number greater than 1. For example, 200% = $\frac{200}{100}$ or just 2. Remember that a number is 100% of itself. Therefore if you add 100 % of something to itself, you end up with 200% of it as a result.
Average (arithmetic mean): $A = \frac{S}{P}$	Average means the total sum of parts divided by the number of parts. The formula is: Average = Sum/Parts. To figure out the average age of three people whose ages are 12, 15, and 30: Average = $\frac{12+15+30}{3}$. Average = $\frac{57}{3} = 19$
Distance-Rate-Time Formula, $D = R \times T$	The D-R-T formula is used when calculating distance, rate, or time. Usually, SAT problems furnish you with two of the three variables, and require you to calculate the third. The formula is: Distance = Rate $\times$ Time or D = R $\times$ T. It can be switched to calculate for rate or time as needed: $R = \frac{D}{T}$ or $T = \frac{D}{R}$
Mean/Median/Mode Mean: Same as average Median: The middle term when a list of numbers is arranged in increasing order. Mode: The most repeated term in a group of numbers.	Often a group or list of numbers is given and you are asked to determine the mean, median and/or mode. It is important that these numbers be separated and listed in increasing order and that repeated values be considered separately. Example: *On a recent SAT math test, three students scored 800s, two students scored 700 and four students scored 600.* Your list of numbers should look like this: *{600,600,600,600,700,700, 800,800,800}* The mean would be the sum of these numbers, 6,200, divided by the number of terms or $\frac{6,200}{9}$ (around 689). The median would be the middlemost number in the ascending list, 700, and the mode would be the most repeated number, 600.

Ratio 12:1 means 12 times as many of one thing as another	A ratio is a fraction that expresses relative quantities in a group or population. For example, a ratio of 3:2 boys to girls means there are 3 boys for every 2 girls. There could be 6 boys and 4 girls, or 30 boys and 20 girls. More information is needed to determine an amount. If you know the total, you can figure out how many of each there are. For a given total (100 students, for example) in a ratio of 3:2 (boys to girls), to figure out the number of each (boys, for example) write $3x + 2x = 100$. This means there are $3x$ (boys) and $2x$ (girls), and a total of 100 students. $5x = 100$. $x = 20$. Since there are $3x$ (boys), there are $3(20)$ or 60 (boys).
Factoring an Algebraic Expression	Simplifying an algebraic expression. A common type of expression looks like this: $x^2 + 5x + 6$. The factored version will be in this form: ( ) ( ). First, factor x^2 into: $(x\ \ )(x\ \ )$. To complete the factoring, the sum of the two numbers you must find will be 5 (the middle number in the equation), and the product will be 6 (the last number in the equation). Thus, the factored form is $(x+3)(x+2)$.
FOIL	Although not a term used in the SAT, it is a necessary skill. FOIL is an acronym for <u>F</u>irst, <u>O</u>uter, <u>I</u>nner, <u>L</u>ast. It refers to a method of changing an algebraic expression in factored form back to its original form. To change an algebraic expression from this form $(x+3)(x+2)$, multiply together **first** two terms, then the **outer** terms, then the **inner** terms then the **last** terms. $[(x \cdot x) + (x \cdot 2) + (3 \cdot x) + (3 \cdot 2)]$ $= (x^2 + 2x + 3x + 6)$ $= \mathbf{x^2 + 5x + 6}$

Definitions: Exercises

Number Sets

(Exercise 1) Which of the following are Integers or can be expressed as Integers?

Integer?	100	0	1	$22/11$	$22/10$	$-51/17$	17.0	$-1/3$
Yes or No								

(Exercise 2) Which of the following are Real Numbers?

Real Number?	$32/33$	$-17/15$	.00089	$5\frac{4}{7}$	22	0	-1	$1/{-1}$
Yes or No								

(Exercise 3) Which of the following are Positive Numbers?

Positive Number?	0	$1/2$	$17/3$	-1	$-2/4$	x^2, $(x=-3)$	x^3, $(x=-3)$	$0/14$
Yes or No								

(Exercise 4) Which of the following are Negative Numbers?

Negative Number?	0	$-1/2$	$-2/1$	-0.7767	3.1415	x^3, $(x=-7)$	x^4, $(x=-7)$	$-3 \bullet 4$
Yes or No								

Answers on the next page

Definitions: Exercises

Answers to Number Sets Exercises

(Exercise 1) Which of the following are Integers or can be expressed as Integers?

Integer?	100	0	1	$22/11$	$22/10$	$-51/17$	17.0	$-1/3$
Yes or No	Yes	Yes	Yes	Yes	No	Yes	Yes	No

(Exercise 2) Which of the following are Real Numbers?

Real Number?	$32/33$	$-17/15$	.00089	$5\frac{4}{7}$	22	0	-1	$1/-1$
Yes or No	Yes	Yes	Yes	Yes	Yes	Yes	Yes	Yes

(Exercise 3) Which of the following are Positive Numbers?

Positive Number?	0	$1/2$	$17/3$	-1	$-2/4$	$x^2,$ $(x=-3)$	$x^3,$ $(x=-3)$	$0/14$
Yes or No	No	Yes	Yes	No	No	Yes	No	No

(Exercise 4) Which of the following are Negative Numbers?

Negative Number?	0	$-1/2$	$-2/-1$	-0.7767	3.1415	$x^3,$ $(x=-7)$	$x^4,$ $(x=-7)$	$-3 \bullet 4$
Yes or No	No	Yes	No	Yes	No	Yes	No	Yes

Definitions: Exercises

Positive/Negative, Even/Odd, Prime, Consecutive Integers

(Exercise 5) Determine which of the following cases yields a Negative or Positive Answer?

Situation	Negative • Negative	Positive • Positive	Negative • Positive	Even • Odd
Negative, Positive or ???				

(Exercise 6) Determine which of the following cases yields an Even or Odd Answer?

Situation	Odd • Even	Even • Even	Odd • Odd	Zero • Odd or Even
Even, Odd or ???				

(Exercise 7) Which of the following are Prime Numbers?

Prime Number?	0	1	88	2	0	101	11	21
Yes or No								

(Exercise 8) Which of the following sets of numbers are Consecutive Integers?

Consecutive Integers?	8, 7, 6	$\frac{1}{2}, \frac{2}{2}, \frac{3}{2}$	$-3, -2, -1$	$-1, 0, 1$	2, 4, 6	1, 2, 1	7, 9, 11	$x, x+1, x+2$ $(x = 11)$
Yes or No								

Answers on the next page

Definitions: Exercises

Answers to Positive/Negative, Even/Odd, Prime, Consecutive Integers

(Exercise 5) Determine which of the following cases yields a Negative or Positive Answer?

Situation	Negative • Negative	Positive • Positive	Negative • Positive	Even • Odd
Negative, Positive or ???	+++Positive+++	+++Positive+++	---Negative---	Tricky! It Could be either

(Exercise 6) Determine which of the following cases yields an Even or Odd Answer?

Situation	Odd • Even (3 x 4 = 12)	Even • Even (4 x 4 = 16)	Odd •Odd (3 x 3 = 9)	Zero • Odd or Even (0 x 3 = 0) (0 x 4 = 0)
Even or Odd	Even	Even	Odd (the only odd case)	Even (0 is even)

(Exercise 7) Which of the following are Prime Numbers?

Prime Number?	0	1	88	2	0	101	11	21
Yes or No	No	No	No	Yes	No	Yes	Yes	No

(Exercise 8) Which of the following sets of numbers are Consecutive Integers?

Consecutive Integers?	8, 7, 6	$\frac{1}{2}, \frac{2}{2}, \frac{3}{2}$	−3, −2, −1	−1, 0, 1	2, 4, 6	1, 2, 1	7, 9, 11	$x, x+1, x+2$ ($x = 11$)
Yes or No	No	No	Yes	Yes	No	No	No	Yes

Definitions: Exercises

Arithmetic and Algebraic Terms and Operations

How well do you read and understand terminology and how are you at following through with operations?

Quiz Yourself on SAT Math Terminology

Fill in

The sum of 3 and 2 =	The sum of 3x and 7x =	The sum of first 5 positive integers is =	The sum of $3/4$ and $7/8$ =	The sum of first 5 prime numbers =	The sum of x^2 and $2x^2$ =
The difference between 7x and 5x =	The difference between 12 and 3 =	The difference between x^2 and $2x^2$ =	The difference between $4/5$ and $7/15$ =	The difference between $3x^2$ and $3x^2$ =	The difference between 0 and $7/4$ =
The product of 3 and $3x^2$ =	The product of 9^2 and 9^3 =	The product of $1/2$ and $2/3$ =	The product of $3x^2$ and $4x^3$ =	The product of 0 and anything =	The product of 1 and $-7/6$ =
The quotient of 4x and 2x =	The quotient of x^2 and x =	The quotient of $7/8$ and $6/7$ =	The quotient of x^4 and x =	The quotient of 5 and $1/2$ =	The quotient of 8x and 4 =
All divisors of 16 are _____	All even divisors of 20 are _____	All odd divisors of 20 are _____	All divisors of 100 are _____	All even divisors of 55 are _____	All odd divisors of 55 are _____
Five multiples of 3 are _____	Is 100 a multiple of 100?	The first 5 positive even multiples of 1 are _____	Is 10 a multiple of 5?	6 is a multiple of which positive numbers?	The first three positive multiples of 9 are _____

Answers on the next page

Definitions: Exercises

Answers to Arithmetic and Algebraic Terms and Operations

The sum of 3 and 2 = **5**	The sum of 3x and 7x = 10x	The sum of first 5 positive integers is = **15**	The sum of $\frac{3}{4}$ and $\frac{7}{8}$ = $\frac{13}{8}$ or $1\frac{5}{8}$	The sum of first 5 prime numbers = **28**	The sum of x^2 and $2x^2$ = $3x^2$
The difference between 7x and 5x = 2x	The difference between 12 and 3 = **9**	The difference between x^2 and $2x^2$ = $-x^2$	The difference between $\frac{4}{5}$ and $\frac{7}{15}$ = $\frac{5}{15}$ or $\frac{1}{3}$	The difference between $3x^2$ and $3x^2$ = **0**	The difference between 0 and $\frac{7}{4}$ = $-\frac{7}{4}$
The product of 3 and $3x^2$ = $9x^2$	The product of 9^2 and 9^3 = 9^5	The product of $\frac{1}{2}$ and $\frac{2}{3}$ = $\frac{2}{6}$ or $\frac{1}{3}$	The product of $3x^2$ and $4x^3$ = $12x^5$	The product of 0 and anything = **0**	The product of 1 and $-\frac{7}{6}$ = $-\frac{7}{6}$
The quotient of 4x and 2x = **2**	The quotient of x^2 and x = **x**	The quotient of $\frac{7}{8}$ and $\frac{6}{7}$ = $\frac{49}{48}$ or $1\frac{1}{48}$	The quotient of x^4 and x = x^3	The quotient of 5 and $\frac{1}{2}$ = **10**	The quotient of 8x and 4 = 2x
All divisors of 16 are **1, 2, 4, 8, 16**	All even divisors of 20 are **2, 4, 10, 20**	All odd divisors of 20 are **1, 5**	All divisors of 100 are **1, 2, 4, 5, 10, 20, 25, 50, 100**	All even divisors of 55 are ∅	All odd divisors of 55 are **1, 5, 11, 55**
Five multiples of 3 are **3, 6, 9, 12, 15**	Is 100 a multiple of 100? **Yes**	The first 5 positive even multiples of 1 are **2, 4, 6, 8, 10**	Is 10 a multiple of 5? **Yes**	6 is a multiple of which positive numbers? **1, 2, 3, 6**	The first three positive multiples of 9 are **9, 18, 27**

Important Math Concepts

Exponents

Squares, Cubes, Powers of 2

In the following pages, we present simple exercises to help you review and reinforce basic concepts of numbers you'll need at the "tip of your brain" as you work through many SAT questions.

<u>Squares of Common Integers</u>

Fill in the square, i.e., ^{2} of each integer below that integer.

n =	0	1	2	3	4	5	6	7	8	9	10	11	12	13	14	15	16
$n^2 =$																	

Tip: *Know them backwards and forwards.* Ex: Know that 121 is the square of 11.

Cubes of Common Integers

Fill in the cube, i.e., ^{3} of each integer below that integer.

n =	0	1	2	3	4	5	6	7
$n^3 =$								

Tip: *Know them backwards and forwards.* Ex: Know that 27 is the cube of 3.

Powers of the Number 2

Fill in these powers of 2.

2^n	2^1	2^2	2^3	2^4	2^5	2^6	2^7	2^8
$2^n =$								

Tip: *Numbers such as 16 and 64 are common in geometry and algebra problems.*

Answers on the next page

Exponents
Solutions to Squares, Cubes, Powers of 2

Squares of Common Integers

Solutions to squares of common integers.

n =	0	1	2	3	4	5	6	7	8	9	10	11	12	13	14	15	16
n^2 =	0	1	4	9	16	25	36	49	64	81	100	121	144	169	196	225	256

Strategy: *You should know the squares through 12^2. For 13^2 and 14^2, reverse last two numbers (169,196). For 15^2, remember $5 \cdot 5 = 25$ (last two numbers in 225).*

Cubes of Common Integers

Solutions to cubes of common integers.

n =	0	1	2	3	4	5	6	7
n^3 =	0	1	8	27	64	125	216	343

Strategy: *Know through at least 5^3.* The others are merely the icing on the cake!

Powers of the Number 2

Solutions to powers of 2 table.

2^n	2^1	2^2	2^3	2^4	2^5	2^6	2^7	2^8
2^n =	2	4	8	16	32	64	128	256

Strategy: *Know through at least 2^6.* The others should come up only in the most difficult questions that are found at the end of SAT math sections.

Exponents
Negatives, Fractions and Algebraic Terms

Powers of Negative Numbers

Fill in these powers of -2

$(-2)^x$	$(-2)^1$	$(-2)^2$	$(-2)^3$	$(-2)^4$	$(-2)^5$	$(-2)^6$	$(-2)^7$	$(-2)^8$
$(-2)^x =$								

Tip: Negative numbers with odd exponents remain negative, but negative numbers are overpowered by even exponents. Even exponents turn negative numbers into positive numbers.

The Effects of Exponents on Fractions

Fill in these powers of common fractions

(x/y)	$(1/2)^2$	$(1/3)^2$	$(1/4)^2$	$(1/5)^2$	$(2/3)^2$	$(3/4)^2$	$(4/5)^2$	$(6/5)^2$
(x/y) =								

Tip: When a fraction is raised to a power, numerator and denominator are raised to that power. Tip: Fractions between 0 and 1 become smaller when raised to a power. The higher the power, the smaller the value.

The Effects of Exponents on Algebraic Terms

Fill in these powers of algebraic expressions

	A	B	C	D	E	F	G	H
simplify these	$(x^2)^3$	$x^3 \cdot x^4$	$(4x^2)^3$	$4x^2 + 4x^2$	x^6 / x^4	$x^6 \div x^2$	$[(x^3)^4]^2$	$2x^8 / 2x^3$
=								

Tip: Know the rules of exponents and the orders of operations (PEMDAS).

Answers on the next page

Exponents Solutions to Negatives, Fractions and Algebraic Terms

Powers of Negative Numbers

Solutions to powers of -2 table

$(-2)^x$	$(-2)^1$	$(-2)^2$	$(-2)^3$	$(-2)^4$	$(-2)^5$	$(-2)^6$	$(-2)^7$	$(-2)^8$
$(-2)^x =$	-2	4	-8	16	-32	64	-128	256

Strategy: Think "N-O-N" Negative number to Odd exponent is a Negative number

The Effects of Exponents on Fractions

Solutions to powers of fractions table

$(x/y)^n$	$(1/2)^2$	$(1/3)^2$	$(1/4)^2$	$(1/5)^2$	$(2/3)^2$	$(3/4)^2$	$(4/5)^2$	$(6/5)^2$
$(x/y)^n =$	1/4	1/9	1/16	1/25	4/9	9/16	16/25	36/25

Strategy: Exponents are democratic: the numerator and denominator receive equal treatment

The Effects of Exponents on Algebraic Terms

Solutions to powers of algebraic expressions table

	A	B	C	D	E	F	G	H
simplify these	$(x^2)^3$	$x^3 \cdot x^4$	$(4x^2)^3$	$4x^2 + 4x^2$	x^6 / x^4	$x^6 \div x^2$	$[(x^3)^4]^2$	$2x^8 / 2x^3$
=	x^6	x^7	$64x^6$	$8x^2$	x^2	x^4	x^{24}	x^5

*Strategy: Take it down a level. When **multiplying** numbers, **add** exponents. When **raising an exponent** to a power **multiply** the exponents.*

The basic rules of exponential equations

- When a power is raised to a power, multiply exponents (A).
- When multiplying numbers with a common base, add exponents (B).
- Exponents outside bracket affect the number and exponent inside (C).
- When adding terms with the same variable and exponent, add the coefficients (D).
- When dividing terms with common base, divide numbers and subtract exponents (E, F, H).
- When multiplying terms with common base, add the exponents (B).
- Always perform the operation within the (inner) brackets first (G).

Exponents
Negative Exponents of Numbers, Fractions, Variables and Algebraic Terms

Negative Powers of 2

Fill in these negative powers of 2.

2^{-x}	2^{-1}	2^{-2}	2^{-3}	2^{-4}	2^{-5}	2^{-6}	2^{-7}	2^{-8}
$2^{-x} =$								

Tip: A negative exponent of the base can be made positive by putting one over the same base to the positive exponent (a positive number raised to negative exponent STAYS positive!).

The Effects of Negative Exponents on Fractions

Fill in these negative powers of common fractions.

$\left(\frac{x}{y}\right)^{-n}$	$\left(\frac{1}{2}\right)^{-3}$	$\left(\frac{1}{3}\right)^{-1}$	$\left(\frac{1}{4}\right)^{-2}$	$\left(\frac{1}{5}\right)^{-2}$	$\left(\frac{2}{3}\right)^{-3}$	$\left(\frac{3}{4}\right)^{-2}$	$\left(\frac{4}{5}\right)^{-3}$	$\left(\frac{6}{5}\right)^{-2}$
$\left(\frac{x}{y}\right)^{-n} =$								

Tip: When a fraction is raised to a negative power, numerator and denominator are swapped and then raised to the positive of that power.
Tip: Fractions between 0 and 1 become bigger when raised to a negative power less than -1. The more negative the power, the greater the value.

The Effects of Negative Exponents on Variables and Algebraic Terms

Fill in these powers of algebraic expressions.

	A	**B**	**C**	**D**	**E**	**F**	**G**	**H**
$\rightarrow$	$(x^2)^{-3}$	$x^3 \cdot x^{-4}$	$(4x^2)^{-3}$	$4^{-1}x^2 + 4x^{-2}$	x^{-6}/x^{-4}	$x^{-6} \div x^2$	$[(x^{-3})^4]^{-2}$	$\dfrac{2(x+1)^{-3}}{2^{-1}x^{-3}}$
$=$								

Tip: Know the rules of exponents and the orders of operations (PEMDAS).

Answers on the next page

Exponents
Solutions to Negative Exponents of Numbers, Fractions, Variables and Algebraic Terms

Negative Powers of 2

Solutions to negative powers of 2.

2^{-n}	2^0	2^{-1}	2^{-2}	2^{-3}	2^{-4}	2^{-5}	2^{-6}	2^{-7}
$2^{-n} =$	1	$\dfrac{1}{2}$	$\dfrac{1}{4}$	$\dfrac{1}{8}$	$\dfrac{1}{16}$	$\dfrac{1}{32}$	$\dfrac{1}{64}$	$\dfrac{1}{128}$
...also	$\left(\dfrac{1}{2}\right)^0$	$\left(\dfrac{1}{2}\right)^1$	$\left(\dfrac{1}{2}\right)^2$	$\left(\dfrac{1}{2}\right)^3$	$\left(\dfrac{1}{2}\right)^4$	$\left(\dfrac{1}{2}\right)^5$	$\left(\dfrac{1}{2}\right)^6$	$\left(\dfrac{1}{2}\right)^7$
or...	$\dfrac{1}{2^0}$	$\dfrac{1}{2^1}$	$\dfrac{1}{2^2}$	$\dfrac{1}{2^3}$	$\dfrac{1}{2^4}$	$\dfrac{1}{2^5}$	$\dfrac{1}{2^6}$	$\dfrac{1}{2^7}$

Strategy: *Know through* 2^{-3}. These alternate ways of expressing negative exponents can be useful on certain problems.

The Effects of Negative Exponents on Fractions

Solutions to negative powers of common fractions.

$\left(\dfrac{x}{y}\right)^{-n}$	$\left(\dfrac{1}{2}\right)^{-3}$	$\left(\dfrac{1}{3}\right)^{-1}$	$\left(\dfrac{1}{4}\right)^{-2}$	$\left(\dfrac{1}{5}\right)^{-2}$	$\left(\dfrac{2}{3}\right)^{-3}$	$\left(\dfrac{3}{4}\right)^{-2}$	$\left(\dfrac{4}{5}\right)^{-3}$	$\left(\dfrac{6}{5}\right)^{-2}$
$\left(\dfrac{x}{y}\right)^{-n} =$	8	3	16	25	$\dfrac{27}{8}$	$\dfrac{16}{9}$	$\dfrac{125}{64}$	$\dfrac{25}{36}$

The Effects of Negative Exponents on Variables and Algebraic Terms

Solutions to powers of algebraic expressions.

	A	B	C	D	E	F	G	H
$\rightarrow$	$(x^2)^{-3}$	$x^3 \bullet x^{-4}$	$(4x^2)^{-3}$	$4^{-1}x^2 + 4x^{-2}$	x^{-6}/x^{-4}	$x^{-6} \div x^2$	$[(x^{-3})^4]^{-2}$	$\dfrac{2(x+1)^{-3}}{2^{-1}x^{-3}}$
$=$	x^{-6}	x^{-1}	$\dfrac{1}{64}x^{-6}$	$\dfrac{1}{4}x^2 + 4x^{-2}$	x^{-2}	x^{-8}	x^{24}	$\dfrac{4x^3}{(x+1)^3}$

Hint: Be on the lookout for alternate presentations of exponent expressions. For example, x^{-1} above can also be expressed as $\dfrac{1}{x}$.

Exponents
Fractional Exponents of Numbers

Fractional Powers of 2
(You may not need to know these for SAT)

Simplify these fractional powers of 2.

$2^{x/y}$	$2^{14/2}$	$2^{36/8}$	$2^{7/21}$	$2^{9/15}$	$2^{9/6}$	$2^{22/4}$	$2^{16/10}$	$2^{32/6}$
$2^{x/y} =$								

Radicals of 2
(You may not need to know these for SAT)

Simplify these radical expressions of 2.

$\sqrt[n]{2^m}$	$\sqrt{2^{12}}$	$\sqrt[21]{2^{22}}$	$\sqrt[5]{2^{11}}$	$\sqrt[18]{2^6}$	$\sqrt[7]{2^{35}}$	$\sqrt[9]{2^{18}}$	$\sqrt[n]{2^{2n}}$	$\sqrt[n]{2^{n+2}}$
$\sqrt[n]{2^m} = 2^?$								

Tip: If no root value is shown above the "elbow" of the radical sign, then the radical is understood to represent a square root, or n = 2.

IMPORTANT**: If the form of your answer does not match the form of the answers on the tests, use your calculator to change forms. For example:**

- **your solution is a fraction, but test answers are decimals, plug the fraction into the calculator.**
- **your answer are decimals, but test answers are in the form of radicals – solve for the radical.**

❖**Strategy:** If solving an equation involving a algebraic expression under a radical, isolate the radical expression and then square both sides. For example, to solve $\sqrt{x} - 3 = 4$, add 3 to both sides, $\sqrt{x} = 7$, and then square both sides to get $x = 49$.

Tip: Radical problems on the SAT involve only square roots and no higher roots. Fractional exponents are used on higher order root problems instead, and they can be solved using rules of exponents.

Answers on the next page

Exponents
Solutions to Fractional Exponents of Numbers

Fractional Powers of 2

Solutions to fractional powers of 2.

$2^{x/y}$	$2^{14/2}$	$2^{36/8}$	$2^{7/21}$	$2^{9/15}$	$2^{9/6}$	$2^{22/4}$	$2^{16/10}$	$2^{32/6}$
$2^{x/y}=$	2^7	$2^{9/2}$	$2^{1/3}$	$2^{3/5}$	$2^{3/2}$	$2^{11/2}$	$2^{8/5}$	$2^{16/3}$

Strategy: Reduce fractions of exponents to lowest terms first before applying them to base. For example, the first step to simplify $2^{9/3}$ would be to reduce the $9/3$ to 3, and then calculate $2^3 = 8$.

Radicals of 2

Solutions to radical expressions of 2.

$\sqrt[n]{2^m}$	$\sqrt{2^{12}}$	$\sqrt[21]{2^{22}}$	$\sqrt[5]{2^{11}}$	$\sqrt[18]{2^6}$	$\sqrt[7]{2^{35}}$	$\sqrt[9]{2^{18}}$	$\sqrt[n]{2^{2n}}$	$\sqrt[n]{2^{n+2}}$
$\sqrt[n]{2^m}=2^?$	64	$2\sqrt[21]{2}$	$4\sqrt[5]{2}$	$\sqrt[3]{2}$	32	4	4	$2\sqrt[n]{4}$

Tip: Root values are only positive, so the "n" values in the table above are understood to be greater than zero.

Percentages

Note: Though few percentage questions appear on the PSAT or SAT, you should nonetheless know all types of percentage questions. You need not spend much time on this section.

1 question per test, on average

Computing a simple percentage using a calculator

 Calculator Strategy:

With any percentage, hit. (point), then the number of the percentage, then x (times), then the number. Remember, the word "of " means times.

Note: Applies only to whole number percentages 10 or greater

Example A: What is 20% of $80.00?
Solution: .2 • 80 = 16

Answer = 16

 Calculator Strategy:

To find out what percentage one number is of a second number, simply divide the first by the second and then interpret the decimal answer as a percentage by shifting the decimal point two places to the RIGHT.

Example B: If 20 out of 45 cars are blue, what percentage of cars are blue?

Solution: 20 ÷ 45 =.44444444 then, shift the decimal two spaces to the right

Answer = 44.4%

Example C: What is 40% of 50?

* Solution: Alternative method: If you are good at keeping answers in perspective (in other words, if you can remember that the answer to the above question cannot be 2 or 200, then you can do this problem in your head. Simply forget the decimal and multiply the first two digits together (4 • 5 = **20**).

Example D: If 15 out of 50 jellybeans are green, what percentage of the jelly beans are green?

Solution: *Alternative method: Recognize that 50 is half of 100; therefore, by doubling both numbers, you will have the percentage ($\frac{15}{50}$ double each term yields $\frac{30}{100}$ which is **30%**).

Computing percentages that are multiples of 10

To do these without writing or using a calculator, multiply first two numbers together

Example E: What is 40% of 70?   (Ex. 4 •7 =)_____

Example F: What is 70% of 30?   _____

Example G: What is 20% of 90?   _____

Example H: What is 60% of 70?   _____

Answers E = 28, F = 21, G = 18, H = 42

Compute the following percentages without paper or calculator

Percentages on left, numbers on top

	10	20	30	40	50	60	70	80	90	100
10%										
20%			2×3=6							
30%										
40%										
50%										
60%				6×4=24						
70%							7×7=49			
80%										
90%										
100%										
200%				20×4=80						

Percentage questions in which the original amount is unknown

Examples of wording from past SATs:

" Mike buys a car from John for **x** dollars...."
" A coat which normally sells for **x** dollars.... "
" **x** increased by 20 % yields y. y decreased by...."

❖Strategy: Since a percentage is part of **100**, plug in the number 100 as the original value. The key is to remember that when you do this, you change the question. If that variable appears anywhere else in the question or in an answer, you must stay consistent by changing the same variable to 100 as well.

Now reread the questions with **100** plugged in for the original value

" Mike buys a car from John for **100** dollars...."
" A coat which normally sells for **100** dollars.... "
" **100** increased by 20 % yields y.   Y (now 120) decreased by...."

Example A: A collector sold a David Ortiz rookie baseball card to Manny for x dollars. Manny added 10% to his cost and sold it to Jack. Jack added 20% to his cost and sold it to Andrew. In terms of x how much did Andrew pay for the card?
(A) 130% x   (B) 125% x   (C) 132% x   (D) x - 30   (E) 70% x
   (Trap↑)

Solution: To solve this question, plug in 100 in place of x. Add 10% by multiplying by 1.1, giving 110. Multiply 110 by 1.2, giving 132.

                                                                    Answer = C

The question above is not only an example of a percentage question in which the original quantity is not known, it is an example of an <u>accumulated percentage question</u>. An accumulated percentage question is one in which the original value is changed by a percentage, then the new amount is changed again. A real life example of this would be money accumulating interest in a bank. Money in a bank earns interest. Then, if you leave the interest in, both the original money and the interest earn interest. A greater explanation of this type of question follows.

Computing accumulated percentages

An accumulated percentage refers to a situation in which an amount changes by a certain percentage, then the new amount changes again by a percentage. Money that earns interest year after year in a bank is one example. A car that depreciates in value several times over several years is another.

❖**Strategy:** The word "of " in a word problem means *"times"* in 99% of all SAT math word problems. When you see the word "of", change it to *times,* then solve the problem as a multiplication problem.

Example A: What is 20% of 30% of 50?

Solution: Hit .2 • .3 • 50 =   **Answer = 3**

▦ **Calculator Strategy:** When <u>adding</u> a percentage to a number, use a one-step calculation. Multiply the number by (1. the percentage). For example to <u>add</u> 22% to the number 40, multiply 40 •1.22. To <u>add</u> 5% to $50.00, multiply 50 •1.05

Example B: A certain bank offers a bond that sells for $50.00, and earns 10% interest per year. If the bond is allowed to accumulate interest for 3 years, how much will it be worth at the end of that time?

Solution: Multiply 50 •$(1.1)^3$ or simply 50 • 1.1 • 1.1 • 1.1

Answer = $66.55

Computing accumulated percentages, cont

▦ **Calculator Strategy:** When subtracting a percentage from a number, multiply the number by the percentage remaining out of 100. For example, to subtract 25% from 250, multiply 250 • .75.

Example C: If a $20,000 car depreciates in value by 25% the first year, and 10% for each of the next two years, what percentage of the original value is the car worth at the end of three years?

Solution: In the example above, the car depreciates by 25%, so the original number should be multiplied by the remaining percentage of 75%. It then depreciates for two years at 10% per year, so the number should be multiplied by the remaining percentage of 90% twice.

$$20,000 \cdot .75 \cdot .90 \cdot .90$$

After determining the dollar value of the car at the end of 3 years, that sum was put over the original value of $20,000 to create the fraction *12,150/20,000*. The percentage of the original value was determined by dividing the new value by the original value.

Answer $12,150/20,000 = 60.75

Now you try!

Example D: What is 30% of 30% of 30?

Example E: Jerry bought a computer for x dollars in 1981. In 1986, the value of the computer decreased by 50%. If over the next five years the value of the computer decreased by the same percentage as in the first five years, in terms of x, how much was the computer worth in 1991?

Answer D: 2.7 $\{30 \cdot (.3)^2\}$
Answer E: 25% Method: plug in 100 for x. $\{100 \cdot 5 \cdot 5 \text{ or } 100 \cdot 5^2\}$

Adding, subtracting and computing percentages with one-step calculator operation

Practice here, using the one-step methods described on the previous pages

Situation:	multiply:	by this:	to get:
Subtract 20% of 80	80	.8	64
Add 65% to 75	75	1.65	123.75
Subtract 40% of 99			
Add 52% to 128			
Subtract 90% of 425			
What is 20% of 60	2	6	12
What is 120% of 120			
Add 50% to 125			
Subtract 10% of 14			

Percentages – Word Problems

1. How much does a coat that was priced at $36.50 sell for if discounted by 30%?

2. Factory A is capable of turning out 250 cars in any given month. Yet, in January of 1997, it produced only 225 cars. What percentage of its production capacity did Factory A achieve during the month of January?

3. Factory A is capable of turning out 250 cars in any given month. Factory B is capable of producing 300 cars per month. In January of 1997, Factory A produced only 225 cars, while Factory B produced 240 cars. The percentage of production capacity of Factory A was how much greater than the percentage of production capacity of Factory B?

4. A team has won 60% of the 20 games it has played so far this season. If the team plays a total of 50 games all season and wins 80% of the remaining games, then the percentage of games it won for the entire season will be......

5. *Note: This is a students produced response question. No multiple choice answers are given*

      m increased by 20% yields *n*
      n decreased by 50% yields *p*
      p decreased by 35% yields *q*

      According to the statements above, q is what percent of m?

6. In 1970 the price of a certain antique car was 30 percent greater than in 1965. In 1975, the price of the same car was 50 percent greater than in 1970. The price of the car was what percent greater in 1975 than in 1965?

Two Difficult Percentage Questions

7. As a fee for his service, a miller kept 10 percent of the flour he ground for a customer. If the customer got 1 ton, how many tons did the miller grind?

8. If 30 percent of 2x is multiplied by 2 percent of x, the result is what percent
of $3x^2$?

Percentages: Word Problems

Answers

1. How much does a coat that was priced at $36.50 sell for if discounted by 30%?

.7 • 36.5	**Answer $25.55**

2. Factory A is capable of turning out 250 cars in any given month. Yet, in January of 1997, it produced only 225 cars. What percentage of its production capacity did Factory A achieve during the month of January?

225 ÷ 250 = .9	**Answer 90**

3. Factory A is capable of turning out 250 cars in any given month. Factory B is capable of producing 300 cars per month. In January of 1997, Factory A produced only 225 cars, while Factory B produced 240 cars. The percentage of production capacity of Factory A was how much greater than the percentage of production capacity of Factory B?

(Factory A) 225 ÷ 250 = .9 90% (Factory B) 240 ÷ 300 = .8 80%	**Answer 10**

4. A team has won 60% of the 20 games it has played so far this season. If the team plays a total of 50 games all season and wins 80% of the remaining games. Then the percentage of games it won for the entire season will be......

60% of the 20 games = 6 • 2 = 12 games won . 80% of 30 remaining games 8 • 3 = 24. This is a total of 36 wins out of 50 games. 36 ÷ 50 = 72.   **Answer 72**

Percentages: Word Problems

Answers, cont.

5.
        m increased by 20% yields *n*
        n decreased by 50% yields *p*
        p decreased by 35% yields *q*

According to the statements above, q is what percent of m?

Since the initial number (m) is not known, assign the number 100 to m. This strategy works really well with percentage questions.
Multiply 100 • 1.2 to yield n, which is 120.
Multiply 120 • .5 to yield p, which is 60
Multiply 60 • .65 to yield q, which is 39

Translate   "q is what percent of m"
into a mathematical expression:

$$39 = \frac{x}{100} \cdot 100 \qquad 39 = \frac{100x}{100} \qquad x = 39$$

Answer 39

---

6. In 1970 the price of a certain antique car was 30 percent greater than in 1965. In 1975, the price of the same car was 50 percent greater than in 1970. The price of the car was what percent greater in 1975 than in 1965?

(1965) car is worth 100. (1970) 100 • 1.3 = 130 (1975) 130 • 1.5 = 195
Answer = 95 (%)

---

7. As a fee for his service, a miller kept 10 percent of the flour he ground for a customer. If the customer got 1 ton, how many tons did the miller grind?

Make x = the amount of grain ground by the miller. Then, .9x = 1 ton Then, solve for x.
x = 1 ton ÷ .9   **Answer = 1.11111 tons or 1 $\frac{1}{9}$**

---

8. If 30 percent of 2x is multiplied by 2 percent of x, the result is what percent of $3x^2$?

Make x = 100 Then translate the sentence:

$$30\% \bullet 2(100) = 60 \qquad \text{and} \qquad 2\% \bullet 100 = 2$$

$$\text{So, } 120 = \frac{x}{100} \bullet 3(100)^2$$

$$x = \frac{120}{30,000} = .004 \qquad \text{Then, move the decimal over two spaces}$$

Answer = .4(%)

Statistics: Mean (Average), Median, Mode

Averages

An average can be thought of as the "medium value" – not necessarily the middle number of a set of numbers.

If three brothers weigh 80, 90 and 103 lbs, their average weight is 91 lbs. Another way of saying that is that their mean weight is 91 pounds.

Example of a weighted average:

If four doctors earn $100.00/hr. $100.00/hr. $100.00/hr. and $200.00/hr their average wage will be between $100.00/hr. and $200.00/hr and will be nearer to the $100.00 side because of the "weighted" value (there are more of them) of the three $100.00 salaries.

It's important that you know the following formulas:

$$Average = Sum/Parts$$
$$Sum = Average \cdot Parts$$

Averages, cont

SAT <u>averages</u> questions usually supply you with two of three components (average, sum, parts) require that you figure out the third, and then sometimes require that you perform an additional step. If you apply the formula, and if you are able to work with the resulting fraction, you should have no problem with even the hardest averages problem.

Example A: Three boxes each weigh no more than 75 lbs. If the average weight of the boxes is 60 lbs, what is the <u>least</u> possible weight of any one of the boxes?

<u>Solution</u>: You are given the average (60 lbs.) and the parts (3 boxes) so you must figure out the sum.

Sum = average • parts, 60 • 3 = 180.

In order to determine the least possible weight of one of the boxes, you must determine the greatest possible weight of the other two. The greatest possible weight of the other two is 150 (75 • 2), so the least possible weight of the third box is 180 - 150.

Answer = 30

Example B: What is the average (arithmetic mean) of all the odd numbers between 1 and 28 that are multiples of 3?

<u>Solution</u>: The odd numbered multiples of 3 between 1 and 28 are (3, 9, 15, 21 and 27). To find their average, add them up (sum), then divide by 5 (parts).

75/5 = 15.

Answer = 15

Example C: The average (arithmetic mean) of 5 integers is greater than 27. If the average of the first four integers is 22 what is the <u>least</u> possible value of the fifth integer?

<u>Solution</u>: Plug into formula: Sum = Average x Parts. In this case, the sum > (27 • 5). The sum is greater than 135. Since the average of the first four integers is 22, the sum of those four numbers is 88, which means that the fifth integer must be an integer greater than 47 (which is135 - 88). The question asks for the least possible value of the fifth integer.

Answer = 48

Example D: m = 80 n = 70. Which is larger:
(A) the average of m and n or
(B) the average of m, n and n?

This next question combines your familiarity with fractions with your knowledge of averages. Hint: a fraction is smallest when its denominator is largest.

Example E : If 2≤ y≤ 3 and 4≤ z ≤ 5 then the <u>least</u> possible average (arithmetic mean) of 1/y and 1/z is?

The answer to D is (A)
The answer to E is 8/30 or 4/15 or .266 repeating

Averages: Word Problems

1. If the average of three numbers is between 6 and 9, then the sum of these three numbers could be any one of the following EXCEPT

    (A) 17   (B) 18 ½   (C) 21   (D) 23   (E) 26 ½

2. Alan is twice as old as Sue and half as old as Joseph. If the average (arithmetic mean) of all three ages is 14, how old is Sue?

3. If the average of two numbers is 7, and the product of the two numbers is 48, then the positive difference between the two numbers is.....?

4. If the average (arithmetic mean) of six numbers is -6 and the sum of four of the numbers is 20, what is the average of the other two numbers?

5. If the average of x, y and 80 is 6 more than the average of y, z and 80, what is the value of x - z?

6. If the average (arithmetic mean) of ten consecutive integers arranged in increasing order is 15 ½, what is the average of the first five of these integers?

7. If the sum of p and r is 18 and if s = 12, what is the average (arithmetic mean) of p, r and s?

8. If the average (arithmetic mean) of four numbers is 37 and the average of two of these numbers is 33, what is the average of the other two?

Averages
Answers to Word Problems

1. If the average of three numbers is between 6 and 9, then the sum of these three numbers could be any one of the following EXCEPT
    (A) 17   (B) 18 ½   (C) 21   (D) 23   (E) 26 ½.

> Sum = average • parts.   So the sum is between 18 and 27.
>
> **Answer (A)**

2. Alan is twice as old as Sue and half as old as Joseph. If the average (arithmetic mean) of all three ages is 14, how old is Sue?

> Make Sue's age = x. Alan's age = 2x. Joseph's age = 4x. Av = sum/parts.
> 7x/3 = 14   7x = 42
>
> **Answer = 6.**

3. If the average of two numbers is 7, and the product of the two numbers is 48, then the positive difference between the two numbers is.....?

> Av = sum/parts. 7 = sum/2   Sum = 14. Try trial and error. The two numbers which have a sum of 14 and a product of 48 are 8 and 6.
>
> **Answer = 2.**

4. If the average (arithmetic mean) of six numbers is -6 and the sum of four of the numbers is 20, what is the average of the other two numbers?

> Av = sum/parts.   -6 = sum/6. Therefore, the sum of the six numbers is -36. If the sum of four of these numbers is 20, then the sum of the other two must be -56, and their average is -56/2.
>
> **Answer = -28**

Averages
Answers to Word Problems, cont

5. If the average of x, y and 80 is 6 more than the average of y, z and 80, what is the value of x-z?

Av = sum/parts. [(x + y + 80) / 3] = [(y + z + 80) / 3] + 6 (Multiply everything by 3) x + y + 80 = y + z + 80 + 18. (Cancel common terms) x = z + 18. x - z = 18

Strategic

Solution: The average of consecutive integers is always equal to the median.

Answer = 18

6. If the average (arithmetic mean) of ten consecutive integers arranged in increasing order is 15 ½, what is the average of the first five of these integers?

Fill in the numbers around 15 ½ .[{11,12,13,14,15} **15 ½**   16,17,18,19,20] . The average of the first five consecutive integers is the number in the middle of those five numbers.

Answer = 13

7. If the sum of p and r is 18 and if s = 12, what is the average (arithmetic mean) of p, r and s?

The sum of p, r, and s = 18 + 12   (30). The average is 30/3.

Answer = 10

8. If the average (arithmetic mean) of four numbers is 37 and the average of two of these numbers is 33, what is the average of the other two?

If the average of four numbers is 37, then their sum = (37 x 4) 148. The sum of the other two numbers is 66. To find the average of the remaining two numbers, find their sum and divide by 2.(148-66)/2

Answer = 41

Median and Mode

Note: These concepts are tested much less often that mean (average).

> ❖ **Strategy:** When all members of a set of number are equally spaced, the median always equals the mean
>
> Example 1: 5, 10, 15, 20, 25
> In the set above the median and mean are both 15.
>
> Example 2: 5, 6, 7, 8, 9
> In the set above the median and mean are both 7.

Mode is the most common term in a set of numbers. If two numbers appear most commonly in a set, the set is said to be bimodal (two modes).

The following set is bimodal.

$$\{1, \underline{2}, \underline{2}, \underline{3}, \underline{3}\}$$

with the modes being 2 and 3

Median is the middle term in a set of numbers arranged in numeric order.

The median of the following set can only be determined once the set is arranged in numerical order.

$$\{11, 17, 1, 3, 6, 8, 10\}$$

Arranged in order, the set looks like this.

$$\{1, 3, 6, \underline{8}, 10, 11, 17\}$$

the median (middle term) of the above set is 8

Mean, Median, Mode Example:

Example A: In June, 2004, the SAT math scores of a group of students were as follows:

480, 540, 710, 800, 710, 690, 570, 600, 730

Which of the following statements is/are true:

  I. The mean is greater than the mode
 II. The median is greater than the mode
III. The mean is greater than the median

    (A) I only
    (B) II only
    (C) III only
    (D) II and III
    (E) None of the above

Answer to Example A is (E).

Distance, Rate and Time

A typical SAT will have no more than one problem that involves distance, rate and time. Where one does appear, it will contain information about two of the three components, and will require you to figure out the missing information. These types of questions can be tricky, and may involve two steps. For example, you might first have to use the formula to figure out to figure out a particular value (total distance of a trip, for example) and then to plug in that value to determine the average rate of travel. Or, it is very common to have a question that involves two different rates, and then to figure out the average rate. Don't be fooled! The average rate is seldom merely the average of the two rates.

It is very useful to know all three forms of the formula:

distance = rate x time $\quad$ d = rt
rate = distance ÷ time $\quad$ r = d/t
time = distance ÷ rate $\quad$ t = d/r

Distance, Rate and Time

Word Problems

Example A (Easy): A racing pigeon that was released at 12:00 noon reached its home loft at 2:30 P.M. the same day having flown a distance of 200 kilometers. What was the pigeon's average speed in kilometers per hour? (A) 40 (B) 50 (C) 80 (D) 100 (E) 160

<u>Solution A</u>: plug in the distance formula for rate (speed). Rate (speed) = distance/time = 200/2.5 Now look at answers. You might be able to see the answer without doing the division. If not, then use your calculator to do the division: 200 ÷ 2.5 = 80.

Answer is (C)

Example B (Hard): A car travels 180 kilometers from A to B at 60 kilometers per hour and returns from B to A along the same route at 90 kilometers per hour. The average speed in kilometers per hour for the round trip is ....?

<u>Solution B</u>: Don't get fooled! This question is very difficult. Your first inclination might be to average the two speeds, 60 and 90, and answer 75 kph. That would be a mistake! For each different rate, distance or time, you must create a separate equation.

Plug in the distance formula for time since the other two numbers (rate and distance) are given. For average speed, you must know **total distance** and divide it by **total time.**

First part: Time = distance/rate   T = 180/60
                          Time = 3 hours
Second part: Time = distance/rate   T = 180/90
                          Time = 2 hours

You can now answer the question. Use the distance formula for rate:
rate = distance/time: r= 360/5   (360 is the total distance and 5 hours is the total time)

Answer = 72 KPH

Now You Try

Example C: Belinda walked up a mountain at the rate of 2 miles per hour and jogged down the same route at the rate of 6 miles per hour. If she traveled a total of 24 miles how many hours did it take her to complete the entire trip?

(A) 24   (B) 18   (C) 16   (D) 8   (E) 6

Example D: A car traveling at an average rate of 55 Kilometers per hour made a trip in 6 hours. If it had traveled at an average rate of 50 kilometers per hour, the trip would have taken how many minutes longer?

(A) 15   (B) 25   (C) 30   (D) 35   (E) 36

Answer to example C: (D: 6 hours up, 2 hours down)
Answer to example E: (E: 6.6 hours total. 60 •.6 = 36)

Ratio, Proportion, Probability

Ratio

3 questions per test, on average

A ratio is a relative measure or comparison of two or more amounts. For example, if the ratio of women to men in the United States is 51:49, then there are 51 women for every 49 men. You could also say that out of 100 people, the average number of men will be 49, and the average number of women will be 51. *The ratio of white tigers to yellow tigers is 1:77,* meaning there are 77 times more yellow than white tigers. Many times, SAT ratio problems supply you with the ratio (the relative number of something compared to another thing) and ask that you find the total.

❖**Strategy: The X-Factor**. Turn a ratio into an equation by attaching "x" to each part of the ratio. For example, if a ratio is 4:1, make it 4x:1x. The sum of these algebraic terms will be equal to the sum of the objects that are being compared (the total number of tigers, people, voters, etc). Then, solve the equation for "x."

Example A: The ratio of red marbles to blue marbles in a bag is 4:1. If there are only blue and red marbles in the bag and there are exactly 20 red marbles how many marbles are in the bag?

X-Factor Solution:

Red marbles = 4x.
Blue marbles =1x
Total marbles = 5x
Since there are 20 red marbles.... $4x = 20$
                                       $x = 5$

Since x = 5 and since there are 5x total marbles,
the number of marbles = 5(5) or 25.

Answer = 25

Example B: There are a total of 140 marbles in a bag all of which are blue or red. If the ratio of blue to red marbles = 5:2 how many red marbles are there?

X-Factor Solution:

$5x + 2x = 140$. Find the value of x.
Since $7x = 140$, $x = 20$. Red marbles = 2 (20)

Answer = 40

Example of a ratio question that involves geometry:

Example C: The measure of the four angles of a quadrilateral are in the ratio 1:2:3:4. What is the positive difference between the measures of the smallest and the largest angles?

X-Factor Solution: All quadrilaterals (four sided geometric figures) have angles totaling 360°
Set up a ratio in terms of "x" as with the previous examples.

$$1x + 2x + 3x + 4x = 360°$$
$$10x = 360°$$
$$x = 36°$$

The positive difference between the largest (4x) and smallest (1x) angles is 3x

Answer: 108°

Example of a difficult ratio question:

Example D: In Dogtown, all adult residents recently voted on a proposal to allow parking on the public beach. The ratio of the vote was 3 : 2 not to allow beach parking. However when 12 people decided to change their votes from not allowing beach parking to allowing it, the voting ratio changed to 1 : 1 How many adults live in Dogtown?

X-Factor Solution: 3x + 2x = all residents of Dogtown. 12 people switch their votes and now the number of people on either side of the issue is equal....

$3x - 12 = 2x + 12$ next, solve for x by adding 12 to both sides,

$3x = 2x + 24$ then, subtract 2x from both sides

$x = 24$ Finally, plug in 24 for x to determine total number of residents

$3(24) + 2(24) = 120$

Answer: 120

Example of a difficult question that combines ratio with average (arithmetic mean).

Example E: Two partners divide a profit of $3000.00 so that the difference between the two amounts is 1/3 of their average (arithmetic mean). What is the ratio of the larger to the smaller amount?

<u>Solution</u>: Since two partners divide a profit of $3000.00, the average is 3000 ÷2 or $1500.00. The difference between the two amounts is 1/3 of the average (which is $1500.00) or $500.00. Since one of the amounts is $500.00 more than the other and the total of the two amounts is $3000.00

$$x + (x + 500) = 3000$$
$$2x + 500 = 3000$$
$$2x = 2500$$
$$x = 1250$$

the amounts then are 1250 (which is x) and 1750 (which is x + 500)

The ratio of the larger to the smaller is 1750 : 1250

Which reduces down to 7:5

Answer 7:5

Proportion

A Proportion is a mathematical statement that two ratios are equal. On the SAT, a proportion usually involves three numbers and one variable, or objects that translate to equations to involve three numbers and a variable.

Example of numerical proportion: $\dfrac{3}{7} = \dfrac{X}{21}$ In this case, you should cross multiply to solve for x.

$$7x = 63$$
$$x = 9$$

Example F: For a certain water heater, the increase in heating expenses is directly proportional to the increase in water-temperature setting. If heating expenses increase by $24 when the water temperature increases by 20 degrees Fahrenheit, by how much will heating expenses increase if the water-temperature setting is increased by 15 degrees Fahrenheit?

❖ Strategy: When setting up a proportion of objects (not numbers) as two equal fractions, make sure that both numerators and both denominators hold the same items or units.

Solution: Set up a proportion.. . . .

$$\frac{\$24}{20\,deg\,rees} = \frac{\$x}{15\,deg\,rees}$$

. . . .then, cross multiply.

$$20x = 24*15$$
$$20x = 360$$
$$x = 18$$

Answer $18.00

Proportion

❖ Strategy: Probability should be expressed as a fraction or ratio. If expressed as a fraction, the denominator is the total that <u>could</u> occur or exist and the numerator is the part that <u>actually</u> occurs or exists. If expressed as a ratio, the left side is the part that <u>could</u> occur or exist and the right side is the total that <u>actually</u> occurs or exists.

Example: The probability of a coin landing as "heads" is ½ or 1:2 (because there is one "head" and two sides of a coin). The probability of getting a red marble from a bag of marbles of different colors would be expressed as:

$$\frac{\# \ of \ Red \ Marbles}{Total \ \# \ of \ Marbles}$$
$$(including \ red)$$

Probability may be thought of as the chance, odds or likelihood of a particular event occurring.
A deck of cards will serve well to explain this concept.

A deck of playing cards contains 52 cards.

The probability of being dealt an ace of spades (there is only one) is 1:52.

Notice that all 52 cards are part of the probability, including the ace of spades

The probability of receiving any ace (there are four) is 4:52 or 1:13
If that card is replaced in the deck, then the odds of picking another ace is again 1:13.

The odds of picking two twos in a row (assuming cards are replaced after picking) is

$$\frac{1}{13} \times \frac{1}{13} = \frac{1}{169}$$

Numbers and Operations

Sequences, Patterns and Series

1-2 questions per test, on average

For purposes of the SAT, a <u>sequence</u> or <u>pattern</u> is an ordered list of numbers (or objects) that follows a rule. Each number in the list is called a <u>term</u>. Three general types of sequences appear consistently on the SAT:

1. <u>Repeating sequences</u>: sequences that repeat themselves after a fixed number of terms. For example, the digits of $0.\overline{12468} = 0.1246812468...$ form a repeating pattern of 12468 over and over again.

2. <u>Arithmetic sequences</u>: sequences in which a term is a fixed amount more or less than the term that immediately precedes it. For example, the rule that the first term is -3 and every term after the first is 5 more than the term immediately preceding it defines an arithmetic sequence, or -3, 2, 7, 12.... If the first term is called a, and the difference between consecutive terms is d, then the nth term, t_n, is given by the formula, $t_n = a + (n-1)d$, which is handy, but often not necessary to know.

3. <u>Geometric sequences</u>: sequences in which consecutive terms are in constant ratio. Hint: if the ratio is negative, the terms of the sequence will alternate signs, e.g., if the first term is -1 and the ratio is $-2:1$, then we have -1, 2, -4, 8, -16... ; if the ratio is between 0 and 1, successive terms will get smaller in magnitude, e.g., if the first term is 150 and the ratio is $1:5$, then we have 150, 30, 6,... ; if the ratio is greater than one, successive terms will get larger in magnitude, e.g., if the first term is 8 and the ratio is $3:2$, then we have 8, 12, 18, 27....

Examples:

Word problems involving <u>exponential growth</u> or <u>decay</u> can be viewed as <u>geometric sequences</u> in which each "term" represents the effect of a fixed period of time passing between one observation and the next; problems of this type are often presented with a formula describing a result after n periods of time.

<u>Bacterial growth, radioactive decay, and interest compounding</u> are all types of these word problems used on the SAT. For example, if a certain population of bacteria doubles every 24 hours (exponential growth), then the bacteria count observed each 24 hours makes a geometric sequence with a ratio of consecutive terms equal to 2.

Sequences, Patterns and Series, cont

<u>Sequences on the SAT are often presented in one of the following types of problems:</u>

- Determining the value of (or the formula to compute) a term not shown.
- Manipulating terms not shown.
- Determining a sum of terms, or series.
- Identifying and manipulating sub-patterns within a main sequence. For example, one might have to determine how many of the first 1,000 numbers in a sequence are odd. To do so, one must figure out the pattern of odds and evens within the main sequence. Another version of this often occurs when a sequence is defined by alternating rules, e.g., rule 1 for terms 1, 3, 5, etc. and rule 2 for terms 2, 4, 6, etc.

Sequence problem involving determining the value of a term not shown:

Example A: The first term of a sequence of numbers is –4. Each term after the first is obtained by adding 4 to the preceding term. What is the 30th term of the sequence?

<u>Solution</u>: create an expression to compute the desired term, recognizing that the 30th term must be 29 increments of 4 more than the first term (this sequence is arithmetic)

$$-4+(30-1)*4=$$
$$-4+116=112$$

Answer: 112

❖Strategy: Write out the first few terms (often 5-10 terms should be sufficient) of a sequence to gain a clear sense of the term's pattern. Often this helps for both better bookkeeping and double-checking an answer.

In the problem above, the first six terms are –4, 0, 4, 8, 12, 16… (are clearly multiples of 4, so the answer, 112, must be a multiple of 4: 112=4 x 28).

Sequences, Patterns and Series, cont

Sequence problem involving determining the value of a term not shown:

Example B: In the repeating decimal,
$$0.\overline{37614} = 0.3761437614...,$$ in which digits 37614 repeat, which digit is in the $1,111^{th}$ place to the right of the decimal point?

❖**Strategy:** Always focus on the last digit in the sequence, since only that number will repeat in a predictable pattern. That number is called **The Repeater.** The other numbers in the pattern will not repeat in a regular pattern. In other words, in the decimal above, every fifth number will be a 4, but every fourth number will not be a 1, every third number will not be a 6, etc.

<u>Solution</u>:. This is a repeater with 5 digits. That means that every fifth digit to the right of the decimal will be a 4. So, the fifth, tenth, hundredth and thousandth digit will be 4s, since those numbers are all multiples of 5. So is 1110. That means that the 1110th digit will be a 4. Simply go to the next number in the repeating decimal to find the 1111th digit.

Answer = 3.

Sequence problem involving manipulating terms not shown:

Example C: -6, -1, 4, 9...
In the above sequence, the first term is -6, and each successive term is found by adding 5 to the prior term. What is the difference between the 45th and 51st terms of the sequence?

<u>Solution</u>: The above sequence is arithmetic, so the difference between consecutive terms is the same, or 5. Since there 6 increments to get from the 45th term to the 51st, the answer is $5 \times 6 = 30$. (note that one can determine the values of the 45th and 51st terms directly and then take the difference, but this is unnecessary).

Answer: 30

Sequences, Patterns and Series, cont

Sequence problem involving determining the value of a series:

Example D: -3, -1, 1, 3, 5, 7
A sequence is formed by repeating the 6 numbers above in the same order indefinitely. What is the sum of the first 42 terms of the sequence?

Solution: this repeating sequence begins with -3 and completes 7 cycles by the 42nd term since 6, the number of terms in the repeating cycle, divides into 42 evenly 7 times with no remainder. Each completed cycle contributes -3 + -1 + 1 + 3 + 5 + *1*, or 12 (notice that the pairs +1 and -1, +3, and -3 cancel each other out, leaving 5 + 7) to the sum. Thus, 12•7=84.

Answer: 84

❖Strategy: When computing series of non-consecutive integers that include both negative and positive numbers, look for, cancel, and exclude pairs of numbers with opposite signs from the sum. For example, to add the consecutive integers from -14 to 16, notice that all numbers from -14 to -1 can be paired with positive numbers of the same magnitude that will cancel out in the sum, so the answer is 15 + 16 = 31.   I

Sequence problem involving manipulating sub-patterns:

Example E: 1, 10, …
In the above sequence, the first term is 1 and the second term is 10.   Each successive term is found by adding 1 to the term two terms before it if the term is odd, and subtracting 1 from the term two terms before it if the term is even.   How many multiples of 3 are in the first 34 terms of the sequence?

Solution: By performing the given operations, you can quickly identify a repeating pattern: (1, 10, 2, 9) (1, 10, 2, 9). Within each of these groups, there is one multiple of 3, which is 9. In the first 34 numbers there are 8 of these groups, plus the first two numbers of the ninth group. Since neither 1 nor 10 (of the ninth group) is a multiple of 3, there are eight numbers that are multiples of 3.

Answer: 8

Algebra and Functions

Direct Variation

1 question per test

<u>Direct variation</u> describes a situation in which two (or more) quantities increase or decrease at the same rate, or are in constant proportion. For example, as one quantity doubles, the other quantity doubles.

Direct variation problems often use particular vocabulary: "x varies directly with y," "x and y vary directly," "x and y are in direct proportion," "x and y are directly proportional," "x and y are in constant proportion...." Once you have identified a direct variation between two variables, you can either set up a proportion of two cases, namely, $\dfrac{x_1}{y_1} = \dfrac{x_2}{y_2}$ or use one case to solve for the constant of variation, k, as either

$x = ky$ or $y = kx$ (where k is the factor of variation)

and then apply to the other case. Review the problem to see which set up is most convenient.

Direct Variation Example

Example A: y varies directly with x. If x is 40 when y is 10, what is x when y is 9?

<u>Solution</u>: Since y varies directly with x, $x=ky$, where k is the *constant of variation*. . In the first case given, $x=40$ when $y=10$, or $40 = 10k$. Thus, $k = 4$, so $x = 4$ x 9, or 36 in the second case.

<u>Alternate solution</u>: Set up a proportion: $\dfrac{40}{10} = \dfrac{x}{9}$, then cross multiply to solve for x.

Answer: x = 36

Direct Variation, cont.

Direct variations can be found masquerading in many word problems involving either two variables in which one is described to vary with the other or three (or more) variables in which one variable is the product of the others.

Common examples of <u>direct variations</u> include:

1. Distance = Rate • Time
   - distances to rates when time is consistent
   - distances to times when rate is consistent

2. Job Completion = Work Rate x Number of workers x Time

3. Spring displacement
   - spring <u>moves</u> when a force is applied

4. Recipe, map scale and proportion problems

Inverse Variation

<u>Inverse Variation</u> describes a situation in which one quantity increases as another quantity decreases, while the product of the quantities remains constant. For example, as one quantity doubles, the other quantity is cut in half.

Inverse variation problems have similar, interchangeable vocabulary: "x varies inversely with y," "x and y vary inversely," "x and y are in inverse proportion," "x and y are inversely proportional...." Once you have identified an inverse variation between two variables, you can either set up the two cases as equal products, namely, $x_1 y_1 = x_2 y_2$ or use one case to solve for the constant of variation, k, as $k = x \Box y$ and then apply to the other case.

Inverse Variation Problem

Example B: h is inversely proportional to g and $h = -1.5$ when g = 30. What is g when h=4.5?

<u>Solution:</u> Since h varies inversely with g, $g \bullet h$ will always equal the same value, k. Therefore, if g increases by a certain factor, h must decrease by the same factor in order to have the product stay consistent. Another way of saying this is that the unknown factor will increase or decrease by the reciprocal of the other.

In the first case given, g = 30 when $h = -1.5$.
In the second case, g is unknown, while h = 4.5

Since, in the second case h is −3 times great than in the first case,
we know that g in the second case must be −1/3 times its value in the first case.
-1/3 times 30 is -10

Answer: -10

Inverse Variation, cont.

Inverse variations can be found masquerading in many word problems involving either two variables in which one is described to vary with the other or three (or more) variables in which one variable is the product of the others.

Common examples of inverse variations include:

1. Unequal-sized gears meshing or pulleys connected by a belt
   - gear teeth counts to rates of revolution
   - radii of gears/pulleys to rates of revolution
   - diameters of gears/pulleys to rates of revolution
   - circumferences of gears/pulleys to rates of revolution

2. Unequal-sized wheels turning on a vehicle, like bicycle, tractor, etc.
   - radii of tires to rates of revolution
   - diameters of tires to rates of revolution
   - circumferences of tires to rates of revolution

Absolute Value

1 question per test, on average

On the SAT, absolute value expressions are most easily interpreted as the distance from zero along the real-number line, e.g., |-3|=3, and |10|=10.

Also, the absolute value of a <u>difference</u> (subtraction) can be readily interpreted as the <u>distance on the number line between the two values</u>. For example, $|3-(-4)|=7$, which is the number line distance between −4 and 3, while $|(-3)-(-4)|=1$ provides the number line distance between −4 and −3.

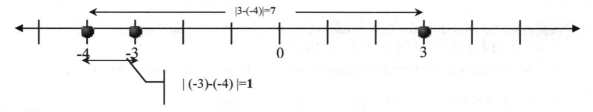

When evaluating the absolute value of a difference (subtraction), it does not matter which term is being subtracted from which:

$$|3-(-4)| = 7 \, and \, |(-4)-3| = 7$$

This is also true when one of the quantities is a variable. For example:

|3-x| = 4 is the same as |x-3| = 4.

Absolute Value, cont.

Example A:
$$|l-4|=2$$
$$|k+12|=14$$

In the equations above, $k<0<l$. What is one possible value of $l-k$?

(A) 28   (B) 6   (C) 4   (D) 0   (E) -10

Solution: By analyzing the first equation, we have l = 6 or 2; similarly, $|k+12|=14 \Rightarrow |k-(-12)|=14$ $k=-26$ or 2.
But according to the information given, k must be less than 0, so k = -26. Thus,

$l-k=6-(-26)$ Answer = 32; not a given solution
or $2-(-26)$ Answer = 28; this is the only one of the
possible answers that is given.

Answer is (A) 28.

Absolute expressions in inequalities

<u>Absolute expressions in inequalities</u> (greater than, less than) often refer to interval solutions, in which one or two ranges of values satisfy the inequality. For example, an answer to a value of some number x could be

$$5 > x > 0$$

meaning that x could be any or all values between zero and 5

To solve inequalities, treat them just like equations (equals). This works for ALL inequality problems, not just for those involving absolute value.

For example, to solve $|x-5| < 3$, we first obtain the two equality solutions to

$$|x-5| = 3$$
$$x = 2 \; or \; x = 8.$$

These two points then become the endpoints (not included as seen below by the hollow circles below) of a line segment that represents the answer to the question.

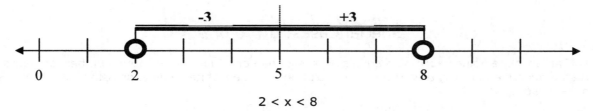

$$2 < x < 8$$

Similarly, to solve $|x+2| \geq 4$, we first solve $|x+2| = 4$, thus $x = -6$ or 2. So one interval of the solution will be $x \leq -6$ and the other will be $x \geq 2$.

The Inequality, $|....| \geq d$ leads to a case in which we have two intervals, each with a closed (number included) endpoint. Thus, the number line solution is as follows

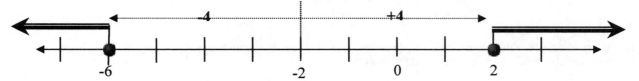

Possible Outcomes of Absolute Value Involving Equations and Inequalities

Common cases
Note: Equations lead to <u>points</u>, while inequalities lead to <u>intervals</u>

Type of Statement	Distance ("$\vert...\vert$"<,=,> d, distance)	Solution
Equality, $\vert...\vert$ = d	d > 0	2 **points** each a distance "d" in opposite directions on a number line from the value inside the absolute value symbols
Inequality, $\vert...\vert$ < d	d > 0	1 **interval** with <u>open</u> endpoints
Inequality, $\vert....\vert \leq$ d	d > 0	1 **interval** with <u>closed</u> endpoints
Inequality, $\vert...\vert$ > d	d > 0	2 **intervals**, each with an <u>open</u> endpoint
Inequality, $\vert....\vert \geq$ d	d > 0	2 **intervals**, each with a <u>closed</u> endpoint

Special Cases: d = 0 or d < 0

I. If an absolute value expression equals or is less than or equal to a negative number, or is less than a negative number, then there is NO solution, since absolute value expressions are ALWAYS non-negative.

Example $\vert$ x - 4 $\vert$ = -2 or $\vert x - 4 \vert \leq$ -2
each has no solution

II. If an absolute value expression is <u>equal to</u> or <u>less than or equal to</u> zero, then the equation will have only one solution.

Examples: $\vert$ x - 4 $\vert$ = 0
$\vert x - 4 \vert \leq 0$
each has one solution

III. If an absolute value expression is greater than 0, than the solution will be all real numbers EXCEPT for the one value of the equality solution.

Example $\vert$ x - 4 $\vert$ > 0
Solution: all real numbers except for x = 4

IV. If the absolute value expression is greater than a negative number or greater than or equal to zero, then the solution is all real numbers.

Example $\vert$ x - 4 $\vert$ > -2 or $\vert$ x - 4 $\vert \geq$ 0
Solution: all real numbers

Functions

2-4 questions per test on average

<u>Functional Notation and Evaluation</u>. A function works like a rule or formula taking whatever number or expression is plugged in ("input"), performing the rule defined by the function on the plug-in, and delivering a single result ("output").

For example, the idea to "multiply by 2" is a function. If you provide a number for this function, say 13, the function would provide 26 back. Early on, you may have been introduced to functions as "black boxes" that take in an "input" number at one end and put out an "output" number at the other end; or, the idea of a function may have been described as a two-column or two-row table:

"Black" Box

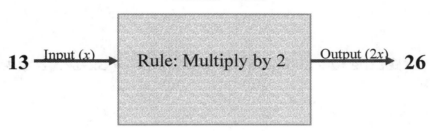

Or....

x (Input)	13	20	-4	$2x$
$f(x) = 2x$ (Output)	26	40	-8	$4x$

Or....

Input x	Output $f(x)=2x$
13	26
20	40
-4	-8
2x	4x

You should be familiar with the shorthand of functional notation: in the above rule, it can be expressed as $f(x)=2x$. $f(x)$ should NOT be misread "f times x." In fact, the x stands for a number or expression that f, the rule, acts on. For example, $f(\sqrt{3}) = 2(\sqrt{3})$, and $f(x^3 - 2) = 2(x^3 - 2)$. In certain problems, a function will be introduced by a word problem including a formula linking the key variables.

Examples of Functions

Example A: A group of students painted walls to raise money. The net amount d, in dollars, raised by painting w walls is given by the function d(w) = 22w-55. If the group painted 11 walls, what is the net amount they raised?

(A) $242   (B) $187   (C) $55   (D) $17   (E) $3

Solution: Simply evaluate d(w) when w(alls) = 11. d(11) = 22•11-55 = 242-55 = 187.

Answer: (B) $187

Example B: Let the function g be defined by g(x) = 3x-12. If g(4q) = g(-q), what is q?

Solution: Evaluate g(x) when x = 4q and when x = -q to get the right and left hand sides of the equation above, respectively, or 3•(4q)-12 = 3•(-q)-12. Rearranging and then solving for q, we have 15q = -12 + 12, or q = 0.

Answer: 0

Interpreting Function Graphs, Graphing Functions and Linear Functions

Functions can be graphed in the *xy*-plane by treating each input-output pair of values from the function as an (*x*, *y*) point in the plane: input or argument values are *x*-coordinates and the output values are treated as *y*-coordinates (see Coordinate Geometry section); therefore, *y* is treated synonymously with *f*(*x*), and can be expressed *y* = *f*(*x*).

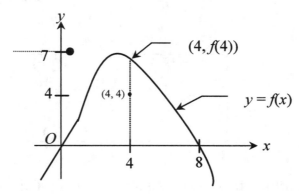

In the portion of the graph shown above, there are several SAT-worthy facts that you should be able to answer in a test question:

1. The graph *y* = *f*(*x*) has positive range values between *x* = 0 and *x* = 8; in fact, the range varies between 0 and 7 when $0 \le x \le 8$.

2. If an area is bounded by the graph *y* = *f*(*x*) and the *x*-axis, then a set of interior points is created, and you should be able to identify them by coordinates. For example (4, 4) is in the interior of the bounded region.

3. *f*(4) > 4, since (4, *f*(4)) lies on the graph itself directly above (4, 4)

4. The maximum value on the portion of the graph shown is *f*(*x*) = 7, and the *x* at which that occurs is just less than 4.

5. A horizontal line *y* = *b*, where 0<b<7 would intersect the graph *y* = *f*(*x*) twice, and if drawn at *y* = 7 would intersect the graph just once, at its maximum.

Linear Functions

One commonly found function on the SAT is the **linear function**, which literally means a function that when graphed describes **a line** in the *xy*-plane. Therefore, all facts about lines from coordinate geometry apply: the coefficient of *x* is the slope and the constant is the *y*-intercept. Conversely, any linear function can be understood to have functional form $f(x) = mx + b$, in which m is the slope and b is the *y*-intercept.

x	**f(x)**
-2	-9
3	6
9	a
b	9

Example C: The table above shows some values for the function *f*. If *f* is a linear function, what is the value of a + b?

(A) 0   (B) 9   (C) 18   (D) 22.5   (E) 28

Solution: Since $f(x)$ is linear, $f(x) = mx+b$, in which b is the y-intercept, not the second variable in the table! $m = (-9-6)/(-2-3) = 3$; and therefore $6 = 3(3) + b \Rightarrow b = -3$, the y-intercept. Plugging in the last points in the table, we have $a = 3 \bullet 9 - 3 = 24$, and $9 = 3 \bullet b - 3 \Rightarrow b = 4$. Thus, $a + b = 24 + 4 = 28$.

Answer: (E) 28

Domain and Range

Know These Terms

The domain of a function is the set of all values for which the function is defined. In problems that refer to domain, especially those that include a formula, watch out for restricted values of the function. Examples would include values that make a square root expression evaluate negative under the radical or a denominator evaluate to zero.

The range of a function is the set of all values that are the output, or result, of applying a function.

Simple Glide Translations

The graph of a function can be shifted, or translated, without changing the shape of the graphed function by making simple additions or subtractions inside or outside of the function's argument. The translated graph is called the image. For example, if a graph y = g(x) (shown below in bold) is to be shifted to the right by two units, one simply subtracts 2 from the function's argument, or y = g(x – 2) shown below (pointed at by arrows)

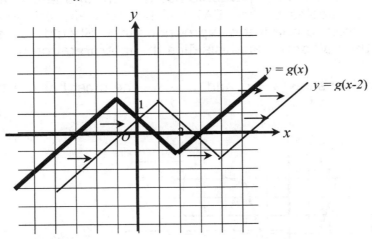

We summarize the following translation effects to a function graph, $y = g(x)$:

Graph y = g(x), and h>0, k>0	Rightward shift of g(x)	No horizontal shift of g(x)	Leftward shift of g(x)
Upward shift of g(x)	y = g(x-h)+k	y = g(x)+k	y = g(x+h)+k
No vertical shift of g(x)	y = g(x-h)	y = g(x)	y = g(x+h)
Downward shift of g(x)	y = g(x-h)-k	y = g(x)-k	y = g(x+h)-k

❖Strategy: To interpret translation effects, choose a unique point like a high or low point on the "before graph" and compare it to its image under the translation and then figure out what horizontal and vertical shift get you from that point.

Parabolas

Parabolas describe the shape of the xy-graph of a quadratic expression in one variable, x or y. If the quadratic expression is in x, then the parabola has an "up and down" shape (it can alternatively be presented as a quadratic function) and is vertically oriented.

If the quadratic expression is in y, then the parabola has a "right and left" shape and is horizontally oriented. Most parabolas on the SAT will be vertically oriented, so the discussion below will confine itself to quadratic expressions in x. Should you encounter a quadratic expression in y, then all of the analysis flips the interpretation of x and y.

The two parabolas graphed below show $y = x^2$ and $y = -x^2$, the most basic "reference" shapes for parabolas.

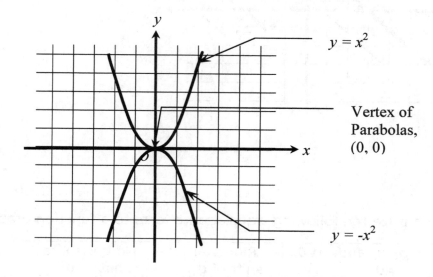

$y = x^2$

Vertex of
Parabolas,
$(0, 0)$

$y = -x^2$

Parabolas, cont.

More general formats for equations of parabolas take one of these three interchangeable forms:

$$y = ax^2 + bx + c \text{ [\underline{standard form}]}$$
$$y = a(x - r_1)(x - r_2) \text{ [\underline{factored or root form}]}$$
$$y = a(x - h)^2 + k \text{ [\underline{completed square form}]}$$

the constants or coefficients of these three equations, a, c, r_1, r_2, h, k, have convenient and revealing interpretations (*b* has a more complex interpretation, however, which depends on the values of *a* and *c*).

The bottommost point of the signature "bowl" of the parabola, no matter which way the parabola is oriented, is called the <u>vertex</u>, located at (*h*, *k*). For vertically opening parabolas, this vertex represents the minimum (lowest, and *a* > 0) or maximum (highest, and *a* < 0) value of the parabola's quadratic equation and represents the endpoint of the *range* of output values; *x* = *h*, vertex' *x*-value describes a vertical <u>axis of symmetry</u> for the parabola, its only one.

If a parabola's graph crosses the x-axis twice, (real r_1, r_2 exist, and $r_1 \neq r_2$) then the points of crossing are called <u>zeroes, roots</u> or <u>x-intercepts</u> of the parabola. If a parabola's graph just touches the x-axis, as in the two parabolas graphed below, it does so at the vertex itself and is called a <u>double root</u> or single zero quadratic equation ($r_1 = r_2$).

Parabolas, cont.

The value of a in $y=ax^2+bx+c$ [standard form] determines the shape of a parabola and whether or not it opens up or down.

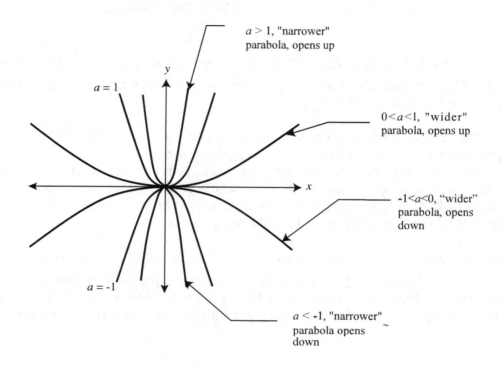

Qualitative Characteristics of Parabolas, based on values of a, c, *h, and k*.			
	> 0	**= 0**	**< 0**
a, the direction of the parabola (more about interpreting *a* appears in the figure below)	Parabola opens up	No parabola, but line instead	Parabola opens down Parabola
c, the y-intercept of the parabola	Parabola intersects *y*-axis above *x*-axis	Parabola passes through origin	Parabola intersects *y*-axis below *x*-axis
h, parabola's horizontal shift	Parabola shifted right from origin, axis of symmetry at *x = h*	Parabola symmetric about *y*-axis	Parabola shifted left from origin, axis of symmetry at *x = h*
k, parabola's vertical shift	Parabola shifted up from origin	Parabola just touches *x*-axis at a double root	Parabola shifted down from origin

Functions – additional information

(This information is for those who desire advanced understanding of the topic)

Functional interpretations of graphed parabolas			
	$y = ax^2 + bx + c$ [standard]	$y = a(x - r_1)(x - r_2)$ [factored or root]	$y = a(x - h)^2 + k$ [completed square]
Vertex in QI, opens up	$a > 0$, $c > 0$	Real roots, r_1, r_2 don't exist (and standard form can't be factored)	$a > 0$, $h > 0$, $k > 0$
Vertex in QI, opens down	$a < 0$, c anything (if $c < 0$, roots positive, y-int < 0; if $c = 0$, 2nd root 0, and parabola passes through origin, y-int = 0; if $c > 0$, one root of each sign, y-int > 0)	Distinct r_1, r_2, at least one positive; $a \bullet r_1 \bullet r_2 = c$. *(see box to left for interpretation)*	$a < 0$, $h > 0$, $k > 0$
Vertex in QII, opens up	$a > 0$, $c > 0$	Real roots, r_1, r_2 don't exist (and standard form can't be factored)	$a > 0$, $h < 0$, $k > 0$
Vertex in QII, opens down	$a < 0$, c anything (if $c < 0$, both roots negative, y-intercept < 0; if $c = 0$, second root 0, and parabola passes through origin, y-intercept = 0; if $c > 0$, one root of each sign, y-intercept > 0)	Distinct r_1, r_2, at least one negative; $a \bullet r_1 \bullet r_2 = c$. *(see box to left for interpretation)*	$a < 0$, $h < 0$, $k > 0$
Vertex in QIII, opens up	$a > 0$, c anything (if $c > 0$, both roots negative, y-intercept > 0; if $c = 0$, second root 0, and parabola passes through origin, y-intercept = 0; if $c < 0$, one root of each sign, y-intercept > 0)	Distinct r_1, r_2, at least one negative; $a \bullet r_1 \bullet r_2 = c$. *(see box to left for interpretation)*	$a > 0$, $h < 0$, $k < 0$
Vertex in QIII, opens down	$a < 0$, $c < 0$	Real roots, r_1, r_2 don't exist (and standard form can't be factored)	$a < 0$, $h < 0$, $k < 0$
Vertex in QIV, opens up	$a > 0$, c anything (if $c > 0$, both roots positive, y-intercept > 0; if $c = 0$, second root 0, and parabola passes through origin, y-intercept = 0; if $c < 0$, one root of each sign, y-intercept > 0)	Distinct r_1, r_2, at least one positive; $a \bullet r_1 \bullet r_2 = c$. *(see box to left for interpretation)*	$a > 0$, $h > 0$, $k < 0$
Vertex in QIV, opens down	$a < 0$, $c < 0$	Real roots, r_1, r_2 don't exist (and standard form can't be factored)	$a < 0$, $h > 0$, $k < 0$
Vertex on positive x-axis	$a > 0$, $c > 0$ if opens up; $a < 0$, $c < 0$ if opens down	$r_1 = r_2 > 0$	$a < 0$, if opens up and $a < 0$, if opens down and , $h > 0$, $k = 0$
Vertex on negative x-axis	$a > 0$, $c > 0$ if opens up; $a < 0$, $c < 0$ if opens down	$r_1 = r_2 < 0$	$a < 0$, if opens up and $a < 0$, if opens down and , $h < 0$, $k = 0$

298

Algebra

This is the largest single category of question on the SAT accounting for almost half of all SAT math questions. Therefore, basic algebraic understanding is essential to SAT performance. Solving for, or manipulating unknown or undefined quantities is the essence of algebra. SAT algebra takes many forms. You'll find algebra in fraction form, in radicals and exponents, and in geometric shapes such as squares and circles. You'll see algebra in standard equation form and in factored form. Use the following examples to become familiar with SAT algebra in all its forms.

Algebra problem involving simple substitution

Example A: If $x = 3$ and $y = -3$, then $x^2 y + y/x =$

Solution: substitution

$$(3^2)\cdot-3 + -3/3 =$$
$$-27 \quad + \quad -1 = -28$$

Answer: -28

Difficult algebra problem involving fractions

Example B: If $\frac{3}{4} x = \frac{2}{3} y$, then $x/y =$

Solution: cross multiply and solve

$\frac{3}{4} x$ may also be written as $\frac{3x}{4}$

$\frac{2}{3} y$ may also be written as $\frac{2y}{3}$

$\frac{3x}{4} = \frac{2y}{3}$

Now, cross multiply

$9x = 8y.$

❖**Strategy.** In an simple equation in which each side has a single coefficient and a variable, use the "Double V" technique. Each variable equals the opposite coefficient.

$9x = 8y.$

$x = 8$ and $y = 9$.

Answer: $\frac{x}{y} = \frac{8}{9}$

Easy algebra problem involving a percentage

Example C: If t = 2r and r is 30 percent of v then t is what percent of v?

Solution: logic only

r = 30% of v,
t= 2r, therefore t = 2 (30% of r)
t = 60% of v.   **Answer: 60**

Algebra problem involving a proportion:

Example D: A basketball player made 12 out of *n* shots attempted which is the same as 2 shots made out of every 3 attempts. What is the value of *n*?

Solution: set up a proportional fraction.

12/n = 2/3. Cross multiply. 2n = 36   **Answer: n = 18**

Algebra problem involving odd/even numbers:

❖**Strategy**: plug in easy numbers. With even/odd questions, all numbers work equally well! When a question says "must be true" you should try to disprove it. Sometimes this involves plugging in several different sets of numbers. For the purpose of determining *odd* and *even* there are no exceptions, so only one set of numbers is needed. The numbers 1 and 2 work as well as any.

Example E: If *x* is an odd integer and *y* is an even integer, which of the following must be true?

      I. x^3 is odd
      II. y^3 is odd
      III. y(x + y) is odd

  A) I only   B) I and II   C) II only   D) I and III only   E) I, II and III

Solution:

  I) All odd integers remains odd when taken to any power, so I is true.

  II) All even numbers stay even when raised to any power, so II is false.

  III) An even number plus an odd number always yields an odd number, and an odd number multiplied by an even number always yields an even number, so III is false

                                            Answer: (A)

Harder Algebra

Algebra problem involving average

Example A: The sum of 8 positive numbers whose average is x is how much greater than the sum of 5 numbers whose average is x -1

Solution: compute the sums of both sets of numbers then subtract

The formula is: average = sum/parts
which becomes sum = average □parts

Sum (set one) = 8x   Sum (set two) = 5x - 5
The words "how much greater" means _difference_ which indicates that subtraction is the operation you'll need to use.
8x - (5x-5) (distribute the negative) becomes 8x - 5x + 5

Answer: 3x + 5

Algebra problem involving percentages (word problem)

Example B: A shopkeeper gave one of his customers a 20% discount on the original price of his purchase then added 10% of the discounted price for sales tax. The result was $9.00 less than the original price. What was the original price of the customers purchase?

Solution:

Original amount is x
x -.2x = .8x   This is the discounted amount

Next, figure out the 10% tax on the discounted amount

(.1 •.8x =.08x) This is the 10% sales tax on the discounted amount

Add these two numbers together to obtain the total cost
.8x = .08x = .88x

Now you know that the discount is 12% of the original amount.
The discounted amount is $9.00, which means that .2x = $9.00
Find the value of x, by dividing both sides by .12

Answer: x = 75

Harder Algebra, Cont.

Algebra problem involving factoring

Example C: If $m^2 - n^2 = 4k^3$, m - n = 12k, and $k \neq 0$
what is m + n in terms of k?

Solution: factor and substitute:

$m^2 - n^2$ is known as a **difference of squares.**
Any difference of squares can be factored this way:

(m - n)(m + n)   (*m - n = 12k was a clue!)

You should learn to recognize, and how to factor, "difference of squares."

Now substitute 12k for (m - n):

$$12k(m + n) = 4k^3$$

To determine the value of m + n, you must <u>isolate</u> it by dividing both sides by 12k:

$$\frac{12k(m+n)}{12k} = \frac{4k^3}{12k}$$

Which leaves only reducing to obtain your final answer:

Answer: $m + n = \dfrac{k^2}{3}$

Algebra problem involving several variables

Example E: x = 2y, y = 3z and 4z = w what is w in terms of x?
(A) $x\!/_{24}$ (B) $2x\!/_3$ (C) $3x\!/_2$ (D) $8x\!/_3$ (E) $6x$

<u>Solution</u>: create one common variable: x. Change all variables to x using standard algebra.

If x = 2y, then y = ½ x.
If y = 3z then 3z also = ½ x
If 3z = ½ x, then to find 4z (which equals w), you should
multiply both sides by $4\!/_3$ Thus

$$3z * 4\!/_3 = \frac{12z}{3} = 4z$$

$$½x * 4\!/_3 = 4\!/_6\,x \text{ which} = 2\!/_3\,x \text{ or } 2x\!/_3 .$$

Answer is (B)

302

Now you try

1. If $q + r + s = 126$, $q = 3r$ and $s = 3r$ then $r =$

2. If $r = 3x$, $s = 4x$, $t = 6x$ and $x > 0$ then which of the following is the greatest?
    A) $\frac{r}{s}$ B) $\frac{r}{t}$ C) $\frac{s}{r}$ D) $\frac{t}{s}$ E) $\frac{t}{r}$

3. John is now x years old. His sister Ann is now twice as old as John was 2 years ago. In terms of *x*, what is Ann's age now?
    A) 2x - 4   B) 2x - 2   C) 2x   D) $\frac{1}{2}x - 2$ E) $\frac{1}{2}x - 4$

4. If $x = 5^y$ and $y = z + 1$, what is $^x/_5$ in terms of z?
    A) z   B) z + 1   C) 5^z D) $5^z + 1$ E) 5^{z+1}

Harder Algebra

Solutions

1. If q + r + s = 126, q = 3r and s = 3r, then r =

| Put everything in terms of 'r'. 7r = 126. | Answer = 18 |

2. If r = 3x, s = 4x, t = 6x , and x > 0, then which of the following is the greatest?

   A) r/s   B) r/t   C) s/r   D) t/s   E) t/r

| Make x = 1. Then r = 3, s = 4, t = 6 | Answer = E |

3. John is now *x* years old. His sister Ann is now twice as old as John was 2 years ago. In terms of *x,* what is Ann's age now?

   A)   2x - 4   B) 2x - 2   C) 2x   D) 1/2x - 2   E) 1/2x - 4

| Two years ago, John was **x - 2** years old. Ann is twice as old. $2(x - 2) = 2x - 4$ |
| Answer = A |

4. If x = 5^y and y = z + 1, what is $^x/_5$ in terms of z?

   A) z   B) z + 1   C) 5^z D) $5^z + 1$ E) 5^{z+1}

| Substitute z +1 for y. As a result, you have x = 5^{z+1} |
| $5^{z+1}/5$ is the same as $5^{z+1}/5^1$. |
| (Subtract exponents when dividing numbers with a common base) [(z +1) -1 = **z**] Thus you are left with 5^z. | Answer = C |

Word Problems

Three Methods of Solving SAT Word Problems

The Direct Method

Explanation: The Direct Method is the best choice when you fully understand a question. It involves setting up an equation or some other way of representing the relationship expressed in the question, then solving the question. You might draw a picture, set up a simple chart, or just write out the important parts of the question.

Warning!!!~~ Make sure you know exactly what the question is asking for. Sometimes, students mistakenly give wrong answers because they do not fully read the question. As an example, let's say a question asks you to solve for the amount of paint remaining in a paint container, you might mistakenly solve for amount of paint used.

Plug-in Method

Explanation: This method is useful in harder questions in which you do not fully understand how to set up an equation. This "backdoor" method involves plugging in the given answers until you find the one that works. In other words, plug in an answer, then determine if that answer could be correct based on other information in the question.

Also, remember this important strategy

❖Strategy: When using the Plug-In Method, start by plugging in the middle answer "C". If that answer is not correct, then move up to a smaller choice ("A" or "B") or down to a larger one "D" or "E"). Numerical answers are always presented in this order.

The Substitution Method

Explanation: The substitution method is useful in solving word problems that have at least one algebraic variable (a letter representing a number). This strategy involves plugging in your own numbers in place of the variable(s), solving the question, then finding your numerical answer among the answer choices. It is important to plug in "good numbers" - numbers that will make your work easy and that make sense to the problem.

Word Problems

Easy Example

1. The Central High School football team played x games in a season. The team won 6, lost 2, and tied the remaining number of games. Which of the following expressions gives the number of tied games.

A) x + 8   B) x + 2   C) x - 4   D) x - 6   E) x - 8

Solution: There are only three possible outcomes to a game, win, lose or tie. Therefore you can determine the number of any *one* of these outcomes (in this case ties) by subtracting the other two outcomes (wins and losses) from the total number of games. In the easy example above, you subtract wins (6) and losses (2) from the total number of games (x).

Substitute a number for "x", such as 10 (although any number greater than 8 will work). Reread the question:

*1. The Central High School football team played **10** games in a season. The team won 6, lost 2, and tied the remaining number of games. Which of the following expressions gives the number of tied games.*
A) x + 8   B) x + 2   C) x - 4   D) x - 6   E) x - 8

With this method, you now end up with a real number as your answer. . . .

> 10 games minus 6 wins and 2 losses
> 10 - (6+2) = **2**

Plug in your number **10**, where you see **x** in the answers until you arrive at the answer **2**.

A)**10** + 8 =18   B) **10** + 2 = 12   C) **10** - 4 = 6   D) **10** - 6 = 4   E) **10** - 8 = 2

Correct answer is E

Word Problems, cont.

In the next example, some students would choose to use the Direct Method, while others would prefer the Substitution Method. . . .

Medium Example

2. A rental library charges a fine of 20 cents per book for each of the first five days that a book is overdue, plus 10 cents per book for each additional day. Which of the following is an expression for the fine, in dollars, for a book that is overdue for d days, where $d > 5$?

A) 0.20 + 0.10d   B) 0.20 + 0.10(5-d)   C) 0.20 + 0.10(d-5)   D) 0.20(5) + .10d
E) 0.20(5) + 0.10(d-5)

Solution 1: the fine for each of the first five days is .20 dollars. So the total fine for the first five days is .20(5). This leaves only (D) and (E) as possible answers.

Then, determine for how many days the .10 dollar (ten cent) fine is counted. It is not d days, since d is the total number of days the book is overdue. It therefore must be (d-5).

Answer E

Solution 2: substitute a number for d, then reread the question. According to the question, d must be greater than 5. If you were to choose the number 6 as a substitute for d, the question would read. . . .

2. A rental library charges a fine of 20 cents per book for each of the first five days that a book is overdue, plus 10 cents per book for each additional day. Which of the following is an expression for the fine, in dollars, for a book that is overdue for **6** *days.*

The answer would be $1.10, since the fine for the first five days (5 days x $.20) is $1.00 and for the sixth day is $.10 (1 day x $.10). When you plug in 6 for d in the answers, the correct answer, E, emerges again.

A) 0.20 + 0.10d   B) 0.20 + 0.10(5-d)   C) 0.20 + 0.10(d-5)   D) .20(5) + .10d
E) 0.20(5) + 0.10(d-5)

Answer E

Word Problems, cont.

Hard Example

3. A blend of coffee is made by mixing Columbian coffee at $8.00 per pound with espresso coffee at $3.00 per pound. If the blend is worth $5.00 a pound, how many pounds of Columbian coffee are needed to make 50 pounds of the blend?
A) 20
B) 25
C) 30
D) 35
E) 40

Solution 1: Did you notice that the cost of the blend is less than the average of the costs of the two types of coffees? The average of the two amounts ($8.00 and $3.00) is $11.00/2, or $5.50. Since the blend is worth less, it must have less than half (25 pounds) of the Columbian Coffee.

The only possible answer is A).

Solution 2: Starting with the middle answer C), plug the answer back into the question. In this case, answer C) indicates that 30 pounds of Columbian Coffee are needed. You can then figure out that 20 pounds of the blend would be Espresso, since there are 50 pounds total.
Use the costs to check this answer.
        50 pounds of a $5.00 per-pound blend should cost $250.00!

Plugging in answer C)   30 pounds Columbian • $8.00 per pound = $240.00
                               20 pounds Espresso   • $3.00 per pound = $ 60.00
                                                                                 $300.00

$300.00 is too much money, so we now know that the answer is either A) or B) since these questions indicate fewer pounds of Columbian (the more expensive) coffee.

Follow the same procedure for either A) or B)
Plugging in answer A)   20 pounds Columbian • $8.00 per pound = $ 160.00
                           + 30 pounds Espresso • $3.00 per pound + $ 90.00
                                                                              $ 250.00

                $250.00 is correct.

                                                        Answer (A)

SAT GEOMETRY

Circles
(2 questions per test, on average)

Circumference -   The distance around a circle's perimeter (in measured units)
Arc -   Part or all of a circle's circumference (measured in degrees)
Diameter -   The distance across the center of a circle
Radius -   The distance from a circle's center to the circle
Pi (п) -   п is approximately 3.14 or 22/7
Chord -   A line segment inside a circle with endpoints on the circle
Secant -   A line that passes through and intersects a circle at two points

Detailed Definitions of Terms

CIRCUMFERENCE:
The distance around the circle, measured in actual units such as inches, centimeters, feet, etc. A circumference of three inches means that the circle is three inches around. A car tire may be thought of as a circle with a circumference of about six feet. A quarter (coin) has a circumference of about three inches. Circumference is also equal to the distance traveled when a wheel (like a car or bicycle wheel) completes one full turn.

ARC MEASURE:
The distance around the circle, measured in degrees. All circles have a total of 360° of arc. A half-circle has measure of 180°, which also means that the arc length is half the circumference. A quarter-circle has 90° of arc. If the arc is formed by two radii that form a central angle, then the measure of the arc is the same as the measure of the central angle.

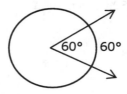

60° central angle corresponds to 60° of arc

continued on next page

Circles

Detailed Definitions of Terms, cont.

DIAMETER:

A line segment that passes through the middle of a circle and has two endpoints on the circle. It may be thought of as the distance across the center of a circle. A full size bike tire has a diameter of about three feet, which means that it measures about three feet across the middle.

RADIUS:

A line segment connecting the center of a circle to any point on the circle. For all circles, radius is ½ the length of the diameter. Within any given circle, all radii are equal. Remember, a radius must originate in the center of a circle and must touch the rim of the circle itself.

PI π

PI (π) equals the ratio of every circle's circumference to its diameter. Each and every circle is 3.14 times as far around as it is across. This is the value known as pi (the symbol for pi is π). For example, if a quarter (coin) is exactly 1 inch across the middle, then it has a circumference of 1 x 3.14 or 1π inches around its circumference. If a bike tire has a circumference of 9 feet, then its diameter is 9 ÷ 3.14 ft. In most cases the solution is expressed as a factor of PI(π). For example, the solution above might simply be $9/\pi$.

CHORD:

A chord is a line segment inside a circle with each of its two endpoints on the circle. The diameter of a circle is a chord; in fact the diameter is the largest chord of any given circle.

SECANT:

A secant is, in fact, a chord whose endpoints are extended to form a line. For the purpose of the SAT, a secant acts just like a chord and should be treated exactly the same way.

Circles

Examples

❖**Strategy**: Finding the radius is often the best way to begin to solving a "circle question" in which the radius is not known. You must know the radius (r) if you are trying to find either area (πr^2) or circumference ($2\pi r$).

Example A

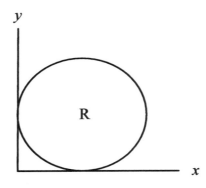

Q. In the figure above, a circle with center R has an area of 36π square units and just touches the x and y axis. What are the coordinates of R?

(A) (3, 12)   (B) (4, 9)   (C) (6, 6)   (D) (18, 18)   (E) (36, 36)

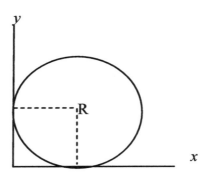

Solution: Draw two radii perpendicular to the x-axis and the y-axis.   The coordinates of R are the distances from R to the x-axis and y-axis, which are also radii of the circle. Since the area of the circle is 36π, $r^2 = 36$, $r = 6$. Since the radii are always equal, the coordinates are (6, 6).

The answer is (C).

Example B

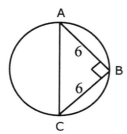

Q. In the figure above, $\overline{AC}$ is the diameter of the circle. The area of semicircle ABC is:

(A) 36π   (B) 18π   (C) 12π   (D) 9π   (E) $\frac{9}{2}\pi$

Solution: The triangle is an isosceles right triangle (45-45-90). In an isosceles right triangle, the hypotenuse is $s\sqrt{2}$ (where s is the length of the leg), which makes the hypotenuse $6\sqrt{2}$. This is also the diameter of the circle.

Since a radius = ½ diameter, the radius = $3\sqrt{2}$.

The formula for the area of a semicircle is $\frac{\pi r^2}{2}$

Plugging in $3\sqrt{2}$ for r, you get $\frac{\pi(3\sqrt{2})^2}{2}$,

which equals 9 ·2π/2, which equals 9π.

The answer is (D).

Example C

Note: This problem was rated "difficult," yet it is easily solved by finding the radius and knowing how to find the circumference.

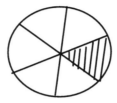

Q. The circle above is divided into six equal regions. If the area of the circle is 36п, what is the perimeter of the shaded region?

   (A) 12п + 6 (B) 6п +12 (C) 6п + 6   (D) 2п + 36   (E) 2п + 12

Solution: The perimeter of the shaded region is equal to **two radii** plus **1/6 of the circumference**. You are told that the area of the circle is 36п, so you know that the radii are each 6 (Area = пr²).

                    The circumference = 2пr (plug in 6 for radius) = 12п.
                    1/6 of the circumference is 2п
                    The perimeter = 12 + 2п.

The answer is (E)

313

Example D

Q. If the figure above, B is the center of the circle with radius r and ABCD is a rectangle.
The length of diagonal AC is

     (A) $\frac{r\sqrt{2}}{2}$ (B) $\frac{r\sqrt{3}}{2}$ (C) r   (D) $r\sqrt{2}$ (E) $r\sqrt{3}$

<u>Solution:</u> You are told the radius is r, yet there is no radius. Draw the radius from B to D. Note that the radius is also a diagonal of rectangle ABCD. Diagonals of rectangles are equal, therefore AC = r.

The answer is (C).

Other Important Properties of Circles

1. A wheel is a circle. The distance a wheel travels in a full turn is equal to the circumference of the wheel.

> Ex. A bicycle has wheels of diameter three feet. How far does the bicycle travel when the wheel makes one complete revolution? Ans. The circumference of the wheel is 3π, which is the distance the bicycle travels.

2. Circles are often used to help determine characteristics of other geometric shapes within a particular problem. For example, the radius or diameter of a circle might be a side of a square, the diagonal of a square, or a side of a triangle.

3. All radii within a circle are equal. This fact has many applications. For example, drawing a second radius might allow you to create an isosceles triangle within a circle - sometimes a useful situation.

4. If you are told the value of the radius, yet no radius is drawn in the diagram, draw it immediately. Draw it so that it connects with other lines or figures within the circle.

Example: In the circle below with center C, the radius = 2, and arc AB = 90°. What is the length of chord AB?

(A) 3   (B) $2\sqrt{2}$ (C) 2.5   (D) 2   (E) $4\sqrt{2}$

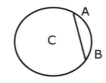

Solution: Draw two radii from the center of the circle to point A and point B. Since chord AB = 90° the angle at the center of the circle (created by drawing these radii) = 90°. This creates a 45-45-90 triangle with chord AB as the hypotenuse. Since the length of sides CA and CB are each 2, AB (hypotenuse) = $2\sqrt{2}$

The answer is (B).

Triangles

(4 per test, on average)

You must know all the following rules of triangles:

1. THE SUM OF THE ANGLES OF ANY TRIANGLE = 180°.

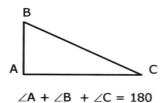

$\angle$A + $\angle$B + $\angle$C = 180

2. AREA OF ANY TRIANGLE = ½ (base • height)

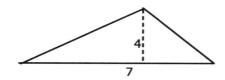

Area = ½ (7 x 4)

EQUILATERAL TRIANGLE: All sides and angles are equal. All angles equal 60°.

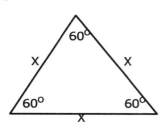

(Two Hidden 30-60-90 Triangles!!!)

Here is a special note about equilateral triangles; if you draw the altitude from the top of the triangle, two 30-60-90 triangles are created! (See figure above on right)

Right Triangles

RIGHT TRIANGLE: A right triangle is any triangle that contains an angle of 90°. In a right triangle, the sum of the squares of the sides equals the square of the "hypotenuse" (which is the side opposite the 90° angle). To determine area of a right triangle, use the lengths of the legs (A and B) as the base and height.

Pythagorean Theorem
$$A^2 + B^2 = C^2$$

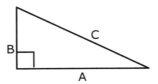

Special Right Triangles

30-60-90. A 30-60-90 triangle is one that has internal angles of 30°, 60°, and 90°. The side opposite the 60° angle equals the length of the short side times $\sqrt{3}$. The length of the hypotenuse is 2 times the length of the short side.

(Strategy: always find the length of the short side, x).

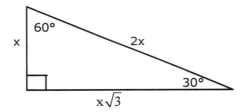

Special Right Triangles, cont.

45-45-90. (These are also called isosceles right triangles). A 45-45-90 triangle is one which has internal angles of 45°, 45°, and 90°. The sides opposite the 45° angles are equal, and the hypotenuse is equal to the side times $\sqrt{2}$. Conversely, each side equals the hypotenuse divided by $\sqrt{2}$.

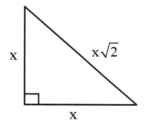

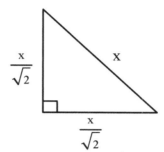

PYTHAGOREAN RIGHT TRIANGLES: 3-4-5 or 5-12-13. Some right triangles have sides in a 3-4-5 or 5-12-13 proportion. They are called Pythagorean Triples. The 3-4-5 version can also appear in multiples of 3-4-5, such as 6-8-10 or 9-12-15. These are worth watching for; there is one on virtually every test and recognizing them can definitely make it easier to solve the question.

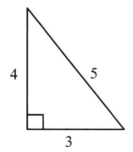

Similarity of Triangles

ANGLE-ANGLE SIMILARITY; SIDE-SIDE SIDE SIMILARITY: If two triangles have two congruent angles, then the triangles are said to be *similar*. This, in turn, means that the three sets of corresponding sides are proportional. Either of these pieces of information are enough to establish triangle similarity. Question: How can you tell that two sets of corresponding angles in figure (below left) are congruent?

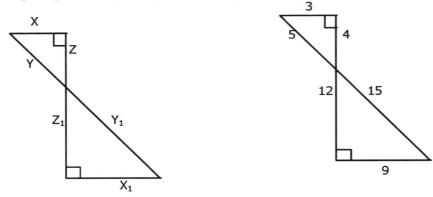

In the set of similar triangles above (left), sides X,Y and Z correspond to sides X_1, Y_1 And Z_1. Likewise, in the set of triangles above (right), the proportions of corresponding sides are the same. Notice how each side of the lower triangle is three times the length of the corresponding side in the upper triangle.

Example:

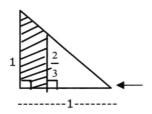

In the figure above, what is the area of the shaded region?

(A) 5/36   (B) 5/18   (C) 1/3   (D) 5/12   (E) 5/6

Solution:
The shaded area is equal to the large triangle minus the small triangle.
The area of the large triangle is ½ •1 • 1 or **½.**

Since the two sides of the large right triangle are equal in length, the triangle is 45-45-90.
The two triangles are similar, because they share an angle (marked ⟵), and both contain a right angle. Thus, the base of the smaller 45-45-90 triangle is $^2/_3$. The area of the smaller triangle is ½($^2/_3$ • $^2/_3$) or $^2/_9$

Subtract: ½ - $^2/_9$ (converting to least common denominator $^9/_{18}$ - $^4/_{18}$)

                                                                    The answer is (B)

Quadrilaterals

A quadrilateral is a closed, four-sided figure in which the angles add up to a sum of 360°. There are several different types of quadrilaterals, each of which has special properties.

Types of Quadrilaterals

Parallelogram

A parallelogram is a four-sided figure in which opposite sides are equal in length and parallel, and in which opposite angles are of equal measure.
Also:

$\overline{AB} \parallel \overline{DC}$ $\overline{BC} \parallel \overline{AD}$

<u>Adjacent angles are supplementary</u> **($m\angle A + m\angle B = 180°$)**
Area of parallelogram = base • height (AD • BE)
Sum of angles = 360° ($m\angle A + m\angle B + m\angle C + m\angle D = 360°$)

Trick: If $m\angle y = 60°$, then)ABE is a 30-60-90 triangle!

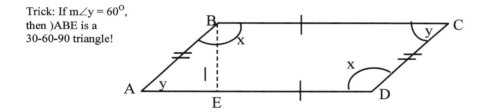

Square

A square is a special kind of a parallelogram. It has all the properties of a parallelogram; in addition it has four equal sides and four 90° angles.

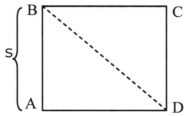

Hint: If a circle is drawn inside the square such that it touches the sides of the square, then the diameter of the circle will equal the length of a side of the square.

Area of square = S^2
Perimeter = 4S
Sum of angles = 360° ($\angle A + \angle B + \angle C + \angle D = 360°$)
Drawing one diagonal (AC) creates two 45-45-90 triangles, so the length of the diagonal is $s\sqrt{2}$.
Drawing two diagonals creates eight 45-45-90 triangles (can you name them?).

Rectangle

A rectangle is another special parallelogram in which opposite sides are equal and which contains four 90° angles.

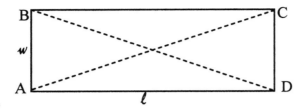

$\overline{AB} \cong \overline{DC}, \ \overline{BC} \cong \overline{AD}$

$\angle A = 90°, \ \angle B = 90°, \ \angle C = 90°, \ \angle D = 90°$
Sum of angles = 360° ($\angle A + \angle B + \angle C + \angle D = 360°$)
Diagonals bisect each other, creating four line segments of equal length
Area $\overline{ABCD} = l \bullet w$ (where l = length and w = width)

Trapezoid

A trapezoid is a quadrilateral with at least one pair of parallel sides.

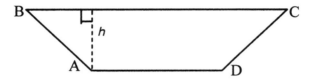

$\overline{BC} \parallel \overline{AD}$

Sum of angles = 360° ($\angle A + \angle B + \angle C + \angle D = 360°$)

Area ABCD = average of the bases time the height $\dfrac{BC + AD}{2} \times h$

Trapezoids are rare on the SAT, but when one does appear, it is almost always question involving *area*.

Polygons

A Polygon is a multi-sided figure. The prefix *poly* means "many." On the SAT, the term pertains to any figure containing more than four sides. A pentagon is an example of a polygon.

Regular, equiangular and equilateral polygon:

A regular polygon has sides of equal length and angles of equal measure. A regular octagon, for example, has eight equal sides and eight equal angles. An equiangular polygon is one in which all angles have equal measure. An equilateral polygon is one in which all sides are of equal length (a stop sign, for example, is both equiangular and equilateral – so therefore it is an example of a regular polygon!!!).

Sum of Angles of a Polygon:

The sum of angles of a polygon is determined by the formula $180° \times (n-2)$, where n is the number of sides. For example, the sum of angles in an octagon (eight-sided figure) is $180° \times (8-2)$ or $1080°$. If the octagon is equiangular (or regular), you could divide $1080°$ by 8 (because there are eight angles) to determine the measure of each angle.

Properties of Solids

(These are relatively rare, only occurring, on average, only once per test.)

Volume: The volume of a solid may be thought of as the amount of space it occupies. There are just a few formulas you'll need to know.

Volume of a Rectangular Solid:

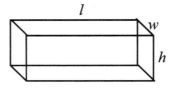

Volume = length • width • height (v=lwh)

Surface Area of a Rectangular Solid:

Surface Area. = 2(l•w) + 2((l•h) + 2(w•h)
Or just add up the areas of all six faces

Volume of a Cube:

Volume = side x side x side (v = s^3) Note: you can use the formula for rectangles, but in the case of a cube, l,w, and h are all the same value

Surface Area of a Cube:

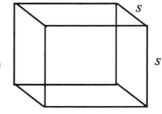

Surface Area = $6s^2$
(since a cube has six faces, each of which has an area of s^2)

A right circular cylinder is a cylinder whose base is perpendicular to its sides. A food can is a good example.

Volume of a right circular cylinder:

Volume = $\pi r^2 h$
Hint: think of it as a circle (πr^2) with height (h)

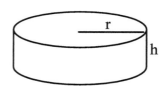

Geometry

Coordinate Geometry

3 questions per test, on average

Coordinate-based problems have grown in importance as the SAT incorporates more algebra, so you will need to properly identify and solve these problems, especially when no graph is present, which occurs about half of the time. Often you will find vocabulary in the problem to tip you off; the following terms all refer to *xy*-graphs:

- *xy*-plane,
- *xy*-coordinate plane
- *xy*-coordinate system
- coordinate plane
- rectangular coordinate system
- Cartesian coordinate system (rarely).

The *xy*-plane works like a giant grid in which each point in the plane is assigned an address, or coordinate location (x, y).

x refers to which direction ($x<0 \Rightarrow$ left or $x>0 \Rightarrow$ right) and how many units to go along the horizontal x-axis (note: the x-value is always the first of the <u>ordered pair</u> just as x always comes before y in the alphabet) in order to reach the point on the x-axis directly above, below or at (x, y).

y describes what direction (up or down), perpendicular to the x-axis and parallel to the y-axis, and how far to go vertically from the prior step to reach (x, y). Each axis can be thought of as its own number line. The two axes divide the plane into four <u>quadrants</u> as shown below, and the point where the two axes meet is called the <u>origin</u>, O, at (0,0). For example, (-5, 1) would describe a point found by going 5 units left along the x-axis and then 1 unit directly above it, and would be located in Quadrant II (see figure below).

For any point (x, y). . . .

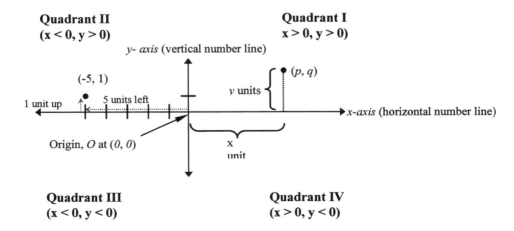

Coordinate Geometry, cont.

Most coordinate-based problems involve describing and manipulating lines. In a coordinate plane, lines are expressed by the simple equation

$$y = mx+b$$

in which $\underline{m}$ represents the slope and $\underline{b}$ represents the y-intercept.

Two points are enough to determine a line and its equation. If two points of a line are given or can be identified, (x_1, y_1) and (x_2, y_2), an easy calculation provides the slope:

$$\frac{rise}{run} = \frac{y_2 - y_1}{x_2 - x_1} = \frac{y_1 - y_2}{x_1 - x_2} = m, \text{ slope.}$$

Rise = the difference of the two points' y-coordinates (doesn't matter which coordinate is subtracted from which as long as x-coordinates are done in the same order), or $y_2 - y_1$.

Run = the difference of the two points' x-coordinates, or $x_2 - x_1$.

For example, if two points are given, (-2, 4) and (3, -3), the slope of the line containing these two points would be $\frac{(-3-4)}{(3-(-2))} = -\frac{7}{5}$. The negative value indicates that the line that slopes downward, to the right.

Once **m** (slope) is known, **b** (y-intercept) can be solved by plugging a point on the line into $y = mx + b$; in this case, we have $y = -\frac{7}{5}x + b$, and can use either point to get b:

$4 = \frac{-7}{5} \cdot -2 + b \Rightarrow b = \frac{6}{5}$. Thus, the equation of the line is $y = -\frac{7}{5}x + \frac{6}{5}$.

Coordinate Geometry

Important facts about pairs of lines in the coordinate plane:

- Two <u>parallel</u> lines always share the same slope, though they have different *y*-intercepts.
- Two lines are <u>perpendicular</u> if the product of their slopes is –1 (which implies that the two slopes are negative reciprocals of each other). For example, if a line has equation $y = 14x + 2$, then a line perpendicular to it will have slope $-\frac{1}{14}$, and $14 \bullet -\frac{1}{14} = -1$.
- <u>Reflections</u> of a line over either axis (or a vertical or horizontal line) simply reverse the sign of the slope, so a line with a slope of $-\frac{7}{5}$ reflected over (or about) the *y*-axis would produce a line with slope of $\frac{7}{5}$.

Example A: In the xy-coordinate plane, line ℓ is perpendicular to line with the equation $y = x - 3$ and passes through the point (-1, 6). Which of the following is an equation of the line ℓ?

(A) $y = -x + 3$
(B) $y = -x + 6$
(C) $y = -x + 5$
(D) $y = x + 5$
(E) $y = x - 1$

<u>Solution:</u> The slope of the perpendicular sought must be –1 since the original line has a slope of 1, and the product of the two must be –1 $\Rightarrow$ eliminate (D) and (E). The equation of the perpendicular must be of the form $y = -x + b$ then, and plugging in (-1, 6) in, we have $6 = -(-1) + b \Rightarrow b = 5$.

Answer: (C)

Example B: Which of the following is a graph of the linear function with a positive slope and negative x-intercept?

(A)

(B)

(C)

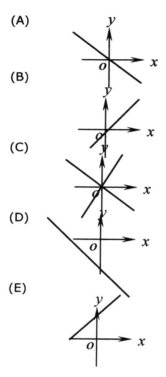

(D)

(E)

<u>Solution:</u> Slopes are negative in (A) and (D)⇒ eliminate. (B) has a positive x-intercept and (C) passes through the origin, making the x-intercept 0, so (E) is the only answer that meets both criteria.

Answer: (E)

Coordinate Geometry, cont

<u>Distance</u> can be found between any two points in the *xy*-plane by computing the number line distances between the corresponding *x*-values and *y*-values and then applying the Pythagorean Theorem (*unless* the segment is parallel to one of axes, in which case you use the number line distance from that axis). These number line distances correspond to a right triangle with horizontal and vertical legs, and a hypotenuse of the distance to be calculated.

For example, you can find the distance between A(-5, 2) and B(-2, 4), as shown in the figure   below:

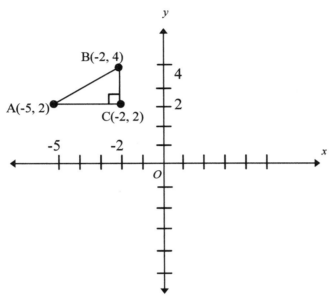

Segment AC and segment BC are both parallel to *x*- and *y*-axes, respectively, so they form the legs of a right angle in △ABC. AC = -2-(-5) = 3, and BC = 4-2 = 2. Applying the Pythagorean Theorem:

$$AB^2 = 3^2 + 2^2$$
$$AB^2 = 13$$
$$AB = \sqrt{13}$$

328

Coordinate Geometry, cont

Distance Formula

In general, if (x_1, y_1) and (x_2, y_2) are two points in the xy-plane, the distance between them is given by the formula:

$$d = \sqrt{(x_2 - x_1)^2 + (y_2 - y_1)^2}$$

Midpoint Formula

You might be asked to find the midpoint of line segments in the coordinate plane. If segment AB has endpoints A(5, 1) and B(-2, 3), then the midpoint of segment AB has coordinates:

$$\left(\frac{5-2}{2}, \frac{1+3}{2} \right) = \left(\frac{3}{2}, 2 \right)$$

The midpoint (x_m, y_m) is simply the average of the x-values and the average of the y-values:

$$\left(\frac{x_1 + x_2}{2}, \frac{y_1 + y_2}{2} \right) = (x_m, y_m), \text{ or } \frac{x_1 + x_2}{2} = x_m \text{ and } \frac{y_1 + y_2}{2} = y_m$$

Some important, basic concepts to remember

Even and Odd

1. Odd + Odd = Even   (no exceptions)
2. Odd x Odd = Odd   (no exceptions)
3. Even + Even = Even (no exceptions)
4. Even x Even = Even (no exceptions)
5. Even + Odd = Odd   (no exceptions)
6. Even x Odd = Even   (no exceptions)

Negative and Positive

1. Positive + Positive = Positive (no exceptions)
2. Positive x Positive = Positive (no exceptions)
3. Negative + Negative = Negative (no exceptions)
4. Positive + Negative = (Larger number's sign)
5. Positive x Negative = Negative (no exceptions)
6. When working with negative numbers, remember:

Example: $-1 > -1,000$
Example: $-5 < -2$

Mean/Median/Mode

1. Mean - the average (total/parts) of all values (numbers) in a data set
2. Median - the middle value when a group of numbers is arranged in numerical order.
3. Mode - the most frequently occurring value in a data set

Digits:

In the number 1234.5678

1 = thousands digit
2 = hundreds digit
3 = tens digit
4 = units digit
5 = tenths digit
6 = hundredths digit
7 = thousandths digit
8 = ten thousandths digit

Set A {12, 12, 14, 18, 19, 77, 88}

Mean $(240 \div 7) = 34.285$
Median   (middle term) 18
Mode   (most common term) 12

Set B {1, 2, 2, 4, 45, 46, 46, 9}

Mean   19.375 ($155 \div 8$)
Median   6.5 (arrange in order 1, 2, 2, 4, 9, 45, 46, 46 then average the middle two terms)
Mode   2, 46 (bi-modal, meaning two modes)

Order of Operations

PEMDAS

P = Parentheses
E = Exponents
M = Multiplication
D = Division
A = Addition
S = Subtraction

MATH QUESTION BANKS:

Advanced Topics for the New SAT

Section 1:
Radical Equations and Expressions

1.

If $\dfrac{z-x}{3} + y^2 = \sqrt{25} + y - 1$, what is the value of $x - z$ when $y = 4$?

    (A) -36
    (B) 3
    (C) 6
    (D) 12
    (E) 24

2.

For what values of z does $\sqrt{9z^2 + 4} = 3z + 2$?

    (A) $z = 0$
    (B) $z > 0$
    (C) $z \geq 0$
    (D) All real numbers
    (E) No real numbers

3.

For what value of x does $\sqrt{xa^2 + 3a} = a$, $a \neq 0$?

    (A) $1 - \dfrac{3}{a}$
    (B) $1 + \dfrac{3}{a}$
    (C) $\dfrac{a-3}{a^2}$
    (D) $\dfrac{a}{a+3}$
    (E) $\dfrac{a}{1+3}$

4.

If $-2 + \sqrt{2n - 3} = 7$, then what is the value of n?

5.

If $3\sqrt{x-2} = 5z^2$ the value of x in terms of z is?

(A) $\dfrac{25}{9}z^2 + 2$

(B) $\dfrac{25}{9}z^4 + 2$

(C) $\dfrac{25}{9}z^2 + 4$

(D) $\dfrac{25}{3}z^2 + 4$

(E) $\dfrac{25}{3}z^2 + 2$

6.

The cube root of the product of -2 and a number is -6. What is the number?

(A) -56
(B) -36
(C) 16
(D) 36
(E) 108

7.

The quotient of the square root of a number and 4 is twice the number. What is one possible value of the number?

(A) $-\dfrac{1}{8}$

(B) $\dfrac{1}{64}$

(C) $\dfrac{1}{32}$

(D) $\dfrac{1}{8}$

(E) $\dfrac{1}{4}$

8.

Which of the following values of m satisfies the equation $\sqrt{\dfrac{2m^2}{5}} - \sqrt{2} = 0$?

(A) -5
(B) -2
(C) $\sqrt{5}$
(D) $\dfrac{5}{2}$
(E) 5

9.

Which of the following values of r satisfies $\sqrt{1+r}-3=-1$?

(A) -5
(B) 0
(C) 2
(D) 3
(E) 8

10.

If $z^2-7=\sqrt{y}$ and $z=4$, what is the value of y?

(A) 81
(B) 9
(C) 7
(D) 4
(E) 3

11.

If $\sqrt{\dfrac{3}{2}z-2}=\dfrac{z}{2}$, then $|z-3|=?$

(A) -1
(B) 1
(C) 2
(D) 6
(E) 12

12.

If $\sqrt{-1-e}=-2f$, where e and f are both real numbers, which of the following statements could be true?

    I. $e>0$
    II. $e=0$
    III. $e<0$

(A) None
(B) I only
(C) III only
(D) I and II only
(E) I, II, and III

13.

The members of set M are the integer solutions of the inequality $\sqrt{10-x} \le 3$, and the members of the set N are the integer solutions of the inequality $\sqrt{3+x} \le 10$. What is one member of the intersection of M and N?

14.

The arithmetic mean of 10, $\sqrt{x}$, and -1 is 7.

What is $\dfrac{x}{16}$?

(A) -1
(B) 9
(C) 10
(D) 12
(E) 16

15.

Which of the following expressions represents the statement: the quotient of the square root of the difference of a and b and the square of a?

(A) $\left(\dfrac{\sqrt{a-b}}{a} \right)^2$

(B) $\sqrt{a-b} - a^2$

(C) $\dfrac{\sqrt{ab}}{a^2}$

(D) $\dfrac{\left(\sqrt{a}-\sqrt{b}\right)}{a^2}$

(E) $\dfrac{\sqrt{a-b}}{a^2}$

16.

Which of the following equations represents the statement: the square root of the difference of x and the product of three and y is equal to the quotient of x and y?

(A) $\sqrt{x-3y} = \dfrac{x}{y}$

(B) $x-3y = \sqrt{\dfrac{x}{y}}$

(C) $\dfrac{y}{x} = \sqrt{x-3y}$

(D) $\sqrt{x}\sqrt{3y} = \dfrac{x}{y}$

(E) $\dfrac{x}{y} = \sqrt{x} - \sqrt{3y}$

17.

If $\sqrt{x-8} = \sqrt{x} - 2$, then $x = ?$

(A) 8
(B) 9
(C) 16
(D) 20
(E) 24

18.

For all $m > 0$, which of the following expressions is equivalent to $5\sqrt{2m^{-3}} - 1$?

(A) $\dfrac{5\sqrt{2}}{m^3} - 1$

(B) $\dfrac{5\sqrt{2}}{m\sqrt{m}} - m$

(C) $\dfrac{5\sqrt{2m} - m^2}{m^2}$

(D) $5\sqrt{2m} - \sqrt{m}$

(E) $\dfrac{5\sqrt{2m} - m^2}{m^3}$

19.

If $\sqrt{4-x} = 3$, then what is the value of x?

(A) 7
(B) 3
(C) −3
(D) −5
(E) −7

20.

If $5\sqrt{z} - 8 = 3\sqrt{z} + 24$, then $z = ?$

(A) 169
(B) 216
(C) 232
(D) 256
(E) 264

Section 2:
Negative & Rational Exponents

1.

If $\dfrac{b^7}{b^x} = b^3$ and $\left(a^{-2}\right)^y = a^{14}$, what is the value of $x - 2y$?

(A)   -2
(B)   9
(C)   10
(D)   14
(E)   18

2.

If $a > 0$ and $a^{\frac{b+3}{4}} = 8$, then $a^{\frac{b+3}{3}} = ?$

(A)   4
(B)   16
(C)   32
(D)   36
(E)   64

3.

If $z > 0$, which of the following is equivalent to $-6z^{\frac{1}{2}}$?

(A) $\sqrt{-36z}$

(B) $-\sqrt{36z^2}$

(C) $-\dfrac{3}{2z}$

(D) $-\sqrt{36z}$

(E) $-\sqrt{\dfrac{36}{z}}$

4.

If $2^{5y-3} = 16^3$, what is the value of $3y$?

(A) 2.25
(B) 3.6
(C) 4.5
(D) 6
(E) 9

339

5.

If $3^{-3y} = 216$, what is the value of 3^{-y}?

(A) $\dfrac{1}{6}$

(B) 6

(C) 9

(D) 27

(E) 36

6.

If $7^{10-x} = 49$, then $x - 10 = ?$

(A) -2

(B) 0

(C) 2

(D) 4

(E) 6

7.

If $\left(2^{-7}\right)^{-x} = 128$, what is the value of x?

8.

If x is a non-zero integer, then $-\left(\dfrac{-1}{(-x)^{-1}}\right)$

cannot be which of the following?

I.   A number between 0 and 1, non-inclusive
II. A number between -1 and 0, non-inclusive
III. A number larger than 1

(A) I only
(B) II only
(C) I and II only
(D) I and III only
(E) I, II, and III

9.
If m and n are integers $\neq 0$ and $m^{-4}n^2 = 9$, what is the smallest value of n possible?

(A)   -9
(B)   -3
(C)   -1
(D)   3
(E)   None of the above

10.
If $3^{-2} = \dfrac{1}{p}$, what is p^{-2}?

(A)   81

(B)   9

(C) $\dfrac{1}{3}$

(D) $\dfrac{1}{9}$

(E) $\dfrac{1}{81}$

11.
If $\left(q^{x/3}\right)^3 = \dfrac{1}{q}$, what is $-3x$?

12.
Which of the following values of a and b satisfy $a^{-1} + b^{-1} = (ab)^{-1}$?

(A) $a = 1,\ b = 1$
(B) $a = -1,\ b = 2$
(C) $a = -2,\ b = 1$
(D) $a = -1,\ b = -1$
(E) $a = 2,\ b = 2$

13.

If $f(x) = x^{-2}$, then when $x{=}3$, $\left(f(x)\right)^{-1}{=}?$

(A)   -6

(B) $-\dfrac{1}{6}$

(C) $\dfrac{1}{9}$

(D)   6

(E)   9

14.

$3\left(f^3 g^{-4} h^5\right)^4 = ?$

(A) $3f^7 h^9$

(B) $\dfrac{3f^{12} h^{20}}{g^{16}}$

(C) $\dfrac{12f^{12} h^{20}}{g^{16}}$

(D) $81f^7 h^9$

(E) $\dfrac{81f^{12} h^{20}}{g^{16}}$

15.

Which of the following expressions are

equivalent to $8z^{-\frac{1}{2}}$?

I. $\dfrac{64z}{8z^{\frac{1}{2}}}$

II. $\left(16z^{-\frac{2}{3}}\right)^{-\frac{3}{4}}$

III. $\left(\dfrac{64}{z}\right)^{\frac{1}{2}}$

(A)   None
(B)   II only
(C)   III only
(D)   I and III only
(E)   I, II, and III

16.

If $c = 3^{3g-3}$ and $d = 9$, then $cd^2 = ?$

(A) 3^{3g+1}
(B) 3^{6g-2}
(C) 3^{3g+15}
(D) 3^{12g-12}
(E) 27^{6g-6}

Section 3:
Rational Equations and
Expressions

1.

If $a > 0$, $a = \dfrac{1}{b}$ and $c = \dfrac{a^2}{2}$, then $b = ?$

(A) $\sqrt{2c}$

(B) $\dfrac{\sqrt{2c}}{2c}$

(C) $2c^2$

(D) $4c^2$

(E) $\dfrac{1}{2c^2}$

2.

If $\dfrac{1}{x+y} = 2$, then $y =$

(A) $\dfrac{1}{2} - x$

(B) $\dfrac{1}{2} - \dfrac{x}{2}$

(C) $1 - 2x$

(D) $\dfrac{1}{2} + x$

(E) $1 + 2x$

3.

If $x \neq y$, then $\dfrac{2}{x-y} + \dfrac{1}{y-x} =$

(A) $\dfrac{-2}{x-y}$

(B) $\dfrac{1}{x-y}$

(C) $\dfrac{1}{x+y}$

(D) $\dfrac{3}{x+y}$

(E) $\dfrac{3}{x-y}$

4.

For all numbers k, where $k \neq -3$, let $g(k) = \dfrac{2k+1}{3+k}$. If $g(k) = 4$, what is k?

(A) $-11\big/2$

(B) $9\big/28$

(C) $9\big/7$

(D) 4

(E) 11

5.

If $3.5x = 17.5$, what is the value of $\dfrac{2}{x+3}$?

6.

For $x > 0$, $\dfrac{x^2 + x - 2}{x^2 + 12x + 20} = ?$

(A) $-\dfrac{1}{10}$

(B) x

(C) $\dfrac{x-2}{x+10}$

(D) $\dfrac{x-1}{x+10}$

(E) $\dfrac{x+2}{12x+20}$

7.

$\dfrac{1}{\dfrac{1}{1+\dfrac{1}{x}}} = ?$

(A) $\dfrac{x+1}{x}$

(B) x

(C) $\dfrac{1}{x}$

(D) $x(x+1)$

(E) $\dfrac{x-1}{x+1}$

8.

If $h = \dfrac{-2}{g}$, where g is not equal to 0 and h is not equal to 2, which of the following is equal to $\dfrac{g+1}{h-2}$?

(A) g

(B) h^{-1}

(C) h

(D) $-h\!\big/\!2$

(E) $h - g$

9.

$\dfrac{x^2 - 2x}{x^2 - 4}$ is equivalent to which expression?

(A) $\dfrac{-x}{x+2}$

(B) $\dfrac{-1}{x+2}$

(C) $\dfrac{x}{x+2}$

(D) $\dfrac{x}{x-2}$

(E) $\dfrac{-x}{x-2}$

10.

For all nonzero values of a, b, and c,

$\dfrac{2a^{-2}b^3c^2}{3^{-3}a^{-1}b^4c^{-6}} = ?$

(A) $\dfrac{54a^2c^8}{b}$

(B) $\dfrac{-18c^8}{ab}$

(C) $\dfrac{54b^7c^4}{a^2}$

(D) $\dfrac{27b^7c^4}{2a^3}$

(E) $\dfrac{54c^8}{ab}$

11.

Which of the following is the most simplified form of the expression $\dfrac{6r^2 - 8rs - 8s^2}{2r^2 - 4rs}$?

(A) $3r + 2s$

(B) $\dfrac{3r^2 - 4rs - 4s^2}{r^2 - 2rs}$

(C) $\dfrac{3r + 2s}{2r}$

(D) $\dfrac{3r + 2s}{r}$

(E) $\dfrac{r^2 - rs - s^2}{r^2 - rs}$

12.

For $|b| > 1$, $\dfrac{2}{b-1} + \dfrac{2}{b+1}$ is equivalent to?

(A) $4b$

(B) $\dfrac{4b}{b^2 - 1}$

(C) $\dfrac{2}{b}$

(D) $\dfrac{1}{b}$

(E) $\dfrac{4}{b^2 - 1}$

13.

If $\dfrac{c^{-2}}{d^2} = \dfrac{c^2}{y}$, what is the value of y, in terms of c and d?

(A) d^2
(B) c^2
(C) $c^4 d^2$
(D) $c^{-4} d^2$
(E) $2d$

14.

If $x = \dfrac{2x^2 + 2y^2}{-4y}$ and $y \neq 0$, then y is equal to which of the following?

(A) $-2x - x^2$
(B) $\dfrac{x^2 - x}{-2}$
(C) $\dfrac{x^2 + x}{-2}$
(D) $-x$
(E) x

15.

If $m = -6$ and $n = m + 2$, what is the value of $\dfrac{m^{-1}(m-n)}{(n-m)^{-1}}$?

(A) -24
(B) $-\dfrac{3}{2}$
(C) $-\dfrac{2}{3}$
(D) $\dfrac{2}{3}$
(E) 2

16.

If $y \neq \dfrac{2}{3}$, then $\dfrac{3y^3 + 7y^2 - 6y}{3y - 2} = ?$

(A) $3y + 3$
(B) $y + 3$
(C) $y^2 + 3y$
(D) $y^2 - 3y$
(E) $3y^2 - \dfrac{7}{2}y$

17.

$$3\left(a^{-7}b^{8}c^{9}\right)^{2} =$$

(A) $\dfrac{3b^{10}c^{11}}{a^{5}}$

(B) $\dfrac{3b^{16}c^{18}}{a^{14}}$

(C) $\dfrac{-9b^{16}c^{18}}{a^{14}}$

(D) $\dfrac{9b^{10}c^{11}}{a^{5}}$

(E) $\dfrac{9b^{16}c^{18}}{a^{14}}$

18.

If a given number is divided by $x+1$, and the result is 4 times the original number, what is the value of x?

(A) $-\dfrac{3}{4}$

(B) $-\dfrac{1}{2}$

(C) $\dfrac{1}{2}$

(D) $\dfrac{3}{4}$

(E) 4

19.

If $x = -a-1$ and $x \neq -1$, then $\dfrac{1}{-1-x} = ?$

(A) a

(B) $-a$

(C) $\dfrac{1}{-1-a}$

(D) $\dfrac{1}{a}$

(E) $-1-a$

348

Section 4:
Direct and Inverse Variation

1.

y varies directly with *x*. If *x* is 30 when *y* is 10, what is *x* when *y* is 9?

(A) 3
(B) 27
(C) 29
(D) $\dfrac{100}{3}$
(E) 35

2.

k is directly proportional to *l* and $l=\dfrac{2}{3}$ when $k=-\dfrac{1}{2}$. What is *l* when *k*=3?

(A) -4
(B) $-\dfrac{4}{3}$
(C) $-\dfrac{1}{3}$
(D) $\dfrac{4}{3}$
(E) 4

3.

h is inversely proportional to *g* and *h*=1.7 when *g*=15.3. What is *g* when *h*=5.1?

(A) 3.4
(B) 5.1
(C) 10.2
(D) 13.6
(E) 15.3

4.

f(x) is directly proportional to x and f(2)=3. What is $f(x)\big/x$ when x=3?

5.

y and z are inversely proportional and $y=1\frac{1}{5}$ when z=2. What is z when $y=\frac{1}{5}$?

(A) $\dfrac{3}{25}$

(B) $3\dfrac{1}{5}$

(C) $10\dfrac{1}{5}$

(D) 12

(E) 22

6.

A tractor has two different size tires, with the rear tire larger than the front. If the rear tire of one such tractor has a circumference of 243 inches, and the front tire a circumference of 144 inches, how many revolutions will the back tire have made if the front tire has made 27 revolutions?

7.

If $x \bullet y=k$, where $3k+3=12$, then when the value of x doubles, y must?

(A) double
(B) halve
(C) triple
(D) none of the above
(E) cannot be determined from the information given

8.

If p^2 varies directly with q and q=8 when p=2, what is p when $\dfrac{q}{p}=18$?

(A) 4
(B) 4.5
(C) 8
(D) 9
(E) 18

9.

The sound produced by blowing air at an angle into a column filled with water varies in frequency inversely with the fraction of the column <u>unfilled</u> with water. If a column $\frac{1}{4}$ full with water produces a 300 frequency sound, what frequency sound will the column produce if it is $\frac{2}{5}$ full?

    (A)   160
    (B)   240
    (C)   300
    (D)   375
    (E)   750

10.

$q=kr$ and k is a member of $\{-5, -3, -2, -1\}$. If $q=-60$, what is the largest possible value of r?

    (A)   300
    (B)   60
    (C)   12
    (D)   -12
    (E)   -60

11.

A belt connects two pulleys and when the belt spins, the pulleys rotate. One of the pulleys has a diameter of 2 feet. If the other pulley rotates 3 times as fast, what is its radius in <u>inches</u>?

12.

$-\frac{3}{2} \le x \le -\frac{1}{2}$ and y is inversely proportional to x. If $y=1$ when $x=-1$, then y could be any of the following EXCEPT?

    (A) $\frac{2}{3}$

    (B) $\frac{3}{4}$

    (C) $\frac{4}{3}$

    (D)   2
    (E)   3

13.

In a certain front row section of a sold out concert, the price of a ticket varies inversely with how far the seat is from the stage. If a $50 ticket is 12 yards from the stage, how many <u>feet</u> from the stage will a $100 ticket be?

(A)　　6
(B)　　8
(C)　　12
(D)　　18
(E)　　24

14.

c varies inversely with d, which of the following <u>cannot</u> be true?

   I. If c doubles, d halves
  II. $c>0$, $d<0$
 III. $c \bullet d = 0$

(A)　III only
(B)　III only
(C)　I and III
(D)　II and III
(E)　I, II and III

15.

x varies directly with z and z varies inversely with y. $x = 2\frac{1}{2}$ when $z=1$ and $z = 2\frac{1}{2}$ when $y=20$. What is $x \bullet y$?

(A)　$2\frac{1}{2}$
(B)　20
(C)　50
(D)　125
(E)　Cannot be determined from the information given

16.

m varies inversely with n and n varies inversely with p. $m=10$ when $n=8$ and $p=20$ when $n=6$. What is p when $m=16$?

(A)　$96/25$

(B)　16

(C)　$50/3$

(D)　24

(E)　$200/3$

Section 5
Absolute Value

1.

If $|2x - 8| = 12$, what is one possible value of x?

(A) −4
(B) −2
(C) 0
(D) 6
(E) 8

2.

If $|3 - x| = 4$, a possible value of x can be found in all the following intervals EXCEPT?

(A) $-7 \leq x \leq -1$
(B) $-3 \leq x \leq 4$
(C) $-4 \leq x \leq 3$
(D) $3 \leq x \leq 7$
(E) $3 \leq x \leq 4$

3.

If $|z - 1| < 2$, then z^2 can be any of the following values EXCEPT?

(A) 0.2
(B) 2.4
(C) 6.3
(D) 8.4
(E) 10.9

4.

If $|2 - 4| + |x - 1| = 3$, then $x = $?

(A) −1
(B) 1
(C) 2
(D) 3
(E) 4

355

5.

Which of the following ordered pairs (x,y) is NOT in the solution set of $||x|-2|-|y|=2$?

    (A) $(2,0)$

    (B) $(4,-1)$

    (C) $(-4,1)$

    (D) $(-6,2)$

    (E) $(10,-3)$

6.

If $y=|x|-4$, what is one possible value of x when $y=-2$?

    (A) -4
    (B) -2
    (C) 0
    (D) 4
    (E) 8

7.

If $x \neq -1$, $\dfrac{|x+1|}{x+1}$ can equal which of the following?

    I. 1
    II. -1
    III. x

    (A) I only
    (B) II only
    (C) III only
    (D) I & II only
    (E) I, II, and III

8.

Let $f(x)$ be defined as the absolute value of the difference between the smallest and largest factors of x greater than 1. For example, $f(12)=|2-12|=10$. What is the value of $f(15)-f(14)$?

9.
Let $g(x)$ be defined as the absolute value of the quotient of x and 3 and $h(x)$ be defined as the absolute value of the product of x and 3. If $g(x) \le h(-1)$, what is the least value of x which satisfies the inequality?

(A) -27
(B) -9
(C) -3
(D) -1
(E) 9

10.
If $x = -7$, then $|3.5 - x| = ?$

(A) -10.5
(B) -3.5
(C) 3.5
(D) 10.5
(E) 24.5

11.
If $f(x) = |2x + 3|$, then $f(-2) = ?$

(A) -7
(B) 1
(C) 4
(D) 7
(E) 12

12.
If $|y| \ne 0$, which of the following statements must be true?

(A) $(y-1)^2$ is positive

(B) $\dfrac{1}{y}$ is positive

(C) $-\dfrac{1}{y}$ is positive

(D) $-y^3$ is negative

(E) y^{-2} is positive

357

13.
If $z = |y-1|+1$, what is z when $y = -2$.

   (A) -3
   (B) -1
   (C) 3
   (D) 4
   (E) 6

14.
If $\frac{1}{2}x = |y|-1$, what is y when $x = -2$?

   (A) -3
   (B) -1
   (C) 0
   (D) 3
   (E) 4

15.
For which value of y is $|y-3| < x-3$ if $x = 2$?

   (A) $y < 3$
   (B) $y > -3$
   (C) all real numbers
   (D) none
   (E) cannot be determined from the information given

16.
If $-1 < -|y| < 0$ and $-2 < -|x| < -1$, which of the following must be true?

   (A) $y < x$
   (B) $x < y$
   (C) $x \cdot y > 0$
   (D) $x \cdot y = 0$
   (E) $x + y \neq 0$

17.

If $|x+y| < 1$ and $x - y = 1$, then y can be any of the following EXCEPT?

(A) $-\dfrac{3}{4}$

(B) $-\dfrac{1}{2}$

(C) $-\dfrac{1}{4}$

(D) $-\dfrac{1}{8}$

(E) 0

18.

If $|x| < 1$ and $|y| > 10$ and x, y are integers, then $x - y$ can be?

(A) 9

(B) 1

(C) 0

(D) -1

(E) -11

19.

If $f(x) = |-2x + 1| - 2|x| - 2$, then $f(-1) - f(1) = ?$

20.

Which of the following gives the solution set for the equation $\left|\dfrac{2}{3}x - \dfrac{3}{2}\right| = \dfrac{7}{2}$?

(A) $\{-3\}$

(B) $\left\{\dfrac{15}{2}\right\}$

(C) $\left\{3, \dfrac{15}{2}\right\}$

(D) $\left\{-\dfrac{15}{2}, -3\right\}$

(E) $\left\{-3, \dfrac{15}{2}\right\}$

21.

Which ordered pair (x, y) satisfies $2x + 2y = 2$ and $|y| = |x| + 1$?

- (A) $(-1, 1)$
- (B) $(-2, 3)$
- (C) $(0, -1)$
- (D) $(1, 0)$
- (E) $(3, -2)$

22.

If $|m - 15| = 2\sqrt{m}$, then m could equal which of the following?

- (A) 9
- (B) 15
- (C) 16
- (D) 30
- (E) 36

23.

If $g = 12$, then $\left|3 - \dfrac{1}{2}g\right| = ?$

- (A) -3
- (B) 3
- (C) 9
- (D) 12
- (E) 15

24.

If $|3 - x| \geq 2$, then x could be any of the following EXCEPT:

- (A) -2
- (B) -1
- (C) 0
- (D) 1
- (E) 2

25.

If $|3n - 8| = 4$, then $n = ?$.

(A) $-\dfrac{4}{3}$ or -4

(B) $\dfrac{1}{3}$ or 4

(C) $\dfrac{4}{3}$ or 4

(D) $\dfrac{8}{3}$ or 8

(E) $-\dfrac{4}{3}$ or 4

Section 6: Functions

1.

If $f(x) = 2x + 9$, what is the value of $f(7) - f(4)$?

2.

If $f(x) = 4x^2 - 2$, then $f(3) = ?$

(A) 1
(B) 4
(C) $\dfrac{\sqrt{10}}{2}$
(D) 10
(E) 34

3.

$f(x)$	x
7	3
12	m
$m + 12$	n

According to the table above, if $f(x) = \dfrac{5x - 1}{2}$, what is the value of n?

(A) 3
(B) 7
(C) 12
(D) 15
(E) 19

4.

If $f(x) = -2x^2 + 11$, for which of the following values of x does $f(x) = 3$?

(A) -4
(B) -2
(C) 0
(D) 1
(E) 4

5.

For all real numbers, $f(x) = \dfrac{(x+1)^2}{2}$. If

$f(a) = 18$ and $f(9) = b$, which of the following could be the value of $b + a$?

(A) 32
(B) 43
(C) 50
(D) 68
(E) 82

6.

If $f(x-3) = x^2 - 6x + 9$, then $f(x) = ?$

(A) x
(B) $x - 3$
(C) x^2
(D) $x^2 - 6x + 6$
(E) $x^2 - 6x + 12$

7.

If $f(x) = 5x - 1$, what is $f(4) + f(2) + 1$?

(A) $f(2)$
(B) $f(4)$
(C) $f(5)$
(D) $f(6)$
(E) $f(8)$

8.

If $f(x) = \dfrac{9x+1}{4} + \dfrac{-5x-7}{4}$, what is the value of $x - f(x)$?

9.

For all positive integers r, $f(r)$ is defined below:

$$f(r) = r^2 \text{ when } r \text{ is prime}$$
$$f(r) = r - 1 \text{ when } r \text{ is } \underline{not} \text{ prime}$$

If $f(3) - f(4) = y$, what is the value of $2y^{-1}$?

10.

Each of the following is within both the domain and range of $f(x) = \dfrac{1}{x^2 - 4}$ EXCEPT:

(A) 1
(B) 2
(C) 3
(D) 4
(E) 5

11.

x	-1	0	1	2	3
$f(x)$	2	5	8	11	14

If $f(x) = ax + b$ and satisfies the above table for the values of x shown, what is $b - a$?

(A) 1
(B) 2
(C) 3
(D) 4
(E) 5

Section 7:
Geometric Sequences/ Growth

1.
A certain population of bacteria doubles every 5 hours. If the number of bacteria in the population initially was 2^{50}, what is the number in the population 5 days later?

(A) 2^{250}
(B) $\left(5^{24}\right)\left(2^{50}\right)$
(C) 2^{75}
(D) 2^{74}
(E) 2^{60}

2.
The first term in a sequence is 27. Every term after the first is obtained by multiplying the term immediately preceding it by $1\frac{2}{3}$. For example, the second term is 45 because $27 \times 1\frac{2}{3} = 45$. What is the 4th term in the sequence?

3.
The number of cells in a certain lab experiment triples every 90 minutes. If there are 50 cells in the culture initially, then what is the number of cells in the culture after 4 hours and 30 minutes?

(A) 150
(B) 225
(C) 450
(D) 1,350
(E) 4,500

4.
The number of stamps in Peter's collection doubles every four months. If after 16 months he has s stamps, then an expression for the number of stamps in his collection after y years is given by?

(A) $2^{y}s$
(B) $2^{3y-4}s$
(C) $2^{3y}s$
(D) $2s^{3y-4}$
(E) $2^{y}s^{y+2}$

5.

If the fifth and sixth terms of a geometric sequence are 162 and 486, what is the average of the second and fourth terms of the sequence?

6.

A certain bacterial cell culture under study quintuples its population every week. If the sample started out with two cells, which of the following expressions would give the population of this culture after 42 days?

(A) 2×5^6

(B) 2×5^7

(C) 2×42^2

(D) 5×7^6

(E) 5×42^6

7.

After the first term in a sequence, the ratio of each term to the preceding term is $2a$. If the first term is b, what is the fourth term?

(A) $4a^2b$

(B) $\dfrac{b}{8a^3}$

(C) $8a^3b^3$

(D) $16a^4b$

(E) $8a^3b$

8.

On a certain day, a Petri dish contained 12 bacteria at 1:00 pm, 48 bacteria at 2:00 pm, and 192 bacteria at 3:00 pm. How many bacteria will be present in the dish at 5:00 pm?

(A) 768

(B) 1,536

(C) 2,072

(D) 3,072

(E) 12,288

9.

Tom opened a savings account that earned a fraction r of its balance in interest every year. Two years ago, Tom deposited $1,600 into the account, and has not deposited or withdrawn any money since. If he has earned $704 on interest so far, what is r?

10.

Denise opened a toy store this year. She wants to have three total, opened and running by the third year and nine total, opened and running by the fifth year. At this continued rate of store openings, how many stores will she open between the ninth and eleventh years?

Section 8: Sets

1.

If *a* is any element from set A, and *b* is any element from set B, how many different values are possible for *a* + *b*?

Set A: {−2, 0, 2, 4}
Set B: {−1, 0, 1, 3}

(A) 5
(B) 7
(C) 10
(D) 12
(E) 16

2.

What is the probability that an integer in set {1, 2, 3, ..., 100} is divisible by 2 and not divisible by 3?

(A) $\dfrac{1}{6}$

(B) $\dfrac{33}{100}$

(C) $\dfrac{17}{50}$

(D) $\dfrac{1}{2}$

(E) $\dfrac{18}{25}$

3.

A set X contains all integers between 11 and 19 inclusive, and set Y contains all integers between −6 and 24 inclusive that are divisible by 6. How many elements are there in the set X ∪ Y?

(A) 13
(B) 14
(C) 15
(D) 38
(E) 40

4.

If A is the set of negative integers that are divisible by 3 and B is the set of even integers from −2 to −100 inclusive, the intersection of A and B contains how many elements?

(A) 15
(B) 16
(C) 21
(D) 23
(E) 24

5.

If set A consists of {4, 8, 12, 16, 20, 24} and set B consists of {6, 12, 18, 24, 30, 36}, how many multiples of 3 are in $A \cap B$?

(A) 0
(B) 2
(C) 3
(D) 6
(E) 8

6.

What is the sum of the elements in set U?

Set U: {11, 17, 19, 23, 34, 57, 92}

(A) 7
(B) 11
(C) 250
(D) 253
(E) 352

7.

Set R: {1, 2, 3, 9, 10, 11}

Which of the following numbers when added to the set above will make the mean of the new set equal to the median of the new set?

(A) 6
(B) 7
(C) 9
(D) 12
(E) 36

8.

Set S is all odd numbers between 13 and 37 inclusive. Set E is all multiples of 5 between 10 and 40. Set T is equal to $S \cap E$. How many numbers in Set T?

(A) 2
(B) 3
(C) 5
(D) 15
(E) 19

9.

How many members are in the set which represents the union of G and Q?

Set G: {1, 4, 9, 16, 25}
Set Q: {1, 8, 27, 64, 125, 216, 343}

10.

If Set X = {1, 4, 9, 16, 25, ..., 100, 121, 144, 169, 196}, what is the probability that a member of the set is a multiple of 3 and 4?

(A) $\frac{2}{7}$

(B) $\frac{1}{2}$

(C) $\frac{1}{7}$

(D) 4

(E) 7

Section 9:
Linear Equations

1.

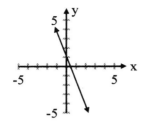

Which of the following is an equation for the graph above?

(A) $y = -\dfrac{1}{3}x + 1$

(B) $y = x + 3$

(C) $y = -3x + 1$

(D) $y = \dfrac{1}{3}x + 1$

(E) $y = 3x + 3$

2.

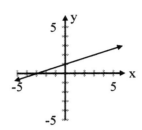

Which of the following equations best describes the line shown in the graph above?

(A) $3x + y = 1$

(B) $x + 3y = 2$

(C) $-3x + y = 1$

(D) $-x + 3y = 3$

(E) $x + 3y = 4$

3.

What is the y-intercept of the line with the equation $2x + 5y = 20$?

(A) -8

(B) -4

(C) 0

(D) 4

(E) 8

4.

What is the slope of a line containing the points $(-6, 2)$ and $(3, 5)$?

(A) -3

(B) $-\dfrac{1}{3}$

(C) $\dfrac{1}{3}$

(D) 1

(E) 3

5.

What is the equation of a line with a slope of 3 containing the point $(2, -5)$?

(A) $y = 3x - 1$
(B) $y = 3x - 11$
(C) $y = 3x + 5$
(D) $y = 3x - 2$
(E) $y = 3x - 5$

6.

What is the slope of the line given by $-2y = 8x - 3$?

(A) -8
(B) -4
(C) $\frac{2}{3}$
(D) 4
(E) 8

7.

Which lines are parallel?

I. $2x + y = 1$
II. $-x + y = -4$
III. $x + y = 5$
IV. $2x - y = 3$

(A) I & II
(B) I & III
(C) I & IV
(D) II & IV
(E) None

8.

Which line is perpendicular to $y = 2x - 4$?

(A) $y = -2x + 4$
(B) $y = -4 - 2x$
(C) $y = -x - 2$
(D) $y = -\frac{1}{2}x + 4$
(E) $y = \frac{1}{2}x - 2$

9.
What is the slope of the line with the equation
$y + 2 = 5(x - 1)$?

(A) -10
(B) 3
(C) 5
(D) 7
(E) 13

10.
Which values are solutions of $y < 2x - 1$?

    I. $(0, 3)$

    II. $(-1, -3)$

    III. $(3, 0)$

(A) I only
(B) II only
(C) III only
(D) I & II only
(E) I & III only

11.
If $y = ax + b$ and $y = cx + d$ are the equations of perpendicular lines and $a \neq 0$, then all of the following must be true EXCEPT

(A) $a = \dfrac{-1}{c}$

(B) $ac = 1$

(C) $a^2 \cdot c^2 = 1$

(D) $|a| = \dfrac{1}{\sqrt{c^2}}$

(E) $ac < 0$

Section 10:
NEW SAT-Mixed
Problems

1.

If $x \neq y$, then $\dfrac{2}{x-y} + \dfrac{1}{y-x} =$

(A) $\dfrac{-2}{x-y}$

(B) $\dfrac{1}{x-y}$

(C) $\dfrac{1}{x+y}$

(D) $\dfrac{3}{x+y}$

(E) $\dfrac{3}{x-y}$

2.

In the xy-coordinate plane, if both x and y are integers, how many points (x,y) lie on the line $2x + 4y = 31$?

(A) None
(B) One
(C) Two
(D) Four
(E) Infinitely many

3.

Each of the following is within both the domain and range of $f(x) = \dfrac{1}{x^2 - 4}$ EXCEPT:

(A) 1
(B) 2
(C) 3
(D) 4
(E) 5

4.

If $x = -2$ satisfies the equation $x^2 - x - c = 0$, where c is a constant, what is another value of x that satisfies the equation?

379

5.

During a tournament, each of the 8 members of a certain chess club plays every other member exactly three times. How many games occur during the tournament?

6.

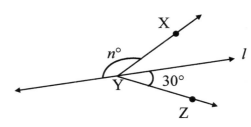

Note: Figure not drawn to scale.

In the figure above, point Y lies on line l and $\angle XYZ$ is bisected by line l. What is the value of $n°$?

7.

If $2^{-x} = 7$, then $2^{2x} = ?$.

(A) $-\dfrac{1}{49}$

(B) $\dfrac{1}{49}$

(C) $\dfrac{1}{7}$

(D) $\dfrac{1}{2}$

(E) 49

8.

If $|3 - x| \geq 2$, then x could be any of the following EXCEPT:

(A) -2
(B) -1
(C) 0
(D) 1
(E) 2

9.

If A is the set of negative integers that are divisible by 3 and B is the set of even integers from −2 to −100 inclusive, the intersection of A and B contains how many elements?

(A) 15
(B) 16
(C) 21
(D) 23
(E) 24

10.

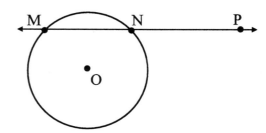

Note: Figure not drawn to scale.

In the figure above, the area of the circle with center O is 4π. If $\overline{MN}$ intersects the circle as shown and $\overline{NP}$ has length equal to the diameter of the circle, the value of $NP \times MN$ cannot be which of the following?

    I.   6
    II. 12
    III. 18

(A) I only
(B) II only
(C) III only
(D) I and II only
(E) I, II, and III

11.

If b is an integer greater than 1, then a^4 must be greater than b^{16} when a is equal to which of the following?

(A) b^4
(B) $4b$
(C) $3b$
(D) $b + 17$
(E) $-b^5$

12.

A certain population of bacteria doubles every 5 hours. If the number of bacteria in the population initially was 2^{50}, what is the number in the population 5 days later?

(A) 2^{250}
(B) $\left(5^{24}\right)\left(2^{50}\right)$
(C) 2^{75}
(D) 2^{74}
(E) 2^{60}

13.

If $|3n - 8| = 4$, then $n = ?$.

(A) $-\dfrac{4}{3}$ or -4

(B) $\dfrac{1}{3}$ or 4

(C) $\dfrac{4}{3}$ or 4

(D) $\dfrac{8}{3}$ or 8

(E) $-\dfrac{4}{3}$ or 4

14.

A set X contains all integers between 11 and 19 inclusive, and set Y contains all integers between −6 and 24 inclusive that are divisible by 6. How many elements are there in the set $X \cup Y$?

(A) 13
(B) 14
(C) 15
(D) 38
(E) 40

15.

x	-1	0	1	2	3
$f(x)$	2	5	8	11	14

If $f(x) = ax + b$ and satisfies the above table for the values of x shown, what is $b - a$?

(A) 1
(B) 2
(C) 3
(D) 4
(E) 5

Question Banks 1-5:
Answer Key

Section 1	Section 2	Section 3	Section 4	Section 5
1. E	1. E	1. B	1. B	1. B
2. A	2. B	2. A	2. A	2. E
3. A	3. D	3. B	3. B	3. E
4. 42	4. E	4. A	4. 3/2	4. C
5. B	5. B	5. 1/4	5. D	5. E
6. E	6. A	6. D	6. 16	6. B
7. B	7. 1	7. A	7. B	7. D
8. C	8. C	8. B	8. D	8. 0
9. D	9. E	9. C	9. D	9. B
10. A	10. E	10. E	10. B	10. D
11. B	11. 3	11. D	11. 4	11. B
12. C	12. B	12. B	12. E	12. E
13. 1, 2, ...10	13. E	13. C	13. D	13. D
14. B	14. B	14. D	14. B	14. C
15. E	15. C	15. D	15. D	15. D
16. A	16. A	16. C	16. D	16. E
17. B		17. B		17. E
18. C		18. A		18. E
19. D		19. D		19. 2
20. D				20. E
				21. B
				22. A
				23. B
				24. E
				25. C

Question Banks 6-10:
Answer Key

Section 6	Section 7	Section 8	Section 9	Section 10
1. 6	1. D	1. C	1. C	1. B
2. E	2. 125	2. C	2. D	2. A
3. B	3. D	3. A	3. D	3. B
4. B	4. B	4. B	4. C	4. 3
5. B	5. 30	5. B	5. B	5. 84
6. C	6. A	6. D	6. B	6. 150
7. D	7. E	7. A	7. E	7. B
8. 3/2	8. D	8. B	8. D	8. E
9. 1/3	9. .2	9. 11	9. C	9. B
10. B	10. 162	10. C	10. C	10. C
11. B	11.	11.	11. B	11. E
12.	12.	12.	12.	12. D
13.	13.	13.	13.	13. C
14.	14.	14.	14.	14. A
15.	15.	15.	15.	15. B

Notes

Notes

Notes

Notes

Notes